B

Nature in the City
SEATTLE

Walks ✴ *Hikes* ✴ *Wildlife* ✴ *Natural Wonders*

Maria Dolan and Kathryn True

THE MOUNTAINEERS BOOKS

Published by
The Mountaineers Books
1001 SW Klickitat Way, Suite 201
Seattle, WA 98134

First edition, 2003

Published simultaneously in Great Britain by Cordee, 3a DeMontfort Street, Leicester, England, LE1 7HD

Manufactured in Canada

Acquisitions Editor: Cassandra Conyers
Project Editor: Kathleen Cubley
Copyeditor: Brenda Pittsley
Cover and Book Design: Kristy L. Welch
Layout Artist: Kristy L. Welch
Mapmaker: Jennifer LaRock Shontz
Illustrator: Judy Shimono

Photography credits: Paul Bannick: page 49, page 207, page 240, page 252, page 258; Maria Dolan: page 17, page 72, page 115, page 237, page 224; Paul Edmondson: page 13, page 44, page 51, page 52, page 58, page 70, page 95, page 123, page 125, page 128, page 133, page 149, page 201, page 222, page 229, page 262, page 265 page 286; Katie Sauter (Seattle Urban Nature Project) page 6, page 11, page 15, page 16, page 61, page 81, page 98, page 102, page 111, page 138, page 140, page 162, page 163; Ruth Taylor: page 34; Kathryn True: page 18, page 29, page 32, page 85, page 156, page 169, page 170, page 181, page 184, page 189, page 196, page 204, page 210, page 214, page 216, page 190.

Cover photograph: © Paul Edmondson and Kathryn True

Library of Congress Cataloging-in-Publication Data

Dolan, Maria.
  Nature in the city : Seattle / Maria Dolan and Kathryn True.
    p. cm.
Includes bibliographical references (p.   ).
  ISBN 0-89886-879-3 (pbk.)
  1. Natural history—Washington (State)—Seattle—Guidebooks. 2.
Seattle (Wash.)—Guidebooks. I. True, Kathryn. II. Title.
  QH105.W2T78 2003
  508.797'772—dc21
                            2003001972

*This one's for the girls: Kathleen and Mary Jane, Emily and Margot—
go outside and stay outside!*
—M.D.

*To Mom and Dad for encouraging my curiosity
and to John and Alex for indulging it, with love*
—K.T.

 CONTENTS

Acknowledgments 10
Introduction 12

Gateway to Puget Sound: Downtown and the International District 19
  1. Seattle to Bainbridge Island: The Watery Wilderness 20
  2. Danny Woo International District Community Gardens 30
  3. Suite 5600: Peregrine Penthouse 33
  4. Space Needle: Cloud Viewing 37
  5. On (and Under) the Waterfront: Myrtle Edwards and Elliott Bay Parks 40

The Forest and the Trees: From the Arboretum to the Central District 45
  6. Frink Park: Woodland Revival 46
  7. Washington Park Arboretum Winter Garden: Green Therapy for Seasonal Blues 54
  8. Nora's Woods: Hushed Tribute 57
  9. Interlaken Park: Making Natural History 60

City Vistas: Queen Anne and Magnolia 73
  10. Walking the Boulevard: An Olmsted Legacy 74
  11. Good Tiding: Beach Walk at Discovery Park 82
  12. Kiwanis Ravine Heron Colony 90
  13. Magnolia's Madrones 92
  14. Eternal Bloom: Lichens at Mount Pleasant 96

Salmon Bay and Beyond: Ballard, Fremont, and Northwest Seattle 103
  15. Carkeek Park Salmon 104
  16. The Big Dig: Hiram M. Chittenden Locks 113
  17. Shilshole Bay: Sea Lions and Sandy Beaches 120

Green Lake Watershed: Green Lake, Ravenna, and the University District 129
  18. Swamp Things: Paddling Lake Washington 130
  19. Green Lake's Birding Bounty 136
  20. Raising the Dead: Ravenna Park and Creek 142
  21. Green Days and Starry Nights: University of Washington Campus 144
  22. Reclaiming Paradise: Union Bay Natural Area 148

Down to Earth: South Seattle   157

23. Dead Horse Canyon: Wild Plant Walk   158
24. Kubota Garden: Idealized Nature   165
25. Bradner Gardens Park: Waiting for Butterflies   171
26. Seward Park Natural History: From Bedrock to Eagles   175
27. Dearborn Park Elementary School: A Forest (and Wetland) of
    Learning   180

Green Peninsula: West Seattle and the Duwamish River   185

28. West Seattle Beach Chronicles: From Broken Earth to
    Storied Sky   187
29. Duwamish River Restoration Bike Tour: Industrial Evolution   193
30. Mushrooming at Camp Long   202
31. Roxhill Bog: Headwaters of a Legacy   209
32. Schmitz Park Preserve: Seattle's Forest Past   214

Carkeek Park beach is the outlet for Piper's Creek, a northwest Seattle salmon stream.

Northeast Seattle: Lakes, Ponds, Springs, and Wetlands   223
    33. Wide Open Spaces: Sand Point Magnuson Park   224
    34. Places for Pondering: Meadowbrook's Wetlands   232
    35. Evening Chorus at Paramount Park Open Space   239
    36. North Seattle Community College Wetlands   242

Farther Afield   253
    37. Renton: Waterworks Gardens   253
    38. Vashon Island: Winter Bird Wonderland   255
    39. Bainbridge Island: IslandWood   257
    40. Bellevue: Wild Wetland in Mercer Slough   259
    41. Kirkland: Orion's Lush Legacy   261
    42. Everett: Jetty Island   263
    43. Everett: Spencer Island   266

Appendixes   268
At-a-Glance Chart   278

MAP KEY

~~	paved road	(P)	parking
+-+-+-+-+-	railroad	(T)	trailhead
- - - - - -	main trail	(R)	restroom
··············	side trail	■	building / site of interest
-··-··-··-	boundary (park or wilderness area)	ᴨ	picnic area
(84)	interstate highway	] [	bridge
(101)	U.S. highway	⬭	lake or pond
(1) (530)	state route	~~~///~~~	river or creek, waterfall
O	city or town	⚘⚘	marsh/wetland

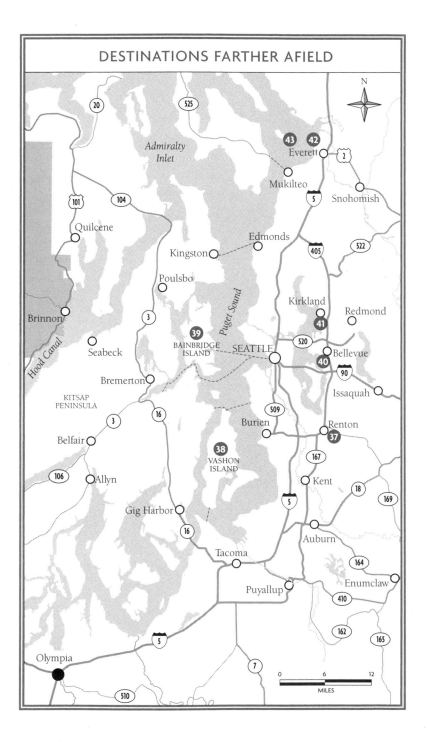

DESTINATIONS FARTHER AFIELD

N

20
525

Admiralty
Inlet

43 42
Everett
2

Mukilteo
5
Snohomish

101
104

Quilcene

Edmonds

Kingston
405
522

Poulsbo

Kirkland
Redmond

41

3

39
BAINBRIDGE
ISLAND
520
Bellevue

Brinnon

SEATTLE
40
90

Seabeck

Bremerton

KITSAP
PENINSULA

Issaquah

Puget Sound

Hood Canal

3
16

509
Burien
Renton
37

Belfair

167

106
Allyn

38
VASHON
ISLAND

Kent
18
169

Gig Harbor

16

Auburn

164

Tacoma
5

Enumclaw

Puyallup
410

165

162

7

0   6   12
MILES

Olympia

510

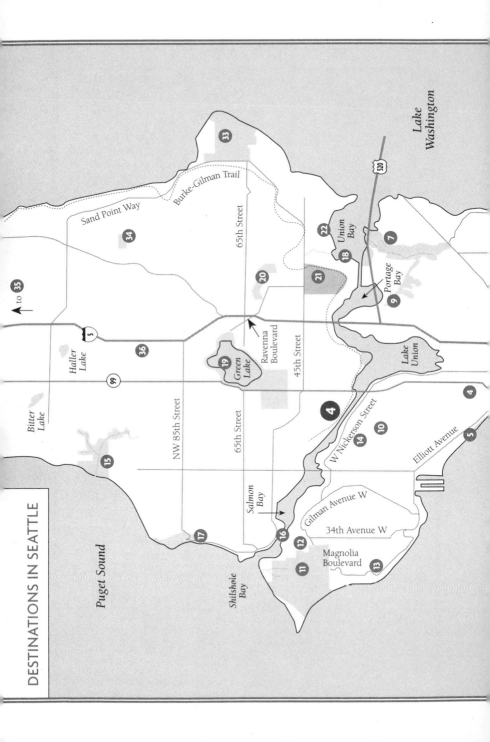

DESTINATIONS IN SEATTLE

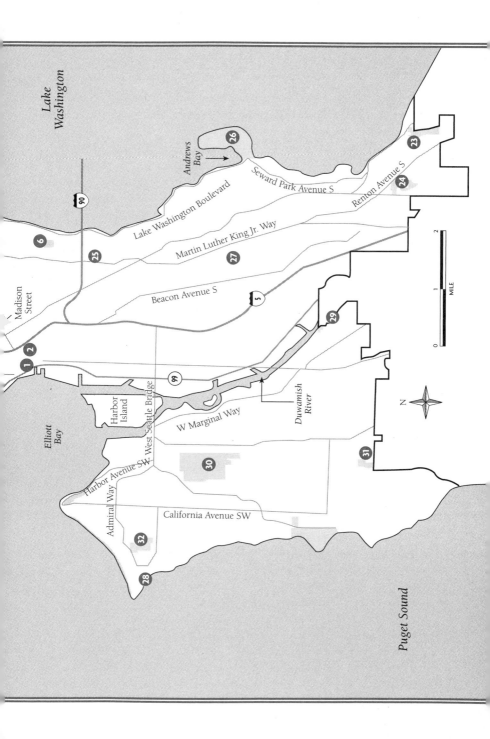

✳ ACKNOWLEDGMENTS

With heartfelt gratitude we would like to thank the following people for generously taking the time to review writing, answer questions, take a walk, or simply offer love and support.

Peter Abrahams, Bud Anderson, Roland Anderson, Marcia Appleton, Rich Appleton, Tom Aversa, John Beal, Chris Behrens, Brian Bell, Jeremy Bell, Curt Black, Connie Blair, Brian Bodenbach, Derek Booth, Patrick Boland, Patty Borman, Jan Bragg, Charles Brennick, Don Brooks, Dru Butterfield, Valerie Cholven, Adam Cole, Brad Colman, Emilie Coulter, Rod Crawford, Eliza Davidson, Brangien Davis, John Dolan, Kathleen Dolan, Claire Hagen Dole, Mike Donahue, Aileen Douglas, Steve Dubiel, Loretta Edwards, Evelyn Fairchild, Karen Fevold, Marcia Fischer, Bob Frazier and the Queen Anne Historical Society, Eric Friedli, Christina Gallegos, Gail Gautestad, Brian Gay, Peggy Gaynor, Pat Gearin, Jamie Glasgow, Stuart Glasoe, Fred Goetz, David Gordon, Terri Griffith and the Roxhill Bog Volunteers, Christian Gronau, Ellen Haas, Kraig Hansen, Cecile Hanson, Lynn Havsall, Jean Hobard, Fred Hoyt, Harriet Huber, Dr. John Huckabee, Janice Hunt, Doug Jackson, Arthur Lee Jacobson, Jon Jaffe, Suzanne Joneson, Lorna Jordan, Kurt Kraemer, Ana Larson, Robin Lesh, Russell Link, Christine Llobregat, Captain Frank Longmate, Peter Lortz, Stuart MacKay, Chris Mayo, Kelly McAllister, Theresa McEwen, Bill McMillan, Mark Mead, Bonnie Miller, Pamela Miller, Joyce Moty, Martin Muller, Jeanie Murphy-Ouellette, Suzanne Nagler and the Upper Skagit School of Botanical Medicine, Kit O'Neill, Kari Olson, Dennis Paulson, Charles Payton, Anne Peterson, Chris Pfeiffer, Cynthia Putnam, Art Rangno, James Rasmussen, Klaus Richter, Penny Rose, Jefferson Saunders, Bob Schafer, Kathy Seider, Sheryl Shapiro, Ken Shaw, Dyanne Sheldon, Brian Sherrod, Constance Sidles, Judith Siefker, Dick Sieger, Bob Spencer, Joe Starstead, Russ Steele, Danny Stratten, Richard Strickland, Woody Sullivan, Terry Swanson, Paul Talbot, Bill Talley, Curtis Tanner, Ruth Taylor, Brian R. Thompson, Sallie Tisdale, Steven Trudell, Carolyn True, Earl True, Fran True, Idie Ulsh, Marian Valentine, Janine Van Sanden, Wade Vaughn, Laura Veirs, Bob Vreeland, Julie Walker, Janet Way, Bruce Weertman, Dan Willsie, John C. Withey, and Chollada Yesuwan.

We offer special thanks to the following people, who went above and beyond to help make this book a reality: Paul Bannick for wildlife photography; David Buerge, whose writings on local Native American history were of great use to our book; Paul Edmondson for professional photography and good cheer; Lyanda Haupt for the words on birds; Alex Koriath for joy and research assistance; John Koriath for keeping the home fires burning with style;

Brenda Peterson for believing it could happen; Katie Sauter and The Seattle Urban Nature Project for photos and consultation on matters of urban green; David Takami, our helpful Seattle Parks reviewer; Elizabeth Wales, our agent, who didn't pull any punches while keeping our chins up; and finally, the people at The Mountaineers Books, for climbing "urban mountains" with us.

Our apologies to any helpful people whose names have been inadvertently left off our long lists, and a grateful thanks.

Slate gray American coots are found at many Seattle ponds and lakes.

INTRODUCTION

Many people offer Seattle's natural beauty as a primary reason they live or visit here. Their nature encounters, however, often take place outside the city—a visit to Paradise on Mount Rainier, for example, or a boat ride to see a pod of spy-hopping orcas in the San Juans. It's undeniable that true wilderness is only available beyond the city limits. Yet many fail to realize just how much wildness survives all around us in Seattle. You don't need to leave town, or ogle a distant view, to experience it. *Nature in the City: Seattle* leads you to woodlands, parks, college campuses, and public shorelines—places where squirrels fly, frogs sing rounds, and peregrine falcons, once at the brink of extinction, now fledge young. Some of these spots are little known, and a few, while not strictly green spaces, offer a chance to see how our built environment interacts with the non-human world. Think of it this way: to some, buildings and streets are one way humans have expressed their "nature"—the results are no less "natural" than nests built by birds or dams built by beavers.

Our city is defined by its exquisite location between mountains, lapped by both salt- and freshwater. Flanked by the Olympic Mountains to the west and the Cascades to the east, Seattle lies at latitude 47.39'N, longitude 122.17'W, approximately 90 air miles east of the Pacific Ocean. Located on the eastern shore of an inland sea, Puget Sound, and with the long stretch of Lake Washington to the east, Seattle is blessed with 53 miles of saltwater shoreline and nearly 148 miles of freshwater in which to dip our toes come summer.

And speaking of water, it does rain a lot here, but take heart—it's less wet than in Eugene, Oregon; Houston, Texas; or Memphis, Tennessee. Seattle's soggy reputation is based mostly on the damp, gray days of fall and winter, but it's this same maritime climate (the mean annual daily temperature is 52 Fahrenheit, and it rarely dips below freezing or rises above 80 Fahrenheit) that makes outdoor activity comfortable year-round.

The moderate climate that now allows trees from all over the world to thrive here (a diversity surpassing most cities in the northern temperate zone) once fostered thick forests of native species. When pioneers first set foot on these shores, Douglas fir, alder, cedar, hemlock, and spruce grew to the water's edge. In 1853, the folks at the Yesler Sawmill, at the foot of what is now Yesler Way, cut the first Seattle tree in the modern era. Twenty-six years later, the last original downtown tree was felled just north of Pike Street.

While settlers cleared the landscape for building, black bears were cruising newly staked backyards. All across the city, native berries hung like fat jewels for the snatching, salmon-thronged pristine streams, and rafts of waterfowl seasonally clogged area wetlands. Shellfish, marine mammals, and hordes of fish were still abundant in the Duwamish River delta, which yawned wide along the south side of Elliott Bay. Before the lower Duwamish was straightened to satisfy the demands of industry, several rivers followed its meander to reach Puget Sound. At that time, Lake Washington still drained via rivers into Elliott Bay, and Lake Union was nearly landlocked.

While some backcountry wilderness in our area has been protected by federal law, the bounty described here was quickly stripped from the city as streams were paved over for development, wetlands were filled in, and even the hydrology of our urban lakes was tampered with in the early twentieth century to accommodate the demands of an expanding metropolis. Thankfully, a few people with forethought fought to preserve parks and other breathing spaces for urban dwellers. In our era, their torch still burns thanks to a cadre of citizens—ecologists, schoolchildren, and dedicated neighbors to name a few—who plant native species along the banks of the Duwamish, tend gardens for butterflies, and tear invasive ivy from old-growth stands. You'll find examples of their projects in this book.

Throughout *Nature in the City: Seattle* you'll find information meant to help answer your nature queries, and perhaps raise new questions for the curious. What do the clouds outside your office window portend? Where are all those crows going that fly over your yard every evening? What is that strange shape in the sand? Read about it, then go out and discover for yourself, letting your sense of community stretch beyond the human realm. Stand within arm's reach of a beaver lodge, harvest an oyster mushroom, or watch a

Canoeing in Union Bay is a good way to quietly observe wildlife.

sharp-shinned hawk de-feather its prey, right here in our city, and you will begin to realize that the wild isn't somewhere out beyond city limits—it is all around you. There's no turning back once your eyes are opened: from now on it's all long lunch breaks and a bookshelf groaning with field guides. The salamanders, foxes, huckleberries, cedars, bats, birds, butterflies, and these two authors will be out there with you.

HOW TO USE THIS BOOK

Nature in the City: Seattle divides the city and nearby environs into eight sections, plus a chapter for areas outside the city limits that deserve exploration. A regional map at the beginning of the book shows all the areas, with each outing in the book highlighted for quick reference.

Each chapter offers a handful of recommended destinations. Guided journeys through a park or other green space are described for some of these, and may take an hour or more to complete. You can use the tours by reading them and viewing the accompanying maps, then charting your own course, or you can follow them faithfully.

Other destinations are descriptions of places where you can experience urban nature, including parks, skyscrapers, college campuses, and sandy beaches. No map is included for these rambles, but all promise an encounter with something wild. Most of these destinations can be explored in thirty minutes to an hour, though many reward longer visits.

A chart on pages 278-281 provides additional details about each destination.

WHAT TO TAKE

In fall, winter, spring, and—let's face it—even in summer, Seattle weather can be unpredictable. In other words, if there are any clouds at all in the sky, consider bringing a rain jacket and wearing warm layers. For footwear you can usually get by with running shoes, but in rainy weather or on a wilder trail you may want hiking boots or trail runners. The type of surface you'll be walking on is mentioned in each write-up, so plan accordingly. You may want to pack water and a snack for longer tours.

Certain items will enliven your experience on nature outings. Binoculars, for instance, are useful on most of these tours and destinations, as birds are a nearly ubiquitous and intriguing city presence. A magnifying hand lens is a good idea for those who enjoy detail and for enriching the experience for kids (binoculars can be used as a makeshift magnifying lens by looking through one of the lenses in the reverse direction). A sketchbook, a notebook, and a pen or a pencil are useful for noting and sketching animal and plant characteristics to help you identify them later. Consider keeping a nature notebook

Black-capped chickadees build nests in tree snags.

for listing species, describing the weather, or otherwise recording your trip. Finally, a good pocket field guide is a handy reference to keep in your backpack. A list of our favorites is in the appendix.

GETTING THERE

Most destinations in this book can be easily reached by bus or bicycle. Natural areas benefit from green modes of transport, and whenever possible, we encourage busing or bicycling to your location. Bus route numbers are listed, but for the latest schedule information call (206) 553-3000, or visit the Metro rider information website at *http://transit.metrokc.gov*. The site includes a trip planner to help you create trip itineraries. All bus routes given begin in downtown Seattle.

Similarly, all driving directions are presumed to have downtown Seattle as a starting point (except for those destinations located downtown).

To find the best bike routes, call for a free copy of the Seattle Bicycling Guide Map from the Seattle Bicycle Alliance, (206) 224-9252. Or visit them on the Internet at *http://bicyclealliance.org/*.

SAFETY

Just as when hiking outside the city, common sense precautions will help you avoid injury on the urban trail. Wear comfortable footwear with good ankle support, and layer clothing appropriate to the season. Trails can be muddy, bridges and steps slippery, and heavy rains can cause flooding on pathways. Although it would be difficult to get lost on most of the trails listed in this book, bring plenty of water to avoid dehydration and a high-protein snack for the return trip. Be mindful of the weather. A walk in the rain can be an enjoyable experience, but be aware of areas prone to landslides and avoid visiting during high winds.

Urban crime can be a concern even in natural areas, and we recommend traveling with a friend. If you choose to explore alone, tell someone where you are going and when you plan to return.

Take special precautions with kids. Stay with children at all times and be mindful of cliffs, ravines, poisonous plants, and other hazards.

Do not eat berries, other plant parts, or mushrooms unless you are 100 percent sure of their identification. Naturalists at park nature centers can help you make a positive identification.

RESPECT ON THE TRAIL

Exploring with respect for the non-human environment will help ensure these places will be part of Seattle's legacy for years to come. A good hiking principle is the classic "take only pictures and memories; leave only footprints." Garbage is a notable problem in many parks, and you may want to bring along a small bag to collect trash along the way.

Dogs can be especially destructive, and we encourage you to follow leash laws at all times. Keep yourself and your dogs on the trail to avoid trampling sensitive undergrowth or bird nests. It's tempting to let children and dogs play in streambeds, but this behavior is highly damaging to sensitive habitat. Unlike wild streams, urban waterways are generally short, shallow, and encroached upon by development, making them especially vulnerable. Stay out of streams and away from their edges.

If your goal is bird watching, leave your dog at home. Dogs will frighten away most animal life. From late spring to late summer, ground nests in bird habitat areas are in danger of being trampled, and brooding birds can be frightened from their nests.

Please be respectful of all wildlife. Do not pester or collect animals. Nesting birds are especially vulnerable. If you find a nest, move quietly away and notify a naturalist. If you pick up a piece of wood in the forest or a rock at the

The pathfinder plant's name comes from the fact that as you brush past, the silvery undersides of its leaves turn over, clearly marking your return route.

Seattle p-patches offer planting space, and sometimes a bountiful harvest, for urban gardeners.

beach to examine the life underneath, gently replace it after you are through.

Many of the destinations in this book border private property. Please be respectful of neighbors and do not enter private property without permission.

SMALL PRINT

Natural areas are in a constant state of flux. For the current status of trails mentioned in this book, check with the contact listed. We apologize for leaving out places we didn't know about or lacked enough space to include, but we hope you will tell us about them for future editions.

A NOTE ABOUT SAFETY

Safety is an important concern in all outdoor activities. No guidebook can alert you to every hazard or anticipate the limitations of every reader. Therefore, the descriptions of roads, trails, routes, and natural features in this book are not representations that a particular place or excursion will be safe for your party. When you follow any of the routes described in this book, you assume responsibility for your own safety. Under normal conditions, such excursions require the usual attention to traffic, road and trail conditions, weather, terrain, the capabilities of your party, and other factors. Keeping informed on current conditions and exercising common sense are the keys to a safe, enjoyable outing.

The Mountaineers Books

Gateway to Puget Sound:
DOWNTOWN AND THE INTERNATIONAL DISTRICT

No other landscape in the city has been as completely overhauled as that of downtown. The edges of Elliott Bay were once mudflats, Pioneer Square was an island, and before being swept into the bay, Denny Hill stood between Capitol Hill and Queen Anne.

After abandoning their first city site at weather-blasted Alki Point in West Seattle, the early pioneers were thankful for this more protected inner-bay location. Puget Sound's first steam-powered log mill rose from a pier at the base of Mill Street (now Yesler Way), and settlers erected elevated wooden troughs to wash fresh spring water from First Hill down to their waiting basins.

The Pioneer Square area had been known by Native Americans as *Zechalalitch*, "the place to pass over." What we know today as Yesler Way was their preferred route between the Duwamish River and Lake Washington. Nearby, where King Street crosses under the viaduct, stood a longhouse 200 feet long and 40 feet wide—in front of which Chief Sealth delivered his famous speech in 1854:

"Every hillside, every valley, every plain and grove, has been hallowed by some sad or happy event in days long vanished. Even the rocks, which seem to be dumb and dead as they swelter in the sun along the silent shore, thrill with memories of stirring events connected with the lives of my people, and the very dust upon which you now stand responds more lovingly to their footsteps than yours, because it is rich with the blood of our ancestors, and our bare feet are conscious of the sympathetic touch."

Certainly a culture driven by the dizzying speed of the Internet and numbed by constant traffic gridlock could find respite in a "sympathetic touch," and noticing nature is a good place to start.

Although locating the wild amidst our burgeoning skyline takes some creativity, there's more than a little to discover downtown. While you're waiting for the ferry, you'd be amazed at the variety of sea creatures you can find making

The Danny Woo Gardens provide a green frame for city views.

their living on dock pilings. Doing time in a skyscraper? Note cloud movement and formations, or try to memorize the names of the visible Olympic or Cascade peaks. For a break from pavement, take a walk through the Belltown P-Patch Garden at Elliott Avenue and Vine Street, try to identify the trees in a building courtyard, or temporarily drown out the noise in your head near a public fountain. During a slow inning at Safeco Field, use binoculars to search for birds—some birder baseball fans make note of species they've spied within the stadium and in the sky above it. Their lists include osprey, bald eagle, red-tailed hawk, and violet-green swallow.

In this chapter, a ferry tour on Elliott Bay from downtown Seattle to Bainbridge Island introduces the wild wonders of Puget Sound. There are four destinations to choose from, or combine several of them to create your own tour. One takes you to a downtown aerie of peregrine falcons, a second heads to the green terraces of the Danny Woo International District Community Gardens, another zips up the Space Needle for glimpses into the habits of clouds, and the final offering introduces you to the natural diversions of Myrtle Edwards Park.

🦎 1. Seattle to Bainbridge Island: The Watery Wilderness

Where:	The Seattle Ferry Terminal is downtown at Pier 52, 801 Alaskan Way
Tour Distance:	1 hour 10 minute round-trip ride
Phone:	(206) 464-6400
Internet:	*www.wsdot.wa.gov/ferries/*
Hours:	Ferry service from 6:20 A.M. to 2:10 A.M.
Disabled Access:	Yes
Dogs:	In cars or on leash on vehicle deck only
Fee:	Call for current prices
Driving:	From I-5 northbound, take Exit 164B into downtown Seattle. From I-5 southbound take Exit 164. Turn right onto Fourth Avenue South, go one block to South Royal Brougham. Turn right and continue four to five blocks to Alaskan Way. Turn right. Travel a little over 1 mile to the ferry terminal on the left. Look for overhead signage. There is a left turn lane for vehicle traffic. No passenger drop-off here.
Bus:	16, 66
Special Note:	Binoculars are recommended. For security reasons, passengers must disembark the ferry at Bainbridge. You may then re-board the same ferry.

The romance of a Seattle ferry ride is bound to the poetry of opposites—the city's beauty retreating in the distance as the boat escapes westward into the horizon-wide embrace of the Olympic Mountains.

> A *Seattle Times* poll found that 89 percent of Seattle residents credit "natural beauty" as the primary reason why they live here.

There are few more convenient and visceral ways to acquaint yourself with the essence of Puget Sound, a wilderness often overlooked by humans. Every day, in view of office towers and freeways, these waters host rituals as foreign to us as ordering a latté would be to a glaucous-winged gull, a Dall's porpoise, or a moon jellyfish. If your timing is right, you can encounter any or all of these creatures on this tour to Bainbridge Island, a thirty-five-minute, one-way trip over Elliott Bay, across a major shipping channel, and into Eagle Harbor on Bainbridge. Board the ferry and head to the Solarium Deck for the best views.

For centuries, the vessel of choice for this passage was a red cedar dugout canoe. Up until 1903 when construction began on the Denny Regrade, these water craft lined the beach near a Native American settlement below Belltown where the Pier 66 marina is located today. Seattle's namesake, Chief Sealth, and his people used canoes to fish, hunt, trade, and visit winter villages on Bainbridge. As Sealth watched steamers chug into his homewaters in the 1850s, it must have been painfully clear that his life would bridge two eras.

The Mosquito Fleet consisted of thousands of steamships carrying everything from cows to love letters, making port at every "whistle-stop" between Olympia and southeast Alaska that could scare up a pier. By the early 1930s, roads had largely replaced water freight service, but passengers and cars still needed a way to cross the Sound.

After San Francisco's Golden Gate Bridge was completed in 1935, a group of diesel-electric auto ferries found a new home in Seattle as the precursors to the Washington State Ferry System. Early regional planners intended the ferry system as a stopgap measure. A 1959 "no" vote by the state legislature terminated a plan to build a network of bridges across Puget Sound. The largest ferry system in the United States, Washington ferries carry more than twenty-six million people each year. The Bainbridge run is the busiest of all, with the two largest boats in the fleet serving more than seven million passengers annually.

As the ferry leaves the dock, step outside for a better view of the water. If the Sound were suddenly drained, it would be a canyon deeper in places than ten Bank of America Centers—the tallest building on Seattle's retreating skyline. During each tidal exchange, 284 billion cubic feet of water comes in with the flood tide and goes out with the ebb tide. Tidal influences are so strong—especially during extreme tides at full moon—that ferry crews adjust their course accordingly. During ebb tide, the tidal outflow from the Duwamish

River creates a surging current around the eastern edge of Elliott Bay so strong that even at 4345 tons the Tacoma ferry makes allowances.

As you make the crossing, look around the boat for whirlpools that occur when water caught between high tide and low tide is spun like a submerged top. A lot of flotsam and jetsam (drift logs and garbage) indicates you're traveling after an extreme high tide, when everything deposited far up on the beach is washed back out to sea. A patch of unusually flat water is often the result of oil discharge or other pollutants. As you enter Eagle Harbor, you can recognize a retreating tide by a large V fanning out in front of channel markers.

Light and wind also change the water's appearance. Extreme winds can also alter the ferry schedule. Occasionally storm winds reaching forty-five–plus knots make it unsafe to make a crossing—mostly due to possible passenger injury (even twenty-knot winds make it hard to keep your balance on deck). Although runs are rarely cancelled, captains regularly alter their routes in winter to steer with high winds and into the waves.

Although more than two hundred fish species dwell in Puget Sound (including seven species of shark and four kinds of skate), we only get glimpses of sea life from the surface. The only "flying fish" in this area are homeward-bound salmon trying to escape a predator (seal, sea lion, or other salmon) or attempting to splash off parasitic isopods. In fall, it's common to see these silvery fish jumping from 3 to 4 feet out of the water.

Another fish phenomenon is the distinctive undulation of a herring ball. Usually seen in the fall and winter when these fish mature, it can be identified at a distance as a "boiling" on the water and by hordes of feasting gulls. Frenzied masses of these 10-inch fish swirl in large circles up to 60 feet across to elude their predators, generally salmon below and gulls above.

Gulls often have "runny noses." They don't have colds, they're just excreting excess salt ingested when drinking seawater. To do this they use a specialized gland above their nostrils. Glaucous-winged gulls prefer island nest sites, and Seattle's gulls have made city buildings their urban islands. These gulls nest alone or in groups on the Cabrini Medical Tower, Sheraton Hotel, Four Seasons Hotel, Century Square Building, St. James Cathedral, and many other downtown buildings.

The gulls hovering above the ferry aren't there just for a lift on the boat's air stream. The most common "ferry rider" is our only year-round resident gull, the large glaucous-winged gull, notable for its pink legs and an absence of black on its wing tips. New chicks use the red spot on an adult bird's bill tip as a pecking target to prompt their parents to regurgitate food. One of the few bird species to thrive in the wake of human development, this gull is an opportunistic omnivore who will eat everything from earthworms to crabs to garbage. They commonly follow groups of mammals such as seals and whales to gobble their leftovers. They see the ferry in the same light: a boatload of mammals tossing popcorn and dropping french fries.

The bird-watching community would like to remove the term "seagull" from our vocabulary because many gull species range far from the ocean. Although eight types can be found in the Seattle area, the only other gulls frequently seen over this part of Puget Sound from fall through spring are the mew and Bonaparte's gulls. The mew gull is about half the size of the glaucous-winged, has yellowish legs and a dainty bill. All-gray glaucous-winged and mew gulls are juveniles. The Bonaparte's is smaller still and has a black dime-size spot behind its eye, except in summer when its head feathers are completely black. Another gull-like bird that's easy to spot because of its vertical dives is the common tern, which hovers over the water, then plunges completely under the surface to snatch small fish.

Other birds commonly seen on this route are the alcids, which leave the water only to nest. Most prevalent here in late fall and winter, they're known to "fly" underwater. Look for the common murre (often confused with a penguin), marbled murrelet, and pigeon guillemot (this year-round resident is easy to spot in the summer with its white wing spot against an all black body). Another year-rounder—the rhinoceros auklet—is a puffin relative named for the whitish horn that grows on its beak during spring and summer. Alcids generally fly single file no more than 5 feet above the water, and typically appear alone or in small groups.

Most common between April and October, jellyfish often can be viewed by looking over the side of the ferry. Shaped like an upended bowl with hanging fringe (stinging tentacles used to catch its prey), what you'll see from your vantage point is a circular mass usually less than 12 inches across. The most common is the fried egg jellyfish—aptly named for a yellowish mass in its center, it can grow to 2 feet in diameter. Ghostly moon jellies are easy to spot and can be recognized by the gonads, four horseshoe shapes in

Moon Jellyfish

Lion's Mane Jellyfish

the center of the body, glowing against the water's dark background. The ferocious lion's mane is yellowish orange to reddish and can pack a powerful sting even after it's washed ashore. The world's largest jellyfish, this species can be deadly to humans and, in Arctic waters, grows to 8 feet with tentacles trailing 60 feet. Don't worry; it's unlikely to top 2 feet locally.

Scan the water for the dark heads of swimming seals or sea lions, which may be seen at any point along the route. Usually appearing singly, you can tell them apart by the sea lion's external ear flaps and solid coloring. Harbor seals are smaller, have smooth, ball-like heads with no earflaps, and large eyes.

Seals frequently "haul out" on Blakely Rocks. Just south of the entrance to Eagle Harbor on Bainbridge, the rocks are most visible at low tide. For the best view, go to the ferry's left front outside deck. Anywhere from fifty to one hundred seals usually can be seen resting here, except in winter when they prefer the relative warmth of the water. Wrongly blamed for salmon gluttony, they prefer bottom fish such as sculpins. Able to carry more oxygen in their bloodstreams than humans, harbor seals can stay under water up to thirty minutes at a time. They are so comfortable there that researchers in airplanes frequently see them relaxing in groups on the Sound floor. Viewed as vermin by the fishing industry, a price was paid for every seal snout collected until the bounty was lifted in 1960. Their comeback was furthered by the 1972 Marine Mammal Protection Act, which made it a federal offense to kill these animals. Approximately two thousand harbor seals make Puget Sound their home.

Steller's and California sea lions prefer to haul out on buoys, but this ferry route does not pass near any. However, you could see a group of the more gregarious Californias forming a large "raft" in springtime where they rest together, tail fins sticking conspicuously out of the water. Sea lions also sleep this way. It is thought to be a temperature-regulating position or a way to maintain balance. Most frequently seen (and heard) are migrant male California sea lions, numbering around one thousand in the Sound compared to fifty resident Steller's. Dark brown to black in color, the Californias can be identified at a distance by the large bump on the foreheads of the males and by their barking voices. With more lion-like golden brown coats and deep roars, Steller's are larger but seldom seen or heard. Agile swimmers, sea lions have been clocked at twenty knots.

In summer months you might be lucky enough to spot one of three resident cetaceans. Often confused with baby orcas because of their black-and-white markings, Dall's porpoises are the fastest and most commonly seen. These wily swimmers are famous for "bow riding" or hitching a ride on the

Dall's Porpoise

pressure wave formed at the front of a boat, though this usually only happens on more northerly ferry routes.

The more streamlined Harbor porpoise was a daily sight here in the 1940s and before, but is a rarity today. More sensitive to urbanization than their cousins, it is thought that because the two share a food source, the Harbors were pushed out by the bolder Dall's. The Harbor porpoise is small, with a shark-like brownish dorsal fin.

Regular commuters will advise that if the boat slows mid-route, start looking for whales. Usually ferry captains will make an announcement, sending passengers scurrying to one side of the boat—a weight shift that registers on the boat's clinometer. The largest member of the dolphin family and the only resident whale of Puget Sound is the orca or killer whale. From the ferry, they are most easily distinguished by their size—males can grow to 30 feet long with huge 6-foot dorsal fins, the female's fin grows to 3 feet. Usually traveling in groups of five to twenty, orcas cover as many as 100 miles every twenty-four hours. Although they have been sighted throughout the year, they are most common along this ferry route during the fall chum salmon run. Usually staying within 200 miles of their San Juan Islands homewaters, members of the "J pod" whale community are most likely to be seen this far south, though K and L pods sometimes pass through as well.

If all other sea life eludes you, look closely at the pilings at the Bainbridge or Seattle ferry docks. Barnacles, mussels, tube worms, and sea anemones make their homes here. Shield-shaped kelp crabs can be seen nibbling kelp as small perch dart at worms and barnacles.

Seattle tide records have been kept since 1899. At the downtown ferry dock, a measuring device bounces sound waves off water in a tube that fills and empties with the tide, continuously sending readings to the Tidal Analysis Branch of the National Oceanic and Atmospheric Administration (NOAA) in Washington, D.C. The data is used to improve tide predictions.

GOING UNDER:
DIVING INTO PUGET SOUND AT THE SEATTLE AQUARIUM

Ever met a spiny lumpsucker, decorated warbonnet, or wolf eel? The Seattle Aquarium at Pier 59 is second only to a scuba dive for up-close-and-personal encounters with many of the more clandestine inhabitants of Elliott Bay and Puget Sound. Free to passers-by, the "Window on Elliott Bay" runs along a wall outside the aquarium and provides a glimpse of perch, rockfish, and cod. Inside the aquarium, the spectacular 400,000-gallon tank of the dome room allows you to walk "under water" to view circling sharks, colorful rockfish, soaring skates, flattened halibut, and flashing salmon. Other exhibits feature the giant octopus, sea dragons, marine mammals, and the salmon life cycle. A short walk from the Seattle ferry terminal, the Seattle Aquarium is located at 1483 Alaskan Way on Pier 59, (206) 386-4300.

PUGET SOUND'S TROUBLED WATERS

Puget Sound has long harbored some of our country's finest shellfish habitat. Archaeological digs around the Seattle area have unearthed huge shell middens—Native American discard piles—revealing the important role oysters, clams, and mussels held at their feasts. But don't head out to gather your own meal just yet. Harvesting these organisms from most urban Puget Sound waters is prohibited, and it's not to protect the bivalves. These filter feeders are ingesting not only saltwater, but fertilizers, pesticides, oil, sewage, and a variety of pollutants you probably wouldn't want at your dinner table. To harvest safely check first with the Department of Health.

Laws enacted in the 1960s and '70s did much to halt industrial dumping of some of the worst contaminants in local waters, but many of those pollutants are still present in sedimentary layers, and it is still legal to discharge some amounts of chemicals, including dioxin and mercury, directly into Puget Sound. Much of the food chain is contaminated to some degree by these poisons. Local orca populations have been declining since the 1990s, a disaster experts blame on shrinking runs of salmon and other prey species combined with toxins found in the marine mammals during laboratory testing.

Obviously, the twentieth century's

The Public Shellfish Sites of Puget Sound guide from the Washington Department of Health (www.doh.wa.gov) offers tips on where and when shellfish can be safely harvested. Since 1980, the first year the situation received a comprehensive study, 25 percent of the already-diminished shellfish tidelands in Puget Sound have closed to production because of pollution.

human population boom here (the Puget Sound area is now home to nearly four million people) is the overreaching problem. Industry is partly to blame, but individuals contribute too. Runoff from roadways, overloaded sewage and septic systems, improperly disposed pesticides and other household chemicals, and oil leaks from cars and boats are all sources of water pollution. Other threats to the health of this waterway include shoreline development—a sensitive area providing important habitat for salmon and other wildlife—and the risk of a major oil spill (as well as the effects of smaller, recurrent spills) from tankers passing through our waters.

Implicated as we are, there is much hope that humans can also find solutions to these problems. For individuals, one way to get involved is to push for changes in government policy, such as demanding stronger laws and enforcement on issues of toxic waste dumping and shoreline management. The nonprofit organization People for Puget Sound also recommends personal changes you can make to help protect our homewaters: use alternative transportation methods, avoid toxic household products such as chemical cleaners and pesticides, and buy chlorine-free (unbleached) paper products. To find out more, or to get involved, contact People for Puget Sound at (206) 382-7007 or *http://pugetsound.org*.

PEERLESS PLANKTON: PUGET'S SOUND'S INVISIBLE WEALTH

You've got three months to live in which you must molt eleven times, reproduce, and survive voracious neighbors ten times your size with powerful jaws and stinging tentacles. Such is life for the copepod, a crustacean belonging to a group of animals and algae called plankton.

Derived from a Greek word meaning "drifter" or "wanderer," many plankters can swim as well as float. The most abundant life forms on earth except for bacteria and other microbes, they are mostly invisible to the naked eye. If the population of Seattle were reduced to their size, we'd fit inside a quart of milk with room to swim around. Some spend their whole life this small while others are the larval form of creatures such as sea cucumbers and jellyfish. Under a microscope, they look like a collection of otherworldly zoo creatures—as local author Jonathan Raban wrote in his book, *Passage to Juneau: A Sea and Its Meanings*,

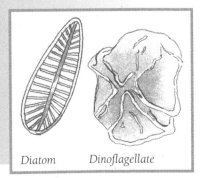

Diatom   *Dinoflagellate*

"If plankton were a little bigger, they would figure in everyone's bad dreams." Puget Sound's daily tidal mixing creates an environment where these organisms thrive. Forceful tidal action breathes oxygen into and lifts nutrients up from the depths to feed these essential first links in the food chain. Puget Sound plankton are ten times more abundant than those found in the deep Pacific Ocean.

Plankton are responsible for sustaining the diverse tide pool life on our beaches, as well as the birds, fish, and even the mighty orcas. Plankton also feed automobiles. Petroleum is largely made up of the geologically altered remains of these ancient denizens of the sea.

Today's drifters generate more than half the earth's oxygen and 95 percent of that in the sea. Scientists use plankton fossils to study climate patterns and changes in plankton populations are used to monitor water quality.

Plankton can also be poisonous. What's known as a "red tide" is a bloom of the dinoflagellate *Alexandrium catenellum*, which is responsible for paralytic shellfish poisoning (PSP). Clams, oysters, and mussels feed on these plankton and the resulting toxic buildup in the shellfish meat can be harmful, even fatal, if eaten by humans.

WATER, WATER EVERYWHERE AND NOT A DROP TO SPARE

Deep in the drizzle of a Northwest winter, it seems ludicrous to consider a water shortage. But the drought of 2001 brought home the seriousness of this concern for many—from salmon to farmers to power companies. As our region's population continues to grow, it's time for a watershed reality check. We need to become savvier about conservation and protecting water resources.

The Cascade neighborhood north of downtown is the only one in the city with guidelines for a sustainable water supply. Interested neighbors started by exploring their watershed—the area drained by a river, lake, or stream system. Cascade lies within the boundaries of the Lake Washington Watershed sub-basin and the South Lake Union Watershed, where water falling on the northwest side of Capitol Hill drains into Lake Union.

Addressing a projected 300-percent use increase for Seattle's centralized water and sewage systems over the next twenty-five years, Cascade residents and business owners focused on alternatives. Instead of increasing the amount of water imported for use and exported for treatment, they developed a handbook with suggestions for conserving, reusing, and biologically treating water in public and private developments. The group was especially concerned about storm-water overflows that wash thousands

Cascade rain barrels collect more than 16,000 gallons of water annually, more than a quarter of that needed for the p-patch gardens.

of gallons of untreated, polluted water from city streets directly into Lake Union during heavy winter rains. In addition, they looked at the rainwater that had to be pumped to Magnolia for treatment as a wasted resource and began to research ways to collect it. Water collection systems are an easy, inexpensive way to address the problem of storm-water overflows and an overtaxed water supply in the dry summer months.

To see their ideas in action, visit the Garden of Happiness and Cascade P-Patch located on Thomas Street between Minor Avenue North and Pontius Avenue North. Forty-eight barrels lined up in a row next to the p-patch collect and store up to 2640 gallons from the roof of the building next door. Forty community gardeners use this water to supplement irrigation. The Giving Garden, located in the northwest corner of the p-patch, is where clients of human service agencies raise their own food and share the abundance with a local food bank.

Next to the p-patch is the Garden of Happiness. Here additional water from the building roof is collected and stored in a 6500-gallon tank located underneath the gazebo. Visitors can take a turn at the Garden of Happiness marine bilge pump that helps distribute water to an entire garden of salvaged, drought-tolerant native plants.

What is a p-patch? Named for the Picardo family, of Picardo Farm in Seattle's Lake City neighborhood, who made the first land available for public cultivation in 1974, a p-patch is a community garden or "passionate people producing peas in public." Seattle's network of gardens includes more than sixteen hundred plots nurtured by forty-five hundred urban gardeners in forty-four Seattle neighborhoods. If you'd like to sign up for your own garden plot or visit a p-patch in your neighborhood, call (206) 684-0264 or go to www.ci.seattle.wa.us/don/ppatch.

THE CEDAR RIVER WATERSHED: QUENCHING OUR THIRST

The next time you sip a cool glass of water, remember that you're sharing it with cougar, elk, black bear, and loons. Just east of North Bend, the Cedar River Watershed spans 90,500 acres of forest and supplies more than one hundred million gallons of water a day to more than two-thirds of King County residents and businesses. Seattle is one of only six large North American cities to use a protected wilderness as a water supply.

This watershed also protects fourteen thousand acres of old-growth forest, and is home to the largest run of sockeye salmon in the contiguous United States. To learn more about the history of the Cedar River Watershed, visit the Volunteer Park Water Tower on Capitol Hill at 1400 East Prospect, off Fifteenth Avenue East, or go to *www.cedarriver.org*. The water tower also features the Olmsted Interpretive Exhibit, an overview of the history of Seattle's park system and the Olmsted legacy. For more information about watersheds, visit the Environmental Protection Agency's "Adopt Your Watershed" website at *www.epa.gov/adopt*.

❀ 2. Danny Woo International District Community Gardens

Where:	In the International District at 620 Main Street, between Sixth Avenue South and Maynard Avenue South
Phone:	(206) 624-1802
Internet:	*www.interimicda.org/*
Hours:	6:00 A.M. to 9:00 P.M.
Disabled Access:	Via South Washington Street, call for details
Dogs:	On leash
Driving:	From I-5 south, take the James Street exit. Continue south on Sixth Avenue past Yesler Way. Turn left onto Main Street. From I-5 north, take the Stadium exit to Dearborn Street. Turn left onto Dearborn. Drive west to Sixth Avenue, turn right and drive north to Main. Turn right. There is parking on Main Street—free two-hour spaces and metered spaces.
Bus:	7, 9, 14
Special Note:	Feel free to sample ripe fruit on the trees, but please don't pick or eat anything else from the gardens unless it is offered to you

Hidden above graceful gates and archways, above a forest of fruit trees and native plants, is one of the International District's best places to stop and breathe. Hollyhocks here mimic the Smith Tower's skyward reach and bean trellises frame the stadiums.

Established in 1975 by the Interim Community Development Association (ICDA) on land donated by the Danny Woo family, the 1.5-acre island of green is the only community garden in this bustling neighborhood. The Danny Woo International District garden plots are available primarily to low-income residents of nearby apartment buildings. According to the ICDA, the neighborhood's large number of elderly residents are mostly Asian immigrants living in one-room apartments with no yards, balconies, or open spaces to grow their own food. Many of these people came from agricultural backgrounds, and their high-rise existence lacks an essential element of home. The Danny Woo Gardens fill that void. The gardens provide recreation and exercise, as well as a chance for these people to practice the farming techniques of their homelands.

Most gardeners in this p-patch are over age sixty-five and speak Mandarin, Cantonese, Korean, or Vietnamese as their first tongue. The two Chinese characters that make up the ICDA logo that appears throughout the garden mean "one" and "heart," "mind," or "spirit," an apt epigraph for a venture that brings together an international community for a common purpose. Though they may speak different languages, these people share gardening know-how, and celebrate together during garden-sponsored potlucks and community gatherings including the annual cider pressing and pig roast.

The gardeners incorporate traditional farming methods such as growing watercress in a small, flooded bed, a heavy focus on seed-saving, and the use of highly effective compost teas made of fish parts and food wastes steeped in 5-gallon buckets. They also allow plants to take care of themselves. With greens such as mustard, arugula, and lettuce, some gardeners let a few of the plants go to seed, then let the vegetables "plant" their own seeds by dropping them naturally into the bed. The gardeners then cut down the spent stalks and place them over new seedlings to protect them from birds.

In addition to apple, plum, Asian pear, and cherry trees, you can find leaf amaranth, mustards, kabocha (Japanese pumpkin), scarlet runner beans, and chrysanthemums grown for their leaves. The ubiquitous bong sun hwa, the national Korean flower, blooms bright shades of purple each summer. In Korea, its flower heads are mashed and used as fingernail polish.

As the only green space in the immediate area, this is a haven for hummingbirds, hawks, and butterflies. Wander through the rows to gain an appreciation for centuries of farming experience. Ponder the Zen-like placement of a fallen apple next to a weathered stepping-stone, then appreciate the juxtaposed views of the garden, city, Puget Sound, and Olympic Mountains.

Most Danny Woo gardeners are over 65 and speak Cantonese, Toisanese, Tagalog, Korean, Mien, Vietnamese, Laotian, Chamorro, or Spanish.

3. Suite 5600: Peregrine Penthouse

Where:	The Washington Mutual Tower downtown at Third and University
Phone:	(206) 461-6475
Internet:	www.frg.org
Hours:	Monday–Friday, 8:00 A.M. to 6:00 P.M.
Disabled Access:	Yes
Dogs:	No
Driving:	From I-5 South, take Exit 165B, Union Street. Stay straight for Union Street. From Union, turn left onto Fifth Avenue. Turn right onto Third Avenue. University is the next street. From northbound I-5, take Exit 156, Seneca Street, which is in the left lane. Take a slight left onto Seneca Street. Turn right onto Third Avenue. University is the next street. Pay parking is available in the building, off Seneca Street between Second and Third Avenues.
Bus:	2, 3, 7, 13, 14, 27, 36, 77

Seattle's only pair of nesting peregrine falcons has a dedicated and extensive fan club. Visitors surrounding a video monitor in the Washington Mutual Tower bank lobby sound as proud and anxious as parents awaiting the arrival of their first child. When the eggs hatch in May, the number of well-wishers visiting the lobby to check on the birds swells to fifty or more at a time. Hundreds more keep daily tabs by visiting "Falco-Cam" on the Falcon Research Group (FRG) website, www.frg.org.

It began in early spring 1994. FRG members noticed two falcons exhibiting nesting behavior by continually swooping near and returning to the ledges of the bank tower. Falcon experts constructed an aerie—a term used for the nests of many birds of prey—to try to encourage a bird they named Stewart and his mate to nest on the ledge the birds seemed to prefer. A comfortable nest to a peregrine is a small shelf with a sprinkling of gravel. The abrupt vertical rise of the skyscraper is an urban substitute for the rocky cliff nest sites that peregrines favor in wild environs. Peregrines are drawn to cities because they host flocks of delicious starlings, pigeons, and the occasional sparrow. Peregrines have an eclectic palate and easily adapt to available prey. Approximately ten peregrines live in and around Seattle—a fairly dense population for a land area of this size. Bremerton and Tacoma also host nesting pairs.

"Suite 5600" is an 18-by-24-inch box lined with pea gravel. The east-facing ledge provides the morning sun that falcons prefer, as well as an exceptional hunting perch. A live video monitor allows people in the bank lobby below to watch every stage of the nesting period—from egg laying to the young peregrines' first leaps into thin air.

Stewart nested the first year with a female falcon named Virginia and since 1995 with Bell. Virginia met a sadly common fate of city-dwelling falcons when she hit a window and died.

For peregrines living in the city or in wild areas, it's tough to obtain adult status. It's estimated that 50 to 90 percent die in their first year. After the young birds learn to avoid the obstacles of windows, buildings, and wires in the city, they must learn to hunt—a skill that can take up to a year to perfect. Of the eyases hatched from thirty eggs at the downtown Seattle nest from 1994 to 2002, three reached adulthood, fifteen died, and the status of twelve birds remains unknown.

Sometimes reaching speeds of more than 250 miles per hour, peregrines are the fastest animals on earth. When the falcon spots her prey, she folds her wings torpedo-tight and does a high-speed dive called a stoop. The bird then grabs her prey, uses a special tooth to break its neck, and simultaneously screeches to a halt to avoid hitting the ground. Next she points her beak skyward and heads to a nearby picnic spot or back to the young in her nest. People working in Seattle skyscrapers have reported seeing clusters

Both peregrine parents share feeding duties.

of feathers floating to the ground—likely the result of a midair peregrine kill.

Peregrines were one of the first creatures to be placed on the federal endangered species list in the 1970s, and their comeback is a pesticide-awareness success story. Like the bald eagle and other birds of prey, peregrines were gravely affected by DDT in the food chain: crops were sprayed with the pesticide to kill insects, small birds ate the insects, and peregrines ate the birds. Among other side effects, DDT ravaged falcon eggs, leaving them paper-thin and unable to hatch. Thousands of falcons died, and the species was almost entirely wiped out. In 1972, DDT was banned for use on U.S. crops. Due to their impressive recovery, peregrines were taken off the endangered species list in 1999.

It's unknown how long these birds will continue to return to the downtown Seattle nest site, but there is evidence that an aerie in Australia was used for more than eleven thousand years and others in England have been used since the 1300s.

SPOTTING FREEWAY FALCONS—FOR PASSENGERS ONLY

Some of the region's fastest roadways are predictable hangouts for peregrine falcons—so much so that bird-watching field trippers hit the highways to check off "peregrine" on their bird lists. These birds brave freeway noise for the starlings and pigeons that roost under bridges.

Next time you drive over the West Seattle Bridge, ask your passengers to be on the lookout for a peregrine that likes to perch on the electrical towers north of the bridge or on the lightpoles above the westbound car lanes. You can identify the crow-size bird by its blocky head on bottle-like shoulders, long wings, and the mature adult's distinctive blue-gray back. In flight, its wing beats are similar to that of a cormorant. Peregrines also can be seen next to the I-5 Ship Canal Bridge on the electrical towers to the west. One famous female peregrine dubbed "Freeway" made the ship canal her home every winter from 1991 to 1998. Another popular hunting perch is the high rigging of the boats in Fisherman's Terminal, visible from the Ballard Bridge. A pedestrian option is Myrtle Edwards Park—peregrines and other birds of prey haunt the grain tower where smaller birds congregate.

Another frequenter of freeways, the red-tailed hawk is slightly larger and uses similar perches, but these birds are usually seen north of the University District and south of downtown. Distinguish them by their football shape, and generally dark head, light bib (chest), and indistinct (often mottled) belly.

THE POOP ON PIGEONS

Unless you're a pigeon fancier, that is, one who races pigeons for sport, you may look askance at the masses of rock doves (*Columba livia*, a.k.a. feral pigeons) sometimes causing foot traffic jams on downtown sidewalks. Raised as barnyard animals for their meat, they accompanied European immigrants to the eastern United States during the 1600s. From there, these birds found their way throughout North America, though their introduction to Seattle is not documented. Originally from northwest Africa and the Mediterranean, rock doves typically nest on cliffsides in the wild, which explains their propensity for window ledges, bridges, and overpasses in adopted urban environs.

Band-Tailed Pigeon

Seattle is also home to a native member of the pigeon and dove family, the band-tailed pigeon (*Columba fasciata*). Preferring tall, coniferous trees in mountainous areas, this bird is commonly found in flocks. Looking like a larger, sleeker version of its urban cousin, they can be distinguished by their yellow bill and legs (rock doves have black bills with white bridges and reddish legs). The back of the band-tailed pigeon's neck is marked with a white collar, and it has a distinctive light gray "band" across its tail. They can be found in area parks, often in their preferred western hemlock trees.

Rock Dove

4. Space Needle: Cloud Viewing

Where:	400 Broad Street on Lower Queen Anne
Phone:	(206) 905-2100
Internet:	*www.spaceneedle.com*
Hours:	Sunday–Thursday, 9:00 A.M. to 11:00 P.M.; Friday and Saturday, 9:00 A.M. to midnight
Disabled Access:	Yes
Dogs:	No
Fee:	Call for current prices, which are subject to change
Driving:	From I-5 north- or southbound, take Exit 167, Mercer Street/ Seattle Center, at downtown Seattle. Follow signs to the Seattle Center. Turn right onto Fairview Avenue North and left onto Valley Street. Valley Street becomes Broad Street.
Bus:	1, 2, 3, 4, 16, or take the monorail from Westlake Center

Before dismissing the Space Needle as tourist territory, consider its prime location and panoramic views akin to those of a fire lookout on an alpine peak. Tall, built structures like these are some of the few places in the city that afford perspective on the land- and waterscapes that define this region. With good visibility, the 360-degree perimeter offers unobstructed views of Mount Rainier, Mount Baker, the Olympic, and Cascade Ranges—and all of the weather churning in between.

As the elevator ascends to the Observation Deck traveling 800 feet per minute (10 miles per hour) you are rising about as fast as a cumulus cloud—those gently billowing masses that so often punctuate the blue skies of spring. Although a trip to the top of the Needle—520 feet above the ground—is thrilling any time of year, March, April, and May offer some of the best sky viewing. During spring, the differences in temperature between the rapidly warming earth and the still wintry upper atmosphere make for some of the most interesting cloud days. The temperature differences also churn away smog, improving visibility.

Although you need decades of cloud watching to predict precipitation to the hour, a few prophetic clouds can help you decide when to pack your bumbershoot. These indicators are most accurate fall through spring.

Named for their lens-like shape, lenticular clouds can be so dramatically saucer-like that they are frequently reported as UFOs. Most often seen above Mount Rainier, they are also one of the surest signs that a cloud system is approaching from the coast. A folk saying purports that "When Mount Rainier puts on her bonnet, it's going to rain, doggone it!" A lenticular cloud is formed when the airflow that precedes a weather front sweeps in, meets "The Mountain," and is forced upward by the cold mountain air. As it reaches a certain altitude, the humidity in this air forms a cloud—it's as if a sky goddess were repeatedly opening a shower door to let the steam out. Clouds stack on top of each other as each new push of coastal air touches Rainier. Together, these tightly stacked clouds make up the noteworthy shape—look closely and you can see the individual layers. Air can be flowing inside the cloud at 35 to 45 miles per hour while the lenticular shape itself stays relatively still, like a kite tethered by the forces of the mountain.

Cirrus clouds, the thin, wispy formations that can be seen trailing tails of falling ice crystals, also herald bad weather. A storm is most likely when these clouds blow in from the south to the west/northwest and cover a large part of the horizon. On a winter day, these clouds guarantee a 70 to 80 percent chance of precipitation within twelve to twenty-four hours.

Another "watch cloud" formation is the altocumulus perlucidus. These honeycomb-like (also described as cotton balls or a tightly herded flock of sheep) clouds span the skies on pre-storm days.

The Space Needle is a good place to witness the birth of local clouds. Most commonly, clouds form when air rises and expands at higher altitudes. The rising air carries water in a gas form, or water vapor. When its temperature lowers to what is known as "dew point," the water vapor condenses, turning into liquid form. The resulting masses of water droplets form clouds that we can see. A cloud is made up of billions and billions of miniscule droplets of water, so small that they literally float on air.

A line or "street" of clouds forms almost every day in virtually the same location over and adjacent to Capitol Hill. Known as "The Capitol Hill Cloud Street," this line of cumulus or stratocumulus clouds develops when the air off Puget Sound meets the mass and heat of the city combined with the lift provided by Capitol Hill. Once started, the series trails off to the eastside of Lake Washington and sometimes extends to the Cascades. Cloud streets are common, and an interesting weather pattern to look for around the city. Cloud streets tend to disappear when larger rain clouds threaten, so the best days to view them are noticeably breezy with broken low clouds or an overcast sky of low clouds.

Also look for cumulus cloud "launching pads" near and west of Winslow on Bainbridge Island, near and west of Poulsbo, and in the vicinity of Issaquah due to the enhanced lift provided by Tiger and Cougar Mountains. With an average life span of 30 minutes or so, these common clouds are usually generated through small rising currents of warm air.

On a spring afternoon over Seattle, cloud scientists routinely measure more than 500,000,000 water droplets per cubic meter of cloud.

The Space Needle is not the only place to get a good look at clouds. Visit a friend with a skyscraper office or pack a lunch and check out the view from Victor Steinbrueck Park at Pike Place Market.

A RAIN BY ANY OTHER NAME...

As David Laskin pointed out in his book on Pacific Northwest weather, *Rains All the Time*—in fact, it doesn't. Although we do experience about 160 days annually

> November 19 is statistically Seattle's most-likely-to-be-rainy day.

with measurable rainfall, more than any other major city, our raindrops don't fall with much intensity—compare Seattle's hundredth of an inch per hour with the 1 to 3 inches commonly dumped on some southern U.S. cities. However, a maritime climate fashioned by the Pacific Ocean, Puget Sound, our latitude, and the prevailing westerly winds places our city near the top of the list for the lowest percentage of possible annual sunshine. Instead, we bask in a variety of clouds and their wet fallout.

When ice crystals form in clouds, there's a 95 percent chance it will rain. To enliven tired weather banter, University of Washington Research Meteorologist Art Rangno describes the finer points to developing a discriminating precipitation palate.

1. Drizzle. One of Rangno's pet peeves is that people wrongly use the term "drizzle." Really more a mist than rain, it's the kind of fine precipitation that can get you soaked faster than any other kind of rain. Like a wet fog, drizzle is made up of a lot of tightly packed drops that float in the air. It falls from very low, shallow, stratiform clouds. Often this name is erroneously confused with very light rain that falls from deep clouds and consists of relatively fast falling drops.

2. Steady rain, called "rain" in official observational jargon, is constant with little or gradual changes in intensity.

3. "Intermittent rain" comes and goes but with little change in intensity. Both rain and intermittent rain fall from deep and relatively homogenous clouds.

4. Showers are created by rain that comes and goes with noticeable changes in intensity, usually from minute to minute or over a few minutes. They usually fall from cumuliform clouds, which are shaped like the letter "A" with tops called "turrets." Each raindrop in such clouds usually starts as an ice crystal that collects drops inside the walls of the cloud as it falls through it. These turreted clouds are to blame when there are vast differences in rain intensity: "Look at it pouring over there!" The heaviest rain occurs just beneath the highest cumulus turret.

5. The heaviest and fastest falling ice particles are called graupel or soft hail. If you feel these, run for cover! A horde of smaller raindrops is likely to soon follow. Also, when you see graupel falling, you might be in for some lightning because it indicates that conditions are active for electrification of the cloud overhead. Graupel falls from cumulus and cumulonimbus clouds.

6. Virga is the "unrain." This is precipitation that never reaches the ground, causing wispy "tails" on rain clouds.

WATERFALLS AND NEGATIVE IONS

If you're stuck behind a desk longing for time in the mountains, one way to temporarily quench your desire is to visit Pioneer Square's Waterfall Gardens. Tucked away in a private courtyard at Second Avenue South and South Main Street, a 22-foot waterfall built to honor the site where the United States Parcel Service was founded in 1907 splashes over granite boulders to the pool at your feet. Sitting at one of the small tables next to the falls can energize even the most Monday of Mondays. If you've ever thought that there's more to that "ahhhh" experience than a waterfall's scenic beauty, an invisible electronic charge may be at work.

Falling water generates electrically charged atoms known as negative air ions, which some scientists believe stimulate the body's resistance to disease. Standing beneath the falls, you breathe in these negative ions, which then enter your bloodstream. The ions are also absorbed through the skin. Though they are not proven to cure disease, it is believed that negative ions are beneficial because they accelerate delivery of oxygen to cells. Studies have shown this "waterfall effect" to help with migraine headaches, respiratory ailments, sleep problems, and even the Northwestern bane: Seasonal Affective Disorder or SAD.

Other waterfalls in the city splash down at the REI store at 222 Yale Avenue North, Westlake Center at Fourth Avenue and Pine Street, and at Waterfront Park at Pier 57 on Alaskan Way.

❋ 5. On (and Under) the Waterfront: Myrtle Edwards and Elliott Bay Parks

Where:	The far north end of the downtown waterfront
Phone:	(206) 684-4075
Internet:	*http://ci.seattle.wa.us/parks/home.htm*
Hours:	Open 24 hours
Disabled Access:	Yes
Dogs:	On leash
Driving:	From I-5 at downtown Seattle, take Exit 167, Mercer Street/Seattle Center. Stay right at a fork in ramp. Go right on Fairview Avenue North, then left on Valley Street. Valley becomes Broad Street. Continue west to Alaskan Way. The park entrance is at Alaskan and Broad.
Bus:	Routes 1 and 24 from downtown stop less than half a mile from the park

Special Note: The bicycle path here is a major commuting route for
cyclists to and from downtown and Magnolia, Ballard,
and Seattle's north end. A separate pedestrian path in
the park is a favorite jogging route. Parking is limited,
so consider biking or hooking up with the trolley cars
that run along Alaskan Way, stopping here.

Run, walk, ride, roll, or trolley your way to this sliver of waterfront peace
beyond the bustle of downtown. With wide, paved trails and a sparkling view
of Elliott Bay, the Olympics, and West Seattle, these linked parks may seem
more like viewpoints than habitat hotbeds, but keep an open mind. Some
prime wildlife viewing opportunities are right in front of you.

First, take another look at that imposing steel structure perched on the
edge of the water. This is Port of Seattle's Terminal 86 grain elevator, a major
holding facility for exported soybeans and corn. Most of what is stored here is
not grown in Washington, but in the Midwest. What is local is the terminal's
bird life. The granary attracts hordes of rock doves (also known as pigeons),
which in turn draw peregrine falcons, their fierce local predator. The area is
within the territory of the downtown resident falcons, Stewart and Bell. They
have been known to bring their young here for hunting lessons. Visiting peregrines may try their luck here in winter. Other raptors sometimes seen at the
park include Cooper's hawks, in nearby trees, and red-tailed hawks, which
occasionally display unusual hunting strategies. Watch for a male red-tailed
hawk forgoing the usual hawk strategy of "perch and wait" for a more aggressive approach—he swoops past the grain elevator scaring pigeons into flight,
snatching up the laggards.

The other place for nature study is underwater—tough to do, however,
if you've forgotten your scuba suit. Try stopping by the Pier 86 public fishing
pier, just west of the grain terminal, to take a look at what locals are catching.
Considering the abundance of Puget Sound life, a variety of fish and crustaceans may be harvested here, but a few are seasonal standbys. Speckled ling-
cod are caught here in May and June, and late summer and fall are the seasons
for king, silver, and chum salmon. Nearly all year long, fisherfolk drop baited
ring nets into the water to bring up rock crabs. Perch come, too, attracted to
barnacles on the pier supports. Jigging, which involves tugging at a line strung
with six or so small hooks, is used to catch herring, which sometimes come to
the pier at night, drawn by the lights.

The squid is another creature drawn by nighttime lighting. If you
are here on a winter evening, you may see jiggers lined up along the
waterfront standing on stools, lines dropped down into the dark water.
They're jigging for opalescent squid, also known as California market

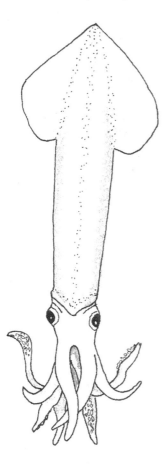

Opalescent Squid

squid (*Loligo opalescens*), which move into the Sound from the open ocean in winter. Squid are a member of the phylum Mollusca, as are clams and mussels, but are in the more rarefied class of cephalopods, a group that includes cuttlefish, the chambered nautilus, and, present in Puget Sound waters, the octopus.

Once you learn about cephalopods, it may be harder to think about catching and eating them. This remarkable group has evolved away from shells toward more sophisticated defense mechanisms. Its members are thought to be some of the ocean's most intelligent life forms. The eyes of squid and octopuses work about the same as human eyes. Both animals can jet propel away from danger by quickly expelling water from their mantles. Both can change skin color and texture for camouflage. Both squid and octopuses can contract their pigment cells to appear lighter, or expand them to darken.

Two kinds of octopuses live in Puget Sound, the giant Pacific octopus (*Octopus dofleini*) and the diminutive red octopus (*Octopus rubescens*). The giant octopus has drawn much attention from scientists for its brainy behavior—they can run mazes, open jars, and have hatched masterful escapes from aquarium holding tanks. They are also fierce predators. The Seattle Aquarium was once stumped by the death of several sharks in a large display tank stocked with several seemingly compatible species, including an octopus. Late night observations revealed the eight-armed cephalopod, with its venomous bite, as the culprit. The aquarium sponsors Octopus Week every year to celebrate this compelling creature, and also conducts annual underwater octopus surveys in Puget Sound, to further study them.

If your typical waterfront visit leaves you yearning for more extensive contact with the waterfront than gift shops and fish and chips stands can

Giant Pacific Octopus

offer, you'll also want to keep tabs on the new project breaking ground just south of here. The Seattle Art Museum is developing an Olympic Sculpture Park, set to open in 2004, on 8.5 acres of waterfront property that is some of the last open space in the area. The park beat out a plan for a condominium tower and will nearly double the size of open space on the waterfront. One of the museum's goals is to restore some of the area's ecology, with tide pools and native plantings.

Female octopuses lay their eggs in a protected lair or "den" whose opening they block with rocks. She moves in pre-fertilized with sperm that can live inside her up to one hundred days. The giant Pacific octopus lays her eggs on the roof of her den, and then strings them together with saliva, gluing them there. For the next several months she cleans them with her suckers and oxygenates them with streams of water until they hatch. She dies soon after.

The Forest and the Trees: FROM THE ARBORETUM TO THE CENTRAL DISTRICT

This chapter encompasses one of the most socioeconomically varied slices of Seattle—from Capitol Hill's imposing mansions along the ridges above Lake Washington to the Central District's mix of low-income housing and gentrified rebuilds. Diversity is the underlying theme from a naturalist's perspective as well. From the Washington Park Arboretum collection—featuring trees and plants from all over the world—to native habitat restoration efforts in several area parks, forests and trees are a natural focus. These areas do more than harbor human sanity, they are safe enclaves for numerous bird species, and homes for animals including bats, mountain beavers, and salamanders, to name a few.

More than any other area of the city, the Olmsted Brothers landscape architecture firm's legacy of preserving our city's natural beauty is evident here. For a walking tour of what could be considered Seattle's lungs, start at Volunteer Park on Capitol Hill—for an overview, visit the Olmsted Interpretive Exhibit at the top of the park's water tower. From the park, continue to Interlaken Boulevard and the Washington Park Arboretum. By bike, take a tree-lined pedal for miles south along Lake Washington Boulevard and through a chain of parks: Lake View, Denny Blaine, Madrona, Leschi (which connects to Frink), Colman, Mount Baker, and Seward.

Capitol Hill residents of the early 1900s caught "green fever"—evident today in the number of large trees looming in yards and overhanging streets. This is said to be the Seattle neighborhood with the richest diversity of trees.

From tiny Nora's Woods to the larger expanses of Interlaken and Frink Parks, this chapter navigates diverse wooded habitats. The tour features the green-filtered respite that is Frink Park. Just two blocks east of the Central District, this unexpected city forest spills down a dramatic hillside above Lake

The common snowberry is easy to spot in winter when its clustered, white berries are brightly visible against a leafless backdrop.

Washington. Trees figure prominently in each of three destinations: Interlaken Park—a neglected greenway recently infused with volunteer energy to preserve notable older trees while nurturing a new generation of conifers; Nora's Woods—formerly a Central District abandoned lot revitalized by native plants; and the Winter Garden—a visual and aromatic cure for the gray-sky blues set within a gardener's dream, the rambling Washington Park Arboretum.

6. Frink Park: Woodland Revival

Where:	Between the Central District and Leschi neighborhoods at South Jackson Street and Thirty-first Avenue South
Tour distance:	0.75 mile loop
Phone:	(206) 684-4075
Internet:	*http://depts.washington.edu/wpac/*
Hours:	4:00 A.M. to 11:30 P.M.
Disabled Access:	No
Dogs:	On leash
Driving:	From downtown Seattle, take Yesler Way east to Martin Luther King Jr. Way South. Turn right and continue to South Jackson Street. Take a left, and follow South Jackson to Thirty-first Avenue South. You will see the Frink Park kiosk at the intersection of South Jackson and Thirty-first Avenue South. Park and enter the park via the trail to the left of the kiosk.
Bus:	14
Special Note:	You can extend this tour by continuing on foot from Frink Park to Leschi Park and on to Lake Washington

"What has 3600 feet and weighs 169 tons?" asks a riddle on the bulletin board at the Frink Park kiosk. The answer is the reconstructed Big Loop Trail—the route for this tour. The tonnage refers to the mountains of gravel and other materials used to widen and improve a trail that was once close to impassable. Although visitors don't come here to see gravel, the riddle is testimony to an amazing volunteer effort that provides inspiration for others and begs the question, "What's happening in my own neighborhood park?"

Located between the Central District and Leschi neighborhoods, Frink's nearly 17-acre urban forest is the closest woodland to Seattle's downtown. You can get here by bus in just a few minutes from Westlake Center. Because the park was inaccessible and overgrown for many years, its steep, slippery

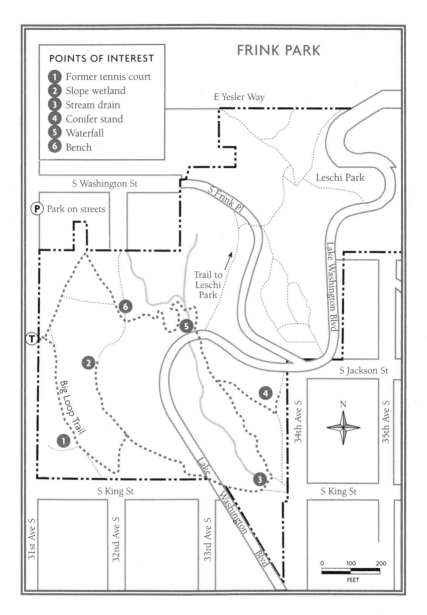

FRINK PARK

POINTS OF INTEREST

1 Former tennis court
2 Slope wetland
3 Stream drain
4 Conifer stand
5 Waterfall
6 Bench

E Yesler Way

Leschi Park

S Washington St

S Frink Pl

P Park on streets

Trail to Leschi Park

Lake Washington Blvd

6

T

5

2

S Jackson St

4

34th Ave S

N

35th Ave S

Big Loop Trail

1

3

S King St

S King St

31st Ave S

32nd Ave S

33rd Ave S

Lake Washington Blvd

0   100   200
FEET

trails only attracted the truly intrepid. A volunteer group called Friends of Frink Park wanted to reclaim this neighborhood resource, and hired an environmental consulting firm to guide them in restoring the area's natural features. Volunteers from all over the city have joined forces with the Parks Department to rehabilitate the neglected woods and recreate an urban retreat.

You'll see their handiwork on your trip. Highlights include a hillside wetland, rhododendron glen, conifer stand, and waterfall.

The area in and around the park has one of the most culturally appealing histories in the city. If hillsides could talk, these slopes would have yarns to knit a thousand nights of stories. Frink connects with Leschi Park to the northeast—which extends down to Lake Washington. Native Americans once camped along the lakeshore there and portaged canoes through a ravine to the north to reach Elliott Bay. Pioneers used this same well-worn path to haul coal and other supplies barged from across Lake Washington to their homesteads in a nascent Seattle.

In the late 1800s, a cable car trestle teetered over these treetops to transport revelers to and from a casino, dance pavilion, zoo, and other attractions at Leschi. John Frink, owner of Washington Iron Works, was a member of the Board of Park Commissioners. In 1906 he purchased and donated the parkland to the city. Landscape designer John Charles Olmsted visited the park that same year, noting he was "pleased with the romantic and secluded ravine." Along with several other Lake Washington area parks, Frink was considered a gem on the "Emerald Necklace"—the Olmsted Brothers landscape architecture firm's plan for a string of Seattle parks connected by a road system, including Lake Washington Boulevard. Over the next several years, the Olmsted Brothers developed plans for the parks, and city commissioners pushed to have them in place for visitors to the Alaskan-Yukon-Pacific-Exposition, the 1909 World's Fair held in Seattle. In the ensuing years, Frink was left to the whims of invasive plants such as ivy, holly, and laurel, and slowly devolved into a somewhat scary garbage dump.

Standing at the trailhead at Thirty-first and Jackson on what's known as Mount Baker Ridge, one of the park's most dramatic wintertime views is visible between bare branches to nearby Lake Washington and Mount Rainier beyond. A deciduous forest of mainly bigleaf maple cascades down a steep embankment created by pre-pioneer landslides that carved a bowl shape out of the hill. As you descend the steps into the park, turn right and walk along the inside of the bowl. Landslides are common on Seattle hillsides, where the underlying geology causes water to collect underground, making it unstable for building. This situation caused landslides in the 1990s on Capitol Hill's west slope above I-5 and above Perkins Lane in Magnolia. Similarly, in 1898 a major mudslide in the Rainier Heights area just south of Frink Park destroyed sixteen houses and a sawmill. Many of Seattle's parklands are situated on or include such unstable slopes, including Fauntleroy, parts of the Duwamish Greenbelt, Discovery, and Carkeek, to name a few.

Continue along the trail to a noticeably flat grassy area with a picnic table (1). This horizontal expanse was once a clay tennis court, where dandies of the early 1900s played sets before visiting Leschi's blithe offerings along the Lake Washington shore below. The cable car, which once ran from the lake up to Jackson Street, saved visitors' knees from a precipitous hike. Volunteers replanted the area around the former court with native plants, such as red flowering currant and kinnikinnick. This trailing evergreen shrub's tongue-twisting name comes from a word that means, "item for mixing in" in the Unami language (a Delaware Native American tribe). Many coastal native groups used its dried leaves for tobacco.

Walk down the stairs to the left. Continue until you come to a side-trail on the left. This spur takes you to one of the most secluded places in the park—one of Frink's nine wetlands. As you pass an old log sprouting white polypores (wood-decaying fungi), you begin to feel a distinct cooling in the air, especially notable in summer, which indicates you're nearing water. The largest wetland in the park, this is a slope wetland (2) adorned with water-loving giant horsetail, Sitka willows, small-fruited bulrush, and ladyfern, whose fiddleheads were enjoyed by Native peoples in early spring. Shallow groundwater, mostly from rainfall and possibly from underground springs, moves under the surface of the soil until it finds an opening—a permeable layer where it can move to the surface, seep out, and flow down the hill to join the creek below. Don't look for a gushing waterfall; this process involves the slow

Steller's jays are mimics and can clear a place at a bird feeder with their convincing red-tailed hawk imitations.

trickling of water as it negotiates a path through soil particles to the surface. Looking up the hill, it's obvious where the wetland begins, just below the maple trees that indicate drier soil.

If you see piles of dead vegetation here and there, it's not because someone forgot to cart it off. Volunteers have begun "spot composting" ivy to save the cost of transporting this material away from the park and to add nutrients to the soil.

Retrace your steps to the main trail and continue downhill to the left. This section of trail is lush in summer with thimbleberries, ocean spray, and hazelnuts. If you hear a woodpecker-like knocking, it could be a brilliantly blue Steller's jay pounding open a hazelnut. Jays are corvids, a family that includes crows and ravens—the Mensa members of the bird world. Corvids have learned to hold a nut with their feet while pounding with the tip of their lower bill to open it. Discarded shells along the trail are evidence of this behavior.

Although casual observers report an increase in songbirds since the rehabilitation efforts, no formal list has been compiled for the park. Based on other area bird sightings, species likely to visit Frink include raptors such as sharp-shinned and Cooper's hawks, which hunt birds and rodents. Woodland species likely to be found here include olive-sided flycatchers, bushtits (small, fluffy, teddy bear-like birds that travel in flocks), northern flickers, and golden-crowned kinglets.

You soon arrive at Lake Washington Boulevard. In spring and summer, this green-canopied curving roadway is beloved of bicyclists, so watch for bikes and cars as you cross the road. The trail continues on the other side and will soon come to a stream flowing unceremoniously into a drain (3). From here it is piped 1000 feet to Lake Washington. Plans for stream channel restoration above this point are part of the Frink recovery plan, but more pressing matters such as developing the trail and rescuing ivy-choked trees have taken precedence.

Continue along this trail to a concrete stairway and take a left at the top. This is a popular place in April when the rhododendrons forming a natural arbor above your head bloom in shades of pink and white. Listen for the stream burbling below, even in the heat of summer. The native rhodies were part of the Olmsted planting plan. A healthy undergrowth of salal lines the pathway to the left, while encroaching ivy laps at the trail's heels to the right. In many places throughout the park, a small pathway separates native undergrowth from the ivy threat. As part of their ivy eradication strategy, volunteers use trails as "firebreaks" to keep invasives at bay until they can get to the next area. The results provide a good "before and after" display for visitors.

IVY: THE GREEN MENACE

Area organizations including EarthCorps and the Washington Native Plant Society are instigating ripping and tearing parties all over the city—ripping up and tearing off ivy, that is. Ivy OUT stands for Ivy Off Urban Trees—an ongoing volunteer campaign to reclaim native habitats.

This nonnative plant can create "ivy deserts" where no other vegetation can survive. It weighs down trees, making them more susceptible to disease and wind, and can reduce the tree's nutrient flow. English ivy does not provide significant food for native wildlife, but does provide rat habitat. It's high time we started intercepting this woody climbing vine because it now covers 70 percent of Seattle's four thousand forested park acres!

If you're familiar with the tenacity of this particular plant, these numbers might prophesize a Sisyphean task, but have heart (and work gloves), ivy can be overpowered. The Fairweather Nature Preserve in Medina just east of the Highway 520 bridge is a good case in point. In the year 2000, the preserve was covered with invasives and in poor health, but EarthCorps volunteers worked with neighbors and the City of Medina to remove almost all of the ivy in this thirteen-acre woodland. The key to sustaining a state of "ivylessness" is in follow-up visits. There is usually 10 percent regrowth the second year, which must be removed. After this, in many cases, the ivy is nearly gone by the third year. Continued checkups are recommended to keep new plants from becoming established.

The Ivy OUT website at *http://ivyout.org* offers details about how to remove ivy, volunteer opportunities, and a list of native plant alternatives to English ivy.

Although it can look innocuous and even pretty, English ivy—which can grow as thick as your arm—is eventually deadly for trees.

As you continue under the arching branches, you'll come to a smaller path on the right. Take this trail under more rhododendrons until you come to a stand of Douglas fir and Western red cedar (4), the only conifer grove in the park. You can't miss a huge madrone that is unfortunately infected with a fungus, the plight of many area trees of this species. Volunteers planted the young cedars, while the native undergrowth of Oregon grape, snowberry, and salal has thrived since it was freed of its ivy net.

Retrace your steps back to the Big Loop Trail and turn right. You will come to a stairway that leads to another Lake Washington Boulevard crossing. Across the road is the aesthetic heart of Frink Park, a 5-foot waterfall designed by the Olmsted Brothers (5). One of the few stream-fed falls in the city (another is just north in Madrona Woods), the water comes from underground springs in the surrounding hillside. The concrete bridge over the creek was also part of the original Olmsted boulevard plan.

Stand under the glorious old-growth cedar tree just west of the waterfall and look across the water to the healthy bank of sword fern on a hill topped by towering madrones. The trees are especially beautiful at sunset when their branches light up golden-red. Volunteers are working to clear invasives from the stream and replace them with native plants.

Continue up the trail where a bench (6) offers a place to catch your breath and listen for birdsong such as the rising "gueeee" of the spotted towhee. More often heard than seen, this bird scratches noisily in the underbrush. You might also hear the tap-tapping of a foraging downy woodpecker, a sparrow-size, black and white bird (the male has a red patch at the back of the head).

A trail heading to the left provides another entrance to the slope wetland discussed in the first part of the tour. To finish the loop, continue up the hill to where you began your walk.

Volunteers with the Friends of Frink Park are restoring the wetlands around this small waterfall.

PARKS FOR THE PEOPLE: THE OLMSTED LEGACY

" . . . In designing a system of parks and parkways the primary aim should be to secure and preserve for the use of the people as much as possible of these advantages of water and mountain views and of woodlands, well distributed and conveniently located."
—*Olmsted Brothers 1903 Report to the Seattle Board of Park Commissioners*

You could say Seattle spun its "emerald" moniker from gold. In 1903, with gold-rush riches burning in their pockets, Seattle city leaders made an investment that would pay out in green dividends for decades to come. They hired the Olmsted Brothers landscape architecture firm of Brookline, Massachusetts, to blueprint the city's parks, boulevards, and playgrounds.

Frederick Law Olmsted Sr. was famous for his impact on urban areas from New York City's Central Park to the Stanford University campus. Known as the father of landscape architecture in this country, Olmsted strongly believed that all people should share in the natural wealth of their cities. He was a visionary of preservation, mapping breathing spaces into urban landscapes long before they were crucial islands of green. His "parks for the people" message was championed in Seattle by his nephew and stepson, John Charles Olmsted. The younger Olmsted traveled the city by streetcar, boat, carriage, and foot. "I do not know of any place where the natural advantages for parks are better than here," remarked John Olmsted. "They...will be, in time, one of the things that will make Seattle known all over the world."

In 1903, the Seattle City Council approved John Charles Olmsted's plan, called "A Comprehensive System of Parks and Parkways," which laid out a 20-mile stretch of parks and boulevards running from Seward Park along Lake Washington and across the city via Woodland Park to Discovery Park. By 1937, the Olmsted Brothers had designed thirty-seven parks and playgrounds, setting Seattle as a city apart for its commitment to green space. The Olmsted legacy includes Colman, Frink, Green Lake, Interlaken, Jefferson, Mount Baker, Seward, Volunteer, Washington, and Woodland Parks, as well as Washington Arboretum, Broadway Playfield, Hiawatha Playground, and Queen Anne, Lake Washington, Magnolia, and Ravenna Boulevards. Capitol Hill's Volunteer Park Water Tower features an interpretive exhibit on the history of the Seattle park system and the Olmsted vision.

7. Washington Park Arboretum Winter Garden: Green Therapy for Seasonal Blues

Where:	2300 Arboretum Drive East in Montlake
Phone:	(206) 543-8800
Internet:	*http://depts.washington.edu/wpa/*
Hours:	Park, 7:00 A.M. to dusk; visitors center, 10:00 A.M. to 4:00 P.M.
Disabled Access:	Yes
Dogs:	On leash
Driving:	From downtown Seattle, take I-5 north. Take one of the first exits you come to, Exit 168B, Bellevue-Kirkland, onto Highway 520. Go approximately 1 mile to the first exit, Montlake Boulevard, and go straight at the light onto Lake Washington Boulevard East. Follow it into the arboretum.
Bus:	11, 43, 48

The Joseph A. Witt Winter Garden at the Washington Park Arboretum is a good place to lose the post-holiday grayness of January, free therapy for the winter blahs that vex even the sturdiest of Northwesterners. Here, protected by an amphitheater of native conifers, the garden provides a sensual concerto. Towering relatives of Oregon grape, Mahonia, known as "Arthur Menzies," spout tropical-looking sprays of yellow flowers. And a veil of Chinese witch hazel (*Hamamelis*) embraces the visitor with branches so golden they could be confused with stray arches of sunlight. These are two of the showiest of this garden's offerings, which has more than one hundred species to help awaken your inner landscape.

Arboretum gardeners who work among the blossoms report an inexplicable sense of well-being, a feeling of being refreshed. The strong scents of the flowers attract more than just human noses. Anna's hummingbirds dart among the florets, sipping nectar, or chatter from high perches standing out in dramatic relief against the white winter sky. Townsend's warblers, the males with arresting black masks over brilliant yellow faces, are also drawn to the abundant blooms.

Witch Hazel

The winter garden has been a feature of the arboretum since 1949. As you meander the garden pathways, sniff for the following standouts.

The tiny flowers of sweet box (*Sarcococca confusa*) belie its powerhouse scent. It overwhelms some people who describe it like being "trapped in an elevator with too much perfume." Others find its deep, powdery, great-grandmotherly aroma appealing. Its dark purple fruit is another winter surprise.

Viburnum (*Viburnum* x *bodnantense*) is a shrub that has earned tree status here where its branches offer pink clusters like tiny bouquets with a subtly spicy smell.

A plant lover's paradise, the Washington Park Arboretum's 230 lush acres have something for everyone, from the Japanese Garden to waterfront trails and classes for children and adults. The internationally known, labeled collections comprise a living plant museum featuring plants and trees hardy in the maritime northwest. For a trail map or details about what's in bloom each season, visit *depts.washington.edu/wpa/ general.htm*, or call the Graham Visitors Center at (206) 543-8800.

Winter-blooming honeysuckle (*Lonicera fragrantissima*) is a partially evergreen shrub whose creamy white flowers have a deep, tangy scent that makes you want to drink it.

A relative of witch hazel, *Chimonanthus praecox* smells deeply tropical, reminiscent of flowers you'd expect to find in a Hawaiian lei.

Several types of witch hazel with blossoms ranging from golden yellow to red-orange in color offer a variety of scents. The garden's signature yellow blooming trees have a fresh, sugary smell with a piquant "aftertaste." Although the plants mentioned here are cold-hardy, witch hazel is the only one that actually closes up its spidery blossoms to prevent them from freezing. (Rhododendrons display this kind of defensive technique by curling their leaves into near scrolls in very cold weather.)

What allows these plants to bloom when many green things are still sleeping is phototropism—the plant's growth in response to changes in available daylight. Each species has its own "biological clock" that triggers the blooming process when the sun offers the prescribed amount of light.

It's more than blossoms that make this garden a visual sensation in a season when many people forget to look at plants. Here you can appreciate subtler attributes of the flora—berries, bark, leaf patterns—when the garden is not as busy

Visit the Seattle Japanese Garden for Children's Day in May or August under the light of the moon for the bi-annual Tsukimi (moon-viewing ceremony), which includes music and dance performances. The Japanese Garden is located in Washington Park Arboretum. For more information on events sponsored by the Japanese Garden Society, call (206) 684-4725.

with color, or completely covered in foliage. This is a garden planted in careful contrast. Layers of texture are created by the raining blooms of the silk tassel, peeling layers of the paperbark maple, and the scribbly branches of the contorted hazelnut.

HUMMINGBIRD MAGIC

When you catch sight of the brilliant fiery red head of a male Anna's hummingbird, you understand why the Maya thought these iridescent colors where a gift of the sun. Many hummingbirds have special, light-reflecting, iridescent feather tips that produce a flash of intense color when viewed from a certain angle. However, hummingbirds are more often heard than seen, jetting by at up to sixty miles per hour, their namesake humming wings pumping an average sixty times per second. Experts at hovering, these avian helicopters are equipped with the unusual ability to move their wings in a figure-eight pattern, allowing them to fly in every direction, including backward and upside-down. Even their nests are magical. Usually well hidden and no larger than a plum, they are woven together with spider's webs, caterpillar silk, and the softest mosses and lichens.

Before 1964, Seattle didn't have any resident hummingbirds. But the Anna's now lives here full time, a shift many attribute to the increase in home hummingbird feeders. Those who feed these birds soon learn that a year-round hummingbird feeder is more responsibility than sport: once a wintering Anna's has established its food source, the bird depends on it.

Just 4 inches long, Anna's are greenish with dark wings. The male has the iridescent head and neck, which looks black when not flashing red. The female has a small red throat patch. In winter and early spring, the males can be seen at the Arboretum Winter Garden fiercely defending

Hummingbird Nest

their territories with fantastic aerial dives that end with a sharp chirp. Although known mostly as nectar lovers, more than half of a hummingbird's diet consists of spiders and insects like aphids, gnats, flies, and mosquitoes. A

If you're lucky and near a pond in the spring, you may see a hummingbird female gathering the seed fluff from last year's cattails for her nest.

hummingbird is "hawking" when it eyes a swarm of insects from a perch, then repeatedly flies out to catch them one by one.

Slightly smaller than the Anna's, the only other regular Seattle hummer is the visiting rufous. It winters in the southern states and northern Mexico and returns to the Northwest in spring seeking the energy-rich nectar of its preferred bright pink, orange, or red flowers such as salmonberry and red-flowering currant. The male rufous is rust-colored with a bright-red throat patch called a gorget, and the female is greenish with rust at the base of her tail and a few iridescent red sprinkles on her throat.

✳ 8. Nora's Woods: Hushed Tribute

Where:	Twenty-ninth Avenue and East Columbia Street in the Central District
Phone:	(206) 684-4075
Internet:	NA
Hours:	24 hours
Disabled Access:	Yes, on two main trails
Dogs:	On leash
Driving:	From downtown, take James Street heading east. James becomes East Cherry Street. Travel 1 mile to Twenty-ninth Avenue and turn left. The park is at the end of the block on your right.
Bus:	3

Perhaps it's the concentration of so many healthy plants oxygenating the pathways, or the fact that founder Nora Wood's ashes are buried here. Or maybe it's an ethereal consequence of thousands of hours of work from many caring volunteers. Whatever the reason, this city corner makes a fine place to clear one's head.

One neighbor says, "There's a feeling of sanctuary here. Even though it's tiny, you feel as if you're moving into a very sacred place, which is magical in the midst of a dense urban neighborhood."

Nora's Woods has come a long way since 1996, when this once neglected trash dump and drug-use area was adopted by neighbors and transformed into a forested garden tribute to our city's green heritage. Hundreds of plants native to the Northwest now grace this varied slope that encompasses a surprising variety of habitats: remnant orchard, fern gully, lowland forest, and meadow. This one-third acre became a Seattle City Park in 1998.

The transformation has created a new home for bird life. Twice a year during migration, a sharp-shinned hawk makes the park a stopover for one to two weeks. Once observed bathing in a neighbor's pond, the hawk is drawn to the healthy supply of local rock doves. Other regular winged visitors include yellow and yellow-rumped warblers, black-capped and chestnut-backed chickadees, bushtits, kinglets, flickers, and downy woodpeckers.

To create a native-species park, volunteers salvaged much of the vegetation seen here from Eastside forests-turned-building sites. Plaques identify the plants in both English and Native American names:

Deer Fern
R'r'ts'bak'kuk (Makah)
Strawberry
T'e'lzq (Puyallup-Nisqually)
Rhododendron
Xawxu'ped (Skokomish)

Local legend recalls that Cherry and Leschi Streets lie over a tribal trail system that native peoples used to move between Puget Sound and Lake Washington. It's remembered that Twenty-ninth Street was a stream, and if that is so, these woods could have been a resting point along the way. A bronze sculpture by Tom Jay called *Homecoming* at the park entrance depicts coho salmon returning to spawning grounds, which years ago quite likely occurred in the near vicinity. Neighbors say it evokes the phantom stream that once ran through the neighborhood.

Nora Wood was a long-time Madrona resident, community activist, and leader. In 1987, along with her husband, Fran, Nora bought this site, one of the last pieces of open space in the neighborhood. Wood loved nature and was a voice of peace known for bringing people together during civil rights clashes of the 1950s. She would have been proud of the fact that her legacy lives on through this park, where neighbors continually come together to care for something greater than themselves.

Practice plant identification at Nora's Woods where hundreds of Northwest natives are packed into a tiny, but abundant, lot.

9. Interlaken Park: Making Natural History

Where: North Capitol Hill at the intersection of East Galer
        Street and Nineteenth Avenue East
Phone: (206) 684-4075
Internet: *www.cityofseattle.net/parks/parkspaces/interlak.htm*
Hours: 4:00 A.M. to 11:30 P.M.
Disabled Access: Yes. For wheelchair access to part of this trail, turn
        right off of Twenty-fourth Avenue East onto East
        Interlaken Boulevard. Park at the turnaround at the
        base of Twenty-first Avenue East. Enter the paved
        boulevard near the park kiosk. The road intersects the
        walking trail at the base of the ravine.
Dogs: On leash
Driving: From downtown Seattle, take I-5 north. Take one of the
        first exits you come to, 168B, Bellevue-Kirkland, onto
        Highway 520. Go approximately 1 mile to the first exit,
        Montlake Boulevard, and turn right at the light onto
        Twenty-fourth Avenue East. Go approximately three-
        quarters of a mile to East Crescent Drive. Turn right
        and continue to East Galer Street and Nineteenth
        Avenue East. The park is on your right. Park on the
        street and enter the park near the kiosk.
Bus: 12

A shining jewel on the Olmsted Brothers's "Emerald Necklace"—a vision of connected urban retreats—is Interlaken Park. This stretch of steep, forested land at the north end of Capitol Hill offers a chance for a shady stroll or bike ride, to commune with the state's tallest redwood tree, discover pocket gopher mounds, or tune your birder's ear to the fluting songs of thrushes. A visit to Interlaken provides a unique blend of a historic walk back in time (in the late 1890s, this park was the main bike and buggy route linking Capitol Hill with Lake Washington), with history in the making—the restoration of an urban forest ecosystem.

At first glance, the mature trees here seem to indicate a healthy forest. But "mature" is the key word, and before reforestation efforts began in 1997, the lack of younger trees meant that Interlaken was a forest in decline. After the park was logged of most of its conifers in the last half of the nineteenth century, deciduous trees like bigleaf maple, alder, and cottonwood grew in their place, none of which can reproduce in its own shade. Many of these trees are nearing the end of their lifespan. The Friends of Interlaken Park, a community group formed in 1994, is working to steward the park's urban forest. Through a Forest Restoration and Public Education Plan and a series of restoration projects, they are helping ensure an enduring refuge for the next generation.

There are many ways to enter the park, but the kiosk at Nineteenth and Galer is a good place to get oriented. Take the easternmost pathway and head down wood steps built into a steep hill and former log skid. This area was once choked with "Tarzan vines" from invasive, nonnative clematis that were painstakingly removed to reveal a more natural forestscape. As you descend into the ravine, you may begin to hear the faint gurgle of the stream while city noises fade

Fringecup is named for its frilly edged petals. In woodland lore this plant was used by elves to help them see in the dark.

into the background. This area has been replanted with Douglas fir and Western red cedars as well as understory plants such as salmonberry, deer fern, and snowberry. Healthy native undergrowth makes it harder for invasive nonnatives to return.

Part of the restoration process involves compromise. Invasive English ivy is the bane of anyone who has been involved in "forest rescue." It damages trees by competing for nutrients and moisture from the soil, adds weight that makes its hosts susceptible to falling, and interferes with a tree's ability to perform photosynthesis. Although volunteers are removing ivy from trees around the park, they opted to leave it on the eastern slope of this ravine for now because its persistent vines help prevent hillside surface erosion.

Because human impact is irrevocable and ongoing, urban habitat becomes a bit like a garden; it needs to be planted and pruned, watered and coddled. Though wilder than a backyard, it doesn't benefit from miles of wilderness buffer like a mountain trail. The Friends of Interlaken have learned that all green is not good, and through a careful selection process, chose sixty-two trees for removal. In order to improve the diversity of the

Bewick's Wren

forest ecosystem, light needed to be let in to dark areas for trees such as Douglas fir to grow. Some trees, like the black cottonwood, which has a propensity to drop limbs, were considered dangerous to people. Native bigleaf maple and alder are the James Deans of the forest, living fast and dying young—so some were taken out to allow longer-lived trees a "roothold." Also on the cut list are imported Norway maple—a lovely but invasive tree that crowds out natives—and the common English laurel, which forms colonies and, unpruned, grows to gargantuan proportions.

At the base of the ravine is a paved boulevard that carried buttoned-up, early twentieth-century bicyclists to a teahouse that provided drinks and snacks for Sunday riders on the way to Lake Washington. Walking left, you soon notice the distinctive red bark and massive trunks of coast redwoods. Standing like sentinels of another era, these were likely planted as part of the Olmsted plan. One of these giants is the tallest of its kind in Washington. Nearby are several old-growth cedars, which were deemed not perfect enough or too small to be logged in the 1800s.

The coffee in your cup could save a bird. In the mid-elevations of Mexico, Central America, the Caribbean, and Colombia, most of the forests still standing are in traditional coffee plantations, which provide the last refuge for birds such as swallows, warblers, and humming-birds that have lost habitat due to the destruction of tropical forests. Shade-loving coffee is a shrub that flourishes under the canopy of larger trees. By purchasing "shade-grown" coffee, you support traditional growing methods that provide long-term environmental benefits. Scientists and birdwatchers have noticed a marked decline in migratory bird populations over the last twenty-five years. Buying "coffee with a conscience" could help reverse this trend.

Interlaken's sixty-two acres form a habitat corridor with the Arboretum and mature trees throughout the Capitol Hill neighborhood, acting as a rest stop for migratory birds on their way south or north. More than one hundred species of birds have been recorded here. In February, males flock to the park in search of nest sites. Birds raising young here include the band-tailed pigeon, downy woodpecker, northern flicker, and pileated woodpecker, as well as several species of warblers and wrens. Area birders report a notable increase in bird activity since the boulevard was closed to vehicle traffic after a landslide in 1986. For the best viewing, pull up a folding chair and sit quietly along the boulevard—and bring a blanket because some of the best birding is in the chilly months of February, March, and April.

As you continue down the road, to your left you will see a stairway heading uphill. This steep trail continues past thriving undergrowth of Oregon grape and sword fern (look for grub-foraging wrens here), through the second restoration area. Along the way, you may pass the distinctive mounds of the Western pocket gopher. These mounds are about the size of molehills with small indentations near their tops, making them look somewhat like miniature volcanoes. Their resident gophers are difficult to spot, however, living mostly underground like the mountain beaver, which also makes its home here. There are more than twenty mammals living in or visiting the park, including the long-eared bat, Trowbridge's shrew, and the Pacific jumping mouse.

Pocket Gopher

Continue on to the upper portion of the restoration area, chosen for its high-profile location and suitability to public education. You have now walked a loop and are near the Galer Street kiosk. Work here focuses on improving the transition from park entrance to forest and establishing a native plant community. These efforts would surely please John Charles Olmsted, who a hundred years ago urged great care in planting choices "to harmonize…with the existing growths," with a goal of keeping Interlaken as natural as possible.

CAPITOL HILL: WHERE THE TREES ARE

No Seattle neighborhood has a richer diversity of trees than Capitol Hill. Arthur Lee Jacobson, noted tree expert and author of *Trees of Seattle* explains why:

Timing. Capitol Hill was not a pioneer neighborhood of the sort that was planted largely with fruit and nut trees, as were Georgetown and South Park. Instead, it was planted right around the time Seattle had an economic boom and financial largess. A planting boom coincided with civic pride in street trees due to the influence of the Olmsted Brothers landscape architecture firm. Thus the neighborhood has numerous old, ornamental trees and has benefited from decades of subsequent enrichment.

Location. Capitol Hill is not as westward and thus as dry as Queen Anne, Beacon, and First Hills. It gets slightly more rainfall. It's also close to the Washington Park Arboretum and the University of Washington, which afford ready access to inspiration and information about trees.

Soil. The soil is less sandy and more water-retentive than that of other Seattle hills, such as Phinney Ridge, Magnolia, and West Seattle. Trees grow bigger here thanks to slightly more rain and better soil conditions.

Space. The lots and planting strips tend to be generously sized, providing ample room for tree growth.

Money. The neighborhood has always been relatively well off, with plentiful funds to buy and maintain trees.

In addition to a wonderful blend of planted and wild trees in Interlaken and Boren Parks, Capitol Hill has a stellar collection of planted trees in Volunteer Park and Lake View Cemetery. The cemetery trees are labeled, making it a great place to learn about trees. Here are a few "don't miss" Capitol Hill trees:

Historic trees. At Louisa Boren Viewpoint, near Fifteenth Avenue East and East Garfield Street, are three English oaks, which grew at Denny Hill's Denny Park before the hill was leveled.

Old trees. Along with the rest of Seattle, Capitol Hill was clear-cut, so a few Western red cedars in Interlaken Park are the only trees alive here today that began their life before Seattle was founded.

Rare trees. With so little "competition," uncommon trees are often of record size partly by default. Practically the only Chinese sweet gum known in Seattle other than at the arboretum, is a street tree on the west side of Twelfth Avenue East between Boston and Lynn Streets. Growing under wires, it is periodically decapitated. Nearby, on the east side of Federal Avenue East just north of Newton Street, is Seattle's only big, old shellbark hickory. With more than 170 tree species, Volunteer Park is full of rare trees. A Japanese flowering cherry named Mikuruma-gaeshi growing north of the bandstand is the only specimen known in Seattle. Its name means "the royal carriage returns," to allow Japan's emperor a second look at its lovely pink flowers.

You can nominate your favorite tree for special recognition through the City of Seattle and Plant Amnesty Heritage Tree Program. Trees are selected based on criteria such as age, size, type, historical association, or horticultural value—a few trees are designated each year. For a nomination form, call (206) 783-9813 or (206) 684-7649. For details about Seattle's Heritage Trees including their locations, visit www.cityofseattle.net/td/heritage.asp.

Big trees. Interlaken Park boasts three of the tallest trees of their species in the city: Mazzard cherry, red maple, and coast redwood, while the adjacent Louisa Boren Park has Seattle's tallest deciduous tree, a black cottonwood. Beyond species that are the biggest in Seattle, there are some Capitol Hill trees of greater renown: Earth's tallest hawthorn of any species anywhere is 67 feet tall in Volunteer Park. Doubtless it dates from the Olmsted era. The largest Chinese scholar tree in the Pacific Northwest grows in the northwest corner of the Broadway Reservoir at Nagle Place and East Denny Way. A locust relative, it bears creamy-yellow blossoms in July or August. On Fourteenth Avenue East, just north of Roy Street, is a unique planting of street trees: in grid fashion are three sweet gums with one tupelo. Tupelo, also called black gum or pepperidge, is the best shade tree for dazzling red fall color. More than 60 feet tall, this specimen is Washington's largest.

Landmark trees. These are the trees that may not be large, old, historic, or rare, but are conspicuous and well loved. A good example is the towering tulip tree at Sixteenth Avenue East and East Aloha Street, where the street, curb, and sidewalk were realigned to accommodate the tree's immense size. Another is the hybrid plane/sycamore in the triangle at Belmont Avenue East and Bellevue Place East, and the American elms on Harvard Avenue East north of East Aloha Street.

RESUSCITATING LAKE WASHINGTON

It wouldn't be Seattle without the 22-mile-long reflecting pool lining her eastern flank. Today people take for granted the cleanliness of Lake Washington, our state's second largest natural lake (Chelan takes first). Many wouldn't guess that in the 1950s sixty-four million gallons per day of inadequately treated sewage were pouring into these beloved waters dubbed "Lake Stinko" by the *Seattle Post-Intelligencer*. Observant lake users noticed an abundance of blue-green algae, which scientists discovered was threatening oxygen supplies essential to plants and fish. Feasting on the heavy phosphate loads of treated effluent, this type of algae bloom is a classic sign of lake deterioration.

Quick action by the Washington State Legislature resulted in the establishment of "Metro"—the Municipality of Metropolitan Seattle, a regional group whose first task was to develop a network of sewage treatment plants. The plan was to discharge treated sewage deep into Puget Sound where tidal action would help dilute and disperse the effluent. In just nine years, Metro installed more than one hundred miles of underground tunnels and four treatment plants to handle sewage that had grown to an average of one hundred

Lake Washington was named Lake Geneva in 1849 by pioneer Isaac Ebey. A few years later, patriots renamed it Lake Washington.

million gallons a day by 1968. At the time, this was the most costly pollution control effort in the nation. By 1967, 99 percent of the treated sewage had been diverted, and Lake Washington rapidly began to recover.

ACCIDENTAL PETS: A MAMMAL PRIMER

Why is it that our pets gain access to beds, food bowls, and plenty of affection, while uninvited mammals make us squirm? Hairy, hungry, and often quite bold, creatures such as rats, raccoons, and opossums visit urban and suburban homes, chewing through insulation, making nests, and leaving their droppings behind. As omnivores, they can eat just about anything, it seems, which has contributed to their success. These wild animals don't really belong in our homes, and may even spread diseases there, so it's not unreasonable to want to keep them outside. But once you've done that, you may find these creatures good candidates for nature study. In cities, dominated by humans, they are wild mammals willing and able to live close enough for observation.

Old World rats and mice, probably the most common urban visitors, have been living close to people for thousands of years. All of the most likely city species originally came here from other places, hitching rides on ships, and are mostly nocturnal. The common house mouse (*Mus musculus*) has a grayish-brown back and belly (some domestic strains may be predominantly white) and a naked tail. They breed continuously in places such as heated houses, producing multiple litters a year with five to six pups per litter. Two kinds of rats may be visiting your home, including the Norway (*Rattus norvegicus*) and the roof rat. If the rat is in your basement, it is most likely a Norway, which is a ground dweller. It's also much bigger than a mouse. Roof rats (*Rattus rattus*), as you might guess, are agile climbers and typically found in your house's upper levels. They are darker and slimmer than Norways, with tails longer than their bodies.

Raccoons (*Procyon lotor*), their masked faces easily recognized by most people, have a cuddly appearance that gives them a leg on the likeability scale. Native to North and South America, their seemingly mischievous nature is probably a result of their exceptionally keen senses. They have terrific night vision, acute hearing, and a refined sense of touch. Breeding season is from late winter through early spring, with three to four babies called "kits," born April to June in a den made in a hollow log or large snag, beneath large rocks, or, in cities, under your front porch, in your attic, or down a chimney. They can be aggressive to house pets or humans—if they are causing problems, do not approach or corner them.

Opossums (*Didelphis virginiana*) are slightly smaller than raccoons, and are frequently seen taking Sunday strolls across our city's roads. They have white or grayish-white fur, pointy faces, and long, rat-like tails. They were introduced to the area from the eastern United States in the early 1900s, and are our only marsupial—like the kangaroo, their young are born nearly embryonic, and spend their first sixty days in their mother's pouch, nursing. Later they ride on their mother's back. Their den locations are similar to those of raccoons. When confronted, opossums either bare their fifty sharp teeth (more than any other mammal) or "play 'possum," falling to the ground with eyes closed and tongues stuck out, as if dead. They are generally non-confrontational.

If any of these mammals are getting into your house, remember that many "pest" control methods are toxic to humans and the environment, or may seem morally unconscionable. Others, such as loud noises and bright lights, work only on some animals. The best cure is prevention. Don't feed pets outside. Inspect your house for holes, and patch them. Block holes around pipes and wires. Cap chimneys with commercial chimney caps or heavy wire mesh. Keep branches, vines, and trellises away from the house. Learn about the particular mammals that concern you, and take steps to keep them from getting in the house in the first place. If you find an injured wild animal, contact the Progressive Animal Welfare Society (PAWS) or a wildlife rehabilitation facility. For more specific tips for calling a truce with your furry visitors, consult your local library, or the wildlife section of the PAWS website at *http://paws.org*.

> The Department of Fish and Wildlife website (*www.wa.gov/wdfw/wildlife.htm*) offers a wealth of information on this and other wildlife subjects in its brochure series, Living with Wildlife in Washington.

GET THE FACTS ON BATS

Most people are surprised to learn that while minding their own business, bats perform more services for humans every night than all of Batman's good deeds combined. Without the pollinating power of bats, mainstays such as coffee, bananas, and agave (think tequila) would be much harder to come by. And in the Northwest, bats are the main predator of night-flying insects—one little brown bat can put away twelve hundred mosquito-size insects in one hour.

Little Brown Bat

These misunderstood animals are our only flying mammals, have excellent vision, usually birth one baby per year, and some species can live to be thirty years old. There are one thousand bat species worldwide and half of these are either endangered or too little is known about them to estimate their numbers. Their precarious status is due to the fact that they are one of the slowest reproducing mammals, a situation exacerbated by human prejudice and habitat loss. There are at least ten bat species in the Puget Sound area. The most commonly reported in Seattle are the little brown bat, big brown bat, Yuma myotis, California myotis, silver-haired bat, and hoary bat. Despite its name, our largest local species, the "big" brown, is so small it could fit into an envelope and be mailed for the price of a first-class stamp. Many local bats hibernate in the winter, while the silver-haired and hoary bats migrate to southern climes.

Many people fear bats because, like all mammals, we can suffer and die from the rabies virus. A small fraction of wild bats carry the disease and only two people have contracted rabies from bats in Washington state since the 1930s. Still, it is a deadly disease that should be taken very seriously. Bats should not be handled by anyone except those with proper training and vaccinations. If you find a sick or injured bat, do not touch it; call the Sarvey Wildlife Center at (360) 435-4817.

Lakes are a good place to watch for bats because they offer both food and water, and the best viewpoint is from the southeastern shore. Just as the sky darkens to the point where reading a newspaper becomes difficult, the setting sun will silhouette the animals as they emerge from roosts in hollow trees, buildings, overpasses, bridges, and under piers. Bats have complicated languages and, while using a larynx like ours, "speak" at frequencies so high we can't hear most species (in Eastern Washington, the spotted bat talks low enough that you can catch a few chirps). Bat detectors allow human ears to pick up on some of their exchanges and help scientists in species identification. Each summer bat walks at Green Lake and Seward Parks allow you to see and listen to bats with experts. For more information, call Bats Northwest at (206) 246-0406 or Seattle Parks and Recreation at (206) 684-4075. With more people learning about the benefits of bats, there has been a surge in interest in creating bat habitat. Bats Northwest has free plans for the most successful bat houses—check with them before you invest in one. Bat Conservation International (*www.batcon.org*) has a "Bat Approved" bat house certification program, and a Bat House Research Project offering citizens a chance to learn more about the needs of Northwest bats.

> Bats have a built-in sonar system called echolocation that allows agility in total darkness. They bounce high-frequency calls off of objects, and use the responding echoes to form mental pictures of the world around them, allowing them to find food while avoiding obstacles and predators.

CREATING A BACKYARD WILDLIFE SANCTUARY

Most homeowners don't consider themselves habitat managers, but as thirty-five thousand acres of Washington's wilderness is lost to development each year, residential yards become more and more essential to the survival of native birds and animals. The Washington Department of Fish and Wildlife (WDFW) sponsors a Backyard Wildlife Sanctuary Program to encourage nurturing the wilderness at your doorstep. There are six thousand such sanctuaries in the state—you may have seen the official WDFW signs recognizing them in front of some of the wilder yards in your neighborhood. Your yard can become a sanctuary when you offer year-round food, water, and shelter sources for wildlife. The WDFW has these suggestions:

1. Plant more trees and shrubs. Vegetation is the key to attracting a variety of wildlife. Dead trees (snags) are especially valuable; try to keep them on your property if they pose no safety hazard.
2. Add a birdbath, garden pond, or other water source. A safe place to bathe and drink will attract many animals.
3. Add bird feeders. A feeder for millet, one for sunflower seeds, and one for suet will appeal to a wide variety of birds.
4. Add birdhouses, or better yet, try to leave snags on your property. Cavity-nesting birds have been especially harmed by urban development. A birdhouse of the proper dimensions can substitute for snags where these birds used to nest.

One element of this Backyard Wildlife Sanctuary, an unmanicured lawn, creates a more diverse habitat (and frees up sunny Saturday afternoons).

5. Cover any openings under the eaves or other places around your house where house sparrows and European starlings may nest. These non-native birds are undesirable competitors for food and nesting cavities, and many native birds have suffered because of their presence. Bird-houses and feeders should be designed to deter use by nonnatives.

6. Cats can be especially harmful to birds that feed or nest on the ground. Consider keeping your cat indoors, especially during nesting season.

7. Interest your neighbors in backyard wildlife. Several adjacent yards with good wildlife resources are even more effective. For more information or to order a Backyard Wildlife Sanctuary packet, contact the Washington Department of Fish and Wildlife, Backyard Wildlife Sanctuary Program, 16018 Mill Creek Boulevard, Mill Creek, WA 98012; (425) 775-1311.

City Vistas:
QUEEN ANNE
AND MAGNOLIA

"And the memory picture will bring nostalgic recollections of hot summer days; a breath-taking climb up the slopes of the 'Hill,' and there in some quiet retreat beside the trail, half hidden through interlacing ferns, was the bubbling spring, invitingly cool and refreshing. And beside that spring, tired bodies were rested, flagging spirits uplifted and there came the peace that passes all understanding."
—L. L. Griffiths, Queen Anne settler's daughter

There's no better place to get the lay of the land than from either of Seattle's tallest slopes: Queen Anne or Magnolia. These are two of the city's seven original hills, which also include First Hill, Capitol Hill, Beacon Hill, West Seattle's central ridge, and the former Denny Hill. Situated just north of downtown and south of the Chittenden Locks and Salmon Bay, Queen Anne's glacial till rises 456 feet from Sound level, while Magnolia's bluffs stretch to 500 feet. In between these neighborhoods, in an area called Interbay, an industrial crazy quilt of much-modified flatlands originally filled in for railroad tracks now holds a bike path, a golf course, a nationally famous community garden, and Fisherman's Terminal, a fine place to watch gulls, surrounded by boats, many just back from or headed up to Alaska.

Neither of these neighborhoods developed quickly. Queen Anne, now the more densely populated of the two hills, was once used as a hunting ground for Native American tribes, some of whom lived at its base. Thomas Mercer, an early settler who claimed a plot on lower Queen Anne in the 1850s, referred to the yet-to-be Queen Anne as "Eden Hill" for its dense woods, bubbling springs, and enviable location between salt- and freshwater. The hill must have lived up to the moniker then, when it was wild and lush enough to provide habitat for bears and cougars. Magnolia was settled by pioneers somewhat later, and particularly rapidly after 1911, when the Army Corps of Engineers dredged

The Doris Chase sculpture Changing Form *frames sunset from Queen Anne's Kerry Park.*

Salmon Bay and began work on the ship canal bordering Magnolia to the north. This lowered water levels and dried up much of the tide flats that became Interbay. Archaeological evidence discovered when the West Point treatment plant was built at Discovery Park show that the west side of Magnolia had been settled at least four thousand years ago. The Duwamish also lived here for hundreds of years before settlers came. The tribe stayed put during the winter months, and, like other regional tribes, followed a nomadic cycle of food gathering and trading around the area in other seasons.

Queen Anne's natural features are mostly preserved in the form of small parks, from the north slope's woody Rodger's Park, one of the city's oldest, to Bhy Kracke Park on the southeast side, with terraced gardens and views east. The only remaining creek on this once spring-filled hill now catalogued by the city is Mahteen Creek, which trickles for only about 15 feet at the bottom of a north-slope ravine before being diverted into a pipe. In general, this hill's natural pleasures are groomed and well visited.

Magnolia has fewer parks, many wide residential streets, and an abundance of meticulously clipped front yards. Nevertheless, it shelters the crown jewel of our city's park system, untamed Discovery Park. You can learn almost everything you want about Seattle's natural history within its boundaries, from the habits of local birds to the geology of our soils. This neighborhood also features unimpeded views west toward the Olympics and San Juan Islands.

This chapter offers a tour around the crest of Queen Anne that gives a perspective on the city's regional setting, but also touches on hilltop subjects such as historical bear trails and the nesting habits of squirrels. A second tour, at Discovery Park, shifts the focus to the close-range subject of tide pools. Three destinations offer three very different experiences: a Queen Anne cemetery provides a crash-course in lichen hunting, the Magnolia Bluffs highlight the uncertain fate of a beloved native tree, and a wooded ravine on Magnolia turns out to be the best place in the city to see herons.

10. Walking the Boulevard: An Olmsted Legacy

Where:	The top of Queen Anne beginning at Kerry Park on West Highland Drive
Tour Distance:	4 miles round trip or 4.5-mile loop
Phone:	(206) 684-4075
Internet:	*www.cityofseattle.net/parks/*
Hours:	See individual park hours. Most of the tour can be walked anytime.
Disabled Access:	Sidewalks with curb ramps on most streets

Dogs:	Yes, leash and scoop
Driving:	Heading north from downtown on Aurora Avenue (S.R. 99), exit just before the Aurora Bridge. The right-hand turn is signed "Queen Anne Next Right." Take an immediate left to loop under the bridge, following signs for Queen Anne U-turn route. At the stop sign, a six-way intersection, stay straight on Queen Anne Drive. Turn left at the stop sign onto Queen Anne Avenue and follow it several blocks through the business district until you begin to head down the south hill. Turn right onto West Highland Drive.
Bus:	2, 4, 13
Special Note:	Walk on a clear day for mountain views

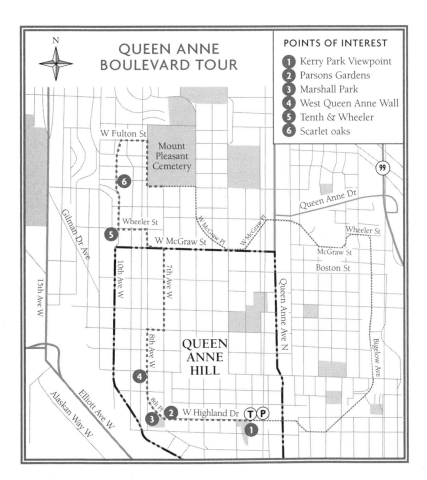

QUEEN ANNE
BOULEVARD TOUR

POINTS OF INTEREST

1 Kerry Park Viewpoint
2 Parsons Gardens
3 Marshall Park
4 West Queen Anne Wall
5 Tenth & Wheeler
6 Scarlet oaks

Queen Anne Hill's upper reaches provide one of the best orientations to the hills, waterways, islands, and mountains that define Seattle. On a clear day, a circular tour of the top of the hill promises Mount Rainier, the Olympic Mountains, Mount Baker, and the Cascade Range. Early last century, from atop the water tower—then a public lookout—at Lee Street and Warren Avenue North, John Charles Olmsted, stepson of famous landscape designer Frederick Law Olmsted Sr., soaked in the 360-degree view while researching what was to become Seattle's current park system.

"The Boulevard" is not actually one thoroughfare but a series of connecting streets that circle the crown of the hill, derived from the original Olmsted plan for Queen Anne. It does not follow Olmsted's wishes for 150-foot-minimum street widths to provide growing room for trees and a footpath lining the entire route. It does follow the streets outlined in the original plan, and its tree-lined avenues are reminiscent of more Olmsted-true boulevards such as those along Lake Washington. When it was first proposed on Queen Anne, real estate developers who had already mapped out housing sites along most of the route made the boulevard concept highly controversial, and for some homeowners, who desire views more than trees, it remains so.

This tour takes you on the south and west sides of the hill. It ends at Mount Pleasant Cemetery, where you can retrace your steps to the starting point at Kerry Park and Viewpoint (4 miles round-trip), or continue along the rest of the boulevard as marked on the map (4.5 miles total).

A Doris Chase sculpture installed at Kerry Park (1) in 1971 provides circular frames for some of the most photographed views of Seattle's icons: Mount Rainier, Elliott Bay, and the Space Needle. Titled *Changing Form*, the top of the steel installation was designed to move in the wind, though it has since rusted to a standstill. The name also applies to the changing form of the city seen through the sculpture's many windows. Chase chose materials for the piece for their likeness in color to madrone bark, to evoke the organic rather than the mechanical environment. She further sprayed the piece with saltwater to speed oxidation.

If you stood here before 1903 and looked out over the city, you would have seen another of Seattle's original hills. Before being scooped away to clear a path for developers, Denny Hill rose 100 feet and covered sixty-two city blocks. By 1928, all 6 million cubic yards of Queen Anne's sister to the south were systematically washed or electrically conveyed into Elliott Bay. The Denny Regrade, as it's known, is one of the most famous human land-moving feats of this region.

"THE STRATOVOLCANO'S OUT!"

Although most Seattleites know exactly where to look when you say, "the mountain's out"—they would probably blink uncomprehendingly at the substitution of the word "stratovolcano" for "mountain." Nevertheless, it can be argued that the exalted wild mama of the Cascades—with her steamy vents and thirty to forty earthquakes each year—is more accurately referred to in volcanic terms. Deep, deep below the relative predictability of our controlled urban environment, Earth's constantly shifting foundation is a humbling reminder of the impermanent nature of nature.

Common along the edges of tectonic plates, stratovolcanoes are steep and conical, their mass comprised of lava flows and volcanic ash. According to the U.S. Geological Survey (USGS), Mount Rainier is the most potentially dangerous volcano in the United States. This dubious honor is attributed to the large population living in her shadow and the frequency of past lahars, or mudflows.

About fifty-six hundred years ago, steam explosions collapsed Rainier's summit (at 14,400 feet; it's now some 1600 feet lower), sending more than 2.7 billion cubic yards of debris flooding down the mountain. The Osceola Mudflow slammed down the White River valley and across the Puget Sound lowlands, eventually covering one hundred square miles and burying the sites of today's Enumclaw, Buckley, Auburn, Kent, Sumner, and Puyallup.

Those who witnessed Mount St. Helen's impressive demonstration in 1980 believe it's possible with Rainier, too—the unanswerable question is when? Mount Rainier is known to have erupted in the early 1800s, and large eruptions are estimated to have occurred about 1000 and 2300 years ago. Since it's impossible to say when it will happen again, how about what will happen when she blows? According to a 1995 USGS report:

"An eruption would probably begin with small steam blasts located at the summit, but could escalate in size and intensity, perhaps leading to a release of new magma (hot, molten rock). Depending on the amount of magma released, the eruptions could have relatively minor effect on the surrounding area or could produce large, destructive floods and debris flows, affecting areas far from the volcano. The shaking by earthquakes or explosions will also dislodge masses of unstable rock . . . Particularly large landslides could also create destructive, far-traveling debris flows."

Lahars, described as looking and acting like walls of concrete, are considered the biggest danger. Seattleites may experience the odd drift of ash (the wind usually blows east), and suffer the loss of our city's most distinctive totem. But those brave souls living in the mountain's shadow might want to keep their cars gassed up and facing toward the road.

Geologists marvel at changes in our landforms that are a little more difficult to picture in your mind's eye. Before the last ice age, which left its final imprints on the Seattle area some 13,500 years ago, the future site of our Emerald City sat at the bottom of a giant lake stretching to the Black Hills south of Olympia. Like Seattle's other hills, a cross-section of Queen Anne Hill reads like a diary of her geologic past. The ancient lake bottom forms the foundation of Seattle's hills. Called Lawton Clay, it ranges in thickness from a few feet to more than 100 feet. Some fifteen thousand years ago, a wall of ice about 3000 feet thick called the Puget Lobe advanced southward from Canada. Countless rivers of sand and gravel poured out in front of the glacier as the ice overran the lake. These deposits of "advance outwash" are called Esperance Sand in the Seattle area, and make up the core of our city's hills. As the weight of the glacier both advanced and retreated over where you're standing, Queen Anne was "steamrolled" with a layer of Vashon Till—a concrete-like deposit of rocks, clay, dirt, and sand lying in wait beneath the topsoil for you to stub your shovel on.

Meanwhile, like a giant fire hose scouring the path of least resistance, massive rivers (comprised of the entire drainage of Washington's Cascade Range) were surging under the glacial ice, carving out what would become the Puget Sound basin. As the great ice mass slowly retreated, the ocean level rose and saltwater filled in the valleys created by a thousand years of glacial occupancy, resulting in one of the world's largest inland seas. The waters west of Magnolia and Alki Point are some of the deepest at more than 200 meters below modern sea level.

Turning your attention back to the present view, the Space Needle and Key Arena tower over what was once known as Potlatch Meadows, a traditional tribal gathering place where feasts honored rites of passage such as a child's naming ceremony and the death of an elder, the return of the salmon and successful hunts.

In the late 1800s, you could also still peer from here into the upper branches of the Powwow Tree, which grew just a few blocks down the hill on Second Avenue West. Queen Anne settler Charles Kinnear noted that Second Avenue was the path favored by black bears as they lumbered down the hill or back up again to and from Elliott Bay.

On a clear day, Mount Rainier can be seen to the right of the Space Needle. The small "hill" to her left is Little Tahoma; fabled to be the only son Tahoma (an English bastardization of a native name for Mount Rainier) took along when she fled her unworthy husband.

Continuing west on Highland Drive for a few blocks, you will come to the formerly private Parsons Gardens (2), open 6:00 A.M. to 10:00 P.M. Once the ornamental garden of the Parsons family, this tranquil spot evokes a secret garden. Get temporarily lost under draping trees along stone pathways while bathing in the springtime aromas of magnolia, pieris, and cherry blossoms.

Kitty-corner and across the street is Marshall Park (3), also called the Betty Bowen Viewpoint, open 4:00 A.M. to 11:30 P.M. This is a good place to watch the waters of Elliott Bay meet Puget Sound. A clear day will afford views of ferries making their way to and from Vashon Island (to the south past West Seattle's Alki Point), and Bainbridge Island to the west, with the Olympic Mountains beyond. Blake Island is the small green patch in between, believed by some to be the birthplace of Chief Sealth. On a windy day, you can watch gulls and crows riding air currents—crows are especially acrobatic and perform aerial dives and somersaults worthy of a circus. In the fall, turkey vultures may be riding the warm updrafts—they have a large, V-shaped wing posture and are wobbly in flight.

SQUIRRELS: A CHARMING NUISANCE

We love 'em for their fluffy-tailed frolics (as long as they perform within park boundaries) and hate 'em when they're raiding our bird feeders or nesting in our attics. Herein lies the paradox of the Eastern gray squirrel— by far the most common of three tree squirrels seen in Seattle. People enamored of their charming qualities imported the Eastern gray squirrel (*Sciurus carolinensis*) and Eastern fox squirrel (*Sciurus niger*) to West Coast city parks, campuses, and estates in the early 1900s. The Eastern gray has a gray back tinged red in summer, and its belly is whitish. The Eastern fox squirrel is slightly larger (both rodents are half tail), with a dark gray-red back and orange to buff-colored belly.

Although the Northwest is home to four native tree squirrels, only the northern flying squirrel (*Glaucomys sabrinus*) is found today in our forested urban areas. This small nocturnal squirrel "flies" by using a natural cape—a flap of skin connecting its front and rear legs—looking more bat than squirrel. Its wide flat tail helps it steer on downward glides that have been recorded reaching lengths up to 200 feet! If you're lucky you might spy this big-eyed creature during scheduled nocturnal hikes at Camp Long in West Seattle. Although its winter diet consists mostly of mosses and lichens, flying squirrels have a weakness for black sunflower seeds and, if you live near a densely wooded area, they may surreptitiously visit your bird feeder while you sleep.

Continuing north on Eighth Avenue West, you'll stroll along an official city landmark, the West Queen Anne Wall (4), formerly known as the Willcox Wall. Designed by city architect Walter Willcox in 1913 and distinguished by its decorative brick detailing (worth a short side trip down the steps), the wall sports five of the city's five hundred stairways. With antique streetlights and sweeping Olympic Mountain views, this is a place where it's easy to understand what Frederick Olmsted Sr. meant when he described landscapes that move us "in a manner more nearly analogous to the action of music than to anything else . . . Gradually and silently the charm overcomes us; we know not exactly where or how."

Moving to a music of their own making, current scientific theories describe how the Olympic Mountains literally rose from the sea some thirty-five million years ago. Underwater volcanic activity formed huge undersea mountains called seamounts. When the plates that made up the ocean floor slowly slid toward North America, some of these masses pushed up under the mainland, forming a dome that would become today's Olympics. Over time, ice and rock were twisted and bent, fractured and folded into their present form.

Fabled to be Mount Rainier's forsaken husband in some Native American myths, the M-shaped "Brothers" are perhaps the most recognizable of the Olympic mountain peaks. The old stories portray the neighboring mountains as Rainier's children. George Davidson of the U.S. Coast Survey named the Brothers for his fiancée's kin in 1857. And as for Ellinor Fauntleroy, the fiancée, her namesake is the southernmost Olympic peak on the horizon. Ellinor's sister was immortalized in Mount Constance, the tallest peak in the range visible from Seattle. Look to the right of the long "valley" north of The Brothers. The highest point you can see from here is Constance at 7743 feet.

The boulevard now jogs up Blaine Street past more of the West Queen Anne Wall on Seventh Avenue and through a residential neighborhood. Note you make turns at McGraw Street, Eighth Avenue, and Wheeler Street—see the accompanying map. At Tenth and Wheeler (5), you're one block north of the site of a large shell midden now buried under Queen Anne homes. The intersections of Tenth and Eleventh West and McGraw streets were a shell "dump" for native tribes—these durable table scraps were uncovered by archeologist Harlan Bretz in 1913. Clams and other shellfish were likely harvested in the tidal flats that used to form Smith Cove between Magnolia, the hill to your west, and Queen Anne.

Looking up Tenth West, the boulevard's famous trees come into view. The scarlet oaks presiding between Halladay to Newell Streets on the east side of Tenth Avenue (6), and from Raye to Newell on the west, are home to one of the city's most prevalent wild mammals, the Eastern gray squirrel. Sated by the acorns these trees produce, and happy to nest in their upper canopies, these nonnative tree dwellers are the most common tree squirrel in the city. Introduced here in the 1900s, their nest or "drey" is a ball-shaped collection of twigs and leaves left starkly visible after the branches become bare in autumn. Preferring large deciduous trees for their protective canopies and—in this case—abundant acorns, squirrels can often be seen burying their food for later or nibbling on the find of the hour. Their sharp front claws and double-jointed back legs enable them to scale trees with ease. These omnivorous rodents also eat seeds, tree bark and buds, eggs, and fungi.

Another nest exposed after the leaves fall is the crow's—a conical home made of sticks and branches located near the top of a tree. When you see one in a lofty perch, you will agree that a ship's "crow's nest" situated high on a mast is aptly named. Squirrel nests are decidedly messier looking, and are usually found lower on the tree and closer to the trunk—although one nest spotted along Tenth Avenue was precariously located on a branch just 2 feet above the bus cable.

Take in your last eyeful of the Olympics before turning right onto West Fulton Street and head up Eighth Avenue West under a long line of yellow birches, with leaves that turn brilliant yellow in the fall. The twigs of these trees taste like wintergreen when chewed. Turn left at Raye, and just around the corner is the entrance to the Mount Pleasant Cemetery. This is an excellent place to go birding, walk among big trees, or examine lichens. The tour ends here. You can choose to spend some time strolling in the quiet of Mount Pleasant, continue along the boulevard following the map, or retrace your steps back to Kerry Park.

This messy pile of tree debris is actually a squirrel drey, or nest.

11. Good Tiding: Beach Walk at Discovery Park

Where:	Magnolia
Tout Distance:	About 3 miles
Phone:	(206) 386-4236
Internet:	*http://discoverypark.org*
Hours:	Park, dawn to dusk; visitor center, Tuesday–Sunday, 8:30 A.M. to 5:00 P.M.
Disabled Access:	Van shuttle service to beach available. Call ahead to schedule.
Dogs:	No dogs allowed on the beach, although they can be walked on leash in most of Discovery Park
Driving:	From the waterfront area in downtown Seattle, take Elliott Avenue north. In a little over a mile it becomes Fifteenth Avenue West. In just under a quarter-mile, take the West Dravus Street exit. You'll see signs for the Daybreak Star Indian Cultural Center, which is in Discovery Park. Turn left onto Dravus Street, crossing over a bridge. In several blocks, turn right onto Twentieth Avenue West. Take Twentieth—which becomes Gilman Avenue West, and then West Government Way—a little over 1 mile to Discovery Park's east entrance. Immediately to the left as you enter the park is the Discovery Park Visitor Center. Stop here if desired or proceed to the north parking lot.
Bus:	33
Special Note:	A 0 or minus tide is necessary to see most tide pools. Consult the phone book or the visitor center for a tide chart, or buy a *Tide and Current Table* at boating stores around town. Summer brings good weather and low tides in the daytime. The unique experience of night tide pooling, and the year's lowest tides, happens only in the winter, when low tide is in the evening. Also, this is a protected area, so you can't bring any sea creatures home.

Discovery Park is Seattle's largest park and a prime destination for any nature lover. Within its 534 acres, most of which was once Fort Lawton Army Base, can be found cool woods, a restored wetland, ancient bluffs, groves of blackberries for summer foraging, and grassy fields slowly being restored with native plants.

This is a favorite destination for bird watchers, who are able to observe birds of many different types of habitat all within park grounds. The Discovery Park Visitor Center sells an inexpensive map that can direct you to miles of trails and other park features. The center offers excellent classes and outings with naturalists on such subjects as mushrooms, snakes, animal tracking, and wetlands.

To hit the beach from the north parking lot, walk west toward the water along the paved road, curving to your left where the road forks, and up a slight hill to the loop trail sign (1). Turn right onto this trail. Walking along woody trails in the park, you might keep watch for coyote tracks, which look much like dog prints but with toenail imprints. Also, their front footprints are very distinct from their rear prints.

The trail will cross a paved road. Keep going. When you get to the next paved road, you'll see just in front and to the right a worn footpath marked North Bluff Area. Follow this, go down wooden steps, and follow signs for North Beach.

As the rockier of Discovery's two beaches, North Beach (2) holds the park's fertile tide pools. Before honing in on these teeming puddles—or if visiting at high tide—get a sense of the larger seashore ecosystem by looking out over the water. Here flock diverse seabirds. At least 279 bird species have been seen from Discovery Park's forests, ponds, meadows, and shoreline. Common and easily identifiable birds along this shore include cormorants,

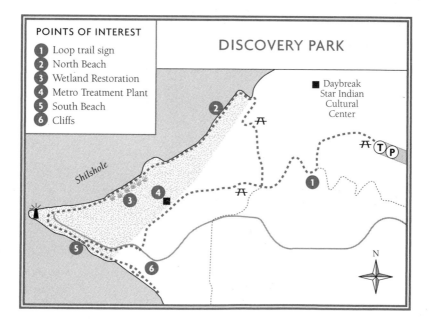

POINTS OF INTEREST

1 Loop trail sign
2 North Beach
3 Wetland Restoration
4 Metro Treatment Plant
5 South Beach
6 Cliffs

DISCOVERY PARK

■ Daybreak
Star Indian
Cultural
Center

Shilshole

N

those graceful, slender necked birds whose wings, spread out to dry, look like a Batman insignia. Cormorants frequently seem to hold this cocky posture. This seabird's wing scaffolding is more open than that of most other birds, a system that helps them dive deeply into the water for fish, but also requires them to hang-dry their wings. You might see wigeons, Western grebes, and certainly gulls—eighteen different species of them have been spotted here.

Discovery Park was closed for four days in the summer of 1981, when a cougar was sighted there. After several sightings, the cougar was finally cornered in a madrone tree on the edge of the south bluff. It was tranquilized and released into the Cascades. Officials theorized that it came into town by walking the corridor of the Burlington Northern railroad tracks from the Cascades.

Looking out at the water you can imagine, if not see, the schools of herring, salmon, flounder, and halibut that inhabit the Sound. Watch—and listen—for sea lions or harbor seals, which might put their heads above water to look at you. If it is winter, keep an eye on the horizon for orca whales migrating past—they are identified in the distance by the spouts of water squirting from their blowholes, and their glistening black backs, tall dorsal fins and white undermarkings, which sometimes arch out of the water. On a promontory in the near distance sits the West Point Lighthouse, the oldest lighthouse in the Seattle area, built in 1881 and operated by the Coast Guard.

If you have come at a mid or low tide, it's time to walk the beach. The place to look for tide pools is in the intertidal zone, that swath of earth, sand, or rock from the farthest spot up the beach that water covers at high tide, to the area exposed to sun and air only at extremely low tides. Since tides do not come and go at the same time every day, most intertidal animals must be able to withstand great changes in their atmosphere on a daily basis. The interlinked nature of all earthly life is rarely more obvious than in a tide pool. You'll find many species using others for camouflage, housing, or a midnight snack. One common example of this opportunistic approach is the barnacle, a crustacean that finds its meals by sticking itself to any hospitable object—even a whale!—with its own version of Superglue. Here it waits, fanlike legs extended, for plankton to wash past. This attentive pose is, in fact, a common one for intertidal creatures, many of which loiter on rocks, under shells, or buried in the sand until plankton or something meatier is sloshed by waves into their vicinity.

The tide zones are divided into low, middle, and high, the latter zone often visible even when the water is just beginning to go out. Creatures living in the very low tide zone are exposed only about a couple of times a month, and must be able to withstand the rough handling of waves. At the far extreme of high tide is the supralittoral or "splash" zone, high rocky areas sprayed

Crabs, sea stars, chitons, anemones, and much other marine life is found on Seattle beaches.

only infrequently by seawater. Here are some of the harshest conditions for any sea life, which must survive both the hottest of summer weather and the coldest of winter, with little of the water's modifying effects.

Two splash zone denizens are the periwinkle and the limpet. Most limpets are recognizable by their conical shells; other sea creatures might recognize them for their radula—a rough tongue with which they scrape up food—or by their strong foot muscles, which can cling tenaciously to a rock or other surface. The periwinkle is a kind of snail, and here at North Beach the checkered variety hides out in its spiraling shell. It's reddish brown or a blue-gray, speckled with white. Lower down in the pools can be found such glamorous sea life as sea stars, anemones, chitons, and moon snails. There are several kinds of crabs on the beach, including purple and green shore crabs, and the red crab. You may also find subtidal creatures such as the sea pen, sea slug, or jellyfish, which can be trapped in pools when the water goes out.

While looking at, touching (gently), and perhaps smelling all of these animals, consider that many sea creatures have not only a sense of sight, but chemo-sensory systems of their own, allowing them to use something between a sense of smell and a sense of taste. This is most often used to avoid predators. The sunflower star is a major beach predator you may find here—like a sea star but with a much softer back and a lot of extra rays. Studies have shown that placing only one tube foot of the sunflower star into water with prey animals will stimulate a flight response in any mobile sea creature, such as snails, most likely because the star secretes a chemical sensed by prey.

PUGET SOUND TIDES

As one of the most complicated phenomena on the planet, tides cannot be explained in a paragraph, or even a page. If you live in Seattle, however, a bit of tidal knowledge is an essential tool for such marine adventures as clamming, tide pooling, and boating.

The basics, useful all over the world, are this: the gravity of both the sun and moon pull at the ocean, creating a wave or bulge. The earth's rotation keeps this wave going, all the way around the planet. There are two daily tides, and this at least explains the fundamentals of one of them.

The second tide sloshing things hither and yon is powered by the centrifugal force created by this sun/moon pulling. Causing headaches for sailors and paddlers, land masses in Puget Sound such as Bainbridge, Vashon, and the Kitsap Peninsula break up this predictable pattern, as does the underwater topography. Then, further complicating matters, there's the mixing of freshwater runoff and saltwater in the Sound.

Other natural forces also leave their mark on the movement of water—as just one example, wind and low barometric pressure can bring higher tides than those listed in the tide table, and, of course, high barometric pressure can have the opposite effect.

While further study of these variables is essential for serious boaters, the beach walker can be content with studying a tide and current table for Puget Sound for the present year, available for a couple of bucks at boating stores around town. The two sections most useful to the beachgoer will be the table listing sunrise and sunset times for each month of the year, and the tide tables for Seattle and nearby towns. And keep in mind a few local tide truths:

The lowest tides of the year happen close to (within about two weeks of) the summer and winter solstices, approximately June 21 and December 21.

Tides on Puget Sound are considered fairly extreme—the range between high and low tide is around 11 feet, compared to, say, 5.4 feet for Los Angeles. That leaves us a lot of beach to explore.

A sense of touch is also important here. One example of how it is used happens within groups of the elegant anemone, a pale green anemone with pink-tipped tentacles you may find in colonies on this beach. The anemone, like the jellyfish, is a member of the *Cnidaria* family, a word that means "nettle" in Greek. Though the nettle-like tendencies of jellyfish are obvious, few people realize that the anemone's tentacles are also equipped with nematocysts that sting. As a carnivore, they use the sting to paralyze hapless prey, but it also works as a curious form of growth management. Anemones reproduce by cloning, and all those in one colony are genetically identical. If one of these colonies bumps into another as a result of too much cloning, the two colonies will be stimulated by this touch to sting each other. This kills off the outer rings of each colony so that they are again separated from one another. The truly adventurous adult beachgoer may wish to touch their tongue to the tip of one of the anemone's petal-like tentacles and feel the benign (to humans) sting.

Walk along the beach toward the lighthouse as far as you want, or you can cut back up to the gravel path, which runs above the beach for its length. Either way, keep your eyes out for the peaceful pond (3), ringed with cattails and red osier dogwoods (a native species identified by its deep red branches) about a half-mile past the start of the beach, beside the upper, gravel path. This wetland was restored in the late 1990s by Seattle Metro as mitigation for installing the West Point Sewage Treatment Plant (4). This famously controversial structure, a destination not only for local sewage but also for diverted city creeks, can be heard humming behind the brush and trees on the hillside. Unfortunately, it also sometimes can be smelled! The wetland, a small sample of what was here before North Point was installed, is planted with many native species, and has become a destination for wildlife, including the mostly nocturnal muskrat, known for its own pungent odor. Watch for a winsome rodent with webbed hind feet and silvery brown or black fur. Observant visitors have seen the muskrat entering holes at the north end of the wetland. This species, native to North America, can stay underwater for more than ten minutes at a time.

Continue on the gravel foot trail, or walk along the beach and around (at high tide you'll have to clamber over rocks) the lighthouse to the South Beach (5). This much different beach is less sheltered from wind than North Beach. It's big and sandy, without tide pools. It does harbor several other interesting features, however, including glacial erratics—boulders left behind when the Puget Lobe of the Cordilleran ice sheet receded at the end of the Ice Age. Look for them dotted around the sandy water at lower tides, and consider that only fourteen thousand years ago the Sound was covered with a massive

Elegant Anemone

Eelgrass

sheet of ice more than 3000 feet thick. Interesting sea life collects around these rocks. You may also see eelgrass beds, visible at very low tide. These mats of very green grass with flat, wide blades grow up in tufts a little like the streamers on a kid's bicycle handlebars. These beds are called the "nursery of the tide pools" because of the many species that begin and sometimes live their lives within this perennial plant. Eelgrass should not be walked on, but kneel in the mud beside a patch and you might find isopods, flat-bodied and segmented. A garden-variety pillbug or "rolly polly" is a kind of isopod. Look for tiny limpets, sea slugs, shrimp, and unusual sea anemones, as well as sea stars and crabs in search of a tender meal. Recent studies have found a correlation between healthy eelgrass beds and healthy salmon populations.

EAGLE STATION

In recent springs, just outside the gates of Discovery Park, eagles have built a nest high up in a Douglas fir. Just as reliably, the park's naturalists have hauled out their high-powered spotting scope and set up an "eagle station" to watch the nesting behavior of these imposing raptors. To join a naturalist at the station, visitors need only call or visit the park nature center in advance to find out when the scope will be in use.

Once at the station, bird watchers will, with luck, catch sight of an eagle delivering fish to its hungry young eaglets. Viewings take place on weekends starting in late March or early April, and each scope session lasts around two hours, enough time to exhaust the naturalist with a gaggle of eagle questions. (Question 1: What do you call a group of eagles?) Some years the birds build their nests within perfect viewing range, while in others they nest among dense branches, leaving bird watchers to wait patiently for the adults to emerge for food.

The 300-foot cliffs (6) rising behind South Beach, are a frequent destination for geology classes because of the strata—layers of soil, clay, sand, and rock revealing two thousand years of geologic history. Holes in the cliffs are nests or damage from foraging by birds such as pigeon guillemots, a small black water bird with red feet and a whistling "peeeee" call, and kingfishers, identified by their swooping flight and high-pitched chittering voice. You may also see red-tailed hawks and bald eagles just above the bluff, riding thermal winds and hunting prey.

This is the end of the walk. When you're ready, head back to the north parking lot. The quickest way from here is to double back from the cliffs to the junction of the beach and cliffs, where a paved road goes uphill. Take this road and turn left at the Hidden Valley Trail. This trail takes you back across meadows and through woods, past restrooms. Turn left at a sign to the north parking lot, eventually take wooden steps, and continue following these signs back to your car.

MOONS IN THE MAKING

While walking Seattle shores during low tide, among the swirls of seaweed and clam geysers you may discover what looks like the business end of a rubber plunger. Before you dismiss this strange stiff creation—also known as a "clergyman's collar"—as so much garbage, look more closely. This donut-like dome is actually home to a half million (or so) moon snail eggs nestled safely between particles of sand. When fully grown, these roundish white carnivorous mollusks roam shallow waters seeking clams or fellow moon snails to munch. They use a small but effective toothy proboscis called a radula to deftly drill through and empty out their prey. A clamshell with a perfectly round hole in it is evidence of a moon snail meal. The egg collar is formed when a moon snail mom secretes her eggs in a gelatinous sheet, which is covered with sand as soon as it leaves the shell. The collar takes its shape from the mollusk's foot, which can be three times as large as its shell. Eventually the egg case crumbles, releasing the free-swimming larvae into the Sound.

Moon Snail
Egg Collar

12. Kiwanis Ravine Heron Colony

Where:	Magnolia
Phone:	(206) 684-4075
Internet:	NA
Hours:	24 hours
Disabled Access:	Yes
Dogs:	On leash, but not conducive to wildlife viewing
Driving:	From the waterfront in downtown Seattle, drive north on Elliott Avenue West. In a little over 1 mile it becomes Fifteenth Avenue West. Travel approximately 1.5 miles and take the last exit before the Ballard Bridge, following signs to Emerson Street. Turn left onto Emerson and go past Fisherman's Terminal to Twenty-first Avenue West. Turn right and stay on Twenty-first as it curves to the left becoming West Commodore Way. Go through an industrial area until you get to the equivalent of Thirty-fourth Avenue West, where you will see a parking lot on the right, on the south side of the Hiram M. Chittenden Locks. Walk east from the parking lot one block to Thirty-third Avenue West and West Harley Street, and go up the hill. In a short block, you will see an alley to the right that ends at a pedestrian bridge over the railroad tracks.
Bus:	Take Routes 44 or 46 to the Hiram M. Chittenden Locks in Ballard. Walk across the locks to Commodore Park and follow walking instructions above.
Special Note:	The best viewing is on the north side of the bridge looking toward Discovery Park. The nests are scattered throughout several large alder and maple trees. The best time to visit the colony is late February through May.

It might seem peculiar to find a nursery of sorts just a stone's throw from the Burlington Northern railroad tracks in Magnolia. But swaying here in the tops of several tall alder and maple trees is one of Seattle's few remaining great blue heron colonies. Known for its pterodactyl-like appearance and unparalleled patience while stalking prey in shallow waters, herons have been raising their gangly broods in Kiwanis Ravine for many years. The ravine is a protected area of nine acres located northeast of the main entrance to Discovery

*Great Blue Heron
in stretch display*

Park. This mostly deciduous stand is home to more than eighty native plant species and is visited by at least fifty-six species of birds

It's an ideal spot for herons because the birds can fish the saltwaters of Puget Sound or the freshwater lakes to the east, both just a short flight away. Although fish is their favorite food, they will also snack on crabs, shrimp, crayfish, frogs, lizards, voles, and insects. The heron's specially adapted foot has four toes; a web joins two of the toes making it easy for the bird to walk on sand and mud without sinking in. A hook on one toe is used in preening the feathers—a cleaning activity essential to smooth flying.

These 4-foot-tall birds have called earth home for the past fifteen million years. They weigh up to 8 pounds with wingspans 6 to 7 feet wide. At this size, watching two adults raise two or more hatchlings to maturity in one nest brings new meaning to the term "shared household."

In 2001, thirty-four nests were counted in Kiwanis Ravine, but because there have been no banding studies it's hard to know how many of the sixty-plus fledglings survived their first winter. There are two other heron colonies in Seattle—one in North Beach and one along the Duwamish River in West Seattle—however, these are harder to view.

The juveniles' heads are dark, while the adults have white crowns. The "kids" are the ones making the loud "braaaack braaaack" sounds you can hear when you visit. One neighbor described the sound of the babies' hunger cries as "a bunch of squeaky doors." Male and female herons look very much alike, but behavior is one way to tell them apart. Some performances to look for during the February and March mating season include:

The Stretch: The heron points its bill and neck up high into the air, then lowers its head down toward its back with the bill still pointing up. This may be accompanied by a long crooning sound. The male uses this move during courtship to attract females to a nest.

The Kiwanis Ravine Heron Habitat Helpers work to restore and protect Kiwanis Ravine. Activities include everything from ivy removal and planting native plants to leading group visits and publicity. If you would like to help, send email to info@heronhelpers.org.

The Bill Duel: During courtship, the male and female sometimes lock the tips of their bills together and move their heads back and forth in a seesawing motion.

The Stick Transfer: The male brings a stick to the female, who places it in the nest.

The herons in our area are resident, meaning they don't migrate, but they don't hang out in the colonies all year long either. The nest sites are used only during breeding season, after which the birds disperse throughout the Seattle area. After the eggs are laid there is a twenty-eight-day gestation period, and about sixty days later the hatchlings begin to fledge. From courtship to fledging, there is always something new going on at the nests, so it's best to return several times during these months. As the spring leaves begin to fill out the trees, the birds become more difficult to locate in the foliage. Please be respectful of the herons' home by staying out of the ravine and keeping noise to a minimum.

13. Magnolia's Madrones

Where:	Magnolia
Phone:	(206) 684-4075
Internet:	http://cityofseattle.net/parks
Hours:	4:00 A.M.–11:30 P.M.
Disabled Access:	Yes
Dogs:	On leash
Driving:	From downtown Seattle, head north on Elliott Avenue West and turn off at the Magnolia Bridge exit. Go uphill. Magnolia Park quickly appears on your left. Just past this park turn left at West Howe Street. Curve left onto Magnolia Boulevard West, soon coming to the Magnolia Boulevard Viewpoints, signed accordingly. There is a little more than one-half mile of bluff viewpoints. Park on the street or in the bluff parking lot near the beginning of the viewpoints.
Bus:	24; get off where Viewmont Way West meets Thirty-sixth Avenue West, and walk a block south toward the water views and Magnolia Boulevard

Damp and cloudy many months of the year, Seattle's climate doesn't seem much like the balmy southern coasts of Spain or France. But that's exactly where most garden specialists will point if you ask for comparable conditions. As evidence, they cite city yards in which such Mediterranean stalwarts as rosemary and sage thrive. Our mild winters benefit from the modifying effects of local waters. Our summers, though not as hot as those of southern Europe, are surprisingly dry, more so in the city, where there's minimal tree canopy and maximum concrete. If gardens full of exotic species don't convince you that our climate is "psuedo Mediterranean," Magnolia Boulevard Viewpoints just might change your mind.

> To view a magnificent, healthy stand of native Madrone at the far reaches of our city, visit the hidden gem Seola Park in Southwest Seattle. The largest madrone in the city is in Seward Park, off the Inner Loop Walk.

The park, stretching along the boulevard with stunning views of Puget Sound and the Olympics, was established, along with the boulevard itself, in 1910. Walk on the paved path or stroll the lawns at the boulevard's southern end, just past Thirty-sixth Avenue West, and you'll soon pass a chain-link fence on the water side of the street. This barrier was erected to keep the reckless from exploring a hillside devastated by storms and flooding in the winter of 1996–97. Downslope, displaced, abandoned houses barely cling to the bluff's edge.

ADOPT-A-MADRONE

The members of Save Magnolia's Madrones worked with a city parks program to plant 135 new trees at Magnolia Viewpoints in the fall of 2000, then "adopted" them to ensure they will remain watered and weed-free for their first few years. As you walk, keep an eye out for the tiny saplings, which look a lot like rhododendrons—another native broad-leafed evergreen—with their glossy, elliptical leaves. While all were planted in groups of four, you may find them in smaller clusters as their survival rate after the first few years is estimated to be around 25 percent. Close at their feet, a native understory of huckleberry, salal, kinnickinnick, and hazelnut is being encouraged as it will benefit the trees by shading their roots and protecting against soil erosion and compaction. It also provides a good opportunity for visitors to practice native plant identification.

While mountain views and rain-washed hills certainly make one think of the Northwest, the trees here, Pacific madrones, transport you to another world entirely. One of our most beloved native tree species, alternately spelled "madrona" or "madrone," these evergreens grow in the sinuous shapes of dancers—perhaps flamenco?—their trunks a smooth red-brown beneath peeling

One of the most prolific of the once ubiquitous Queen Anne springs was located on the south slope at Fourth Avenue North and Ward Street. In the 1880s, it was the source for the Union Water System, one of the largest water supply systems in Seattle, yielding around eighty thousand gallons per day. Now most of Queen Anne's wealth of water is diverted into pipes bound for sewage treatment.

bark, their leaves dark and glossy. If you squint a little, you might see how a Navy botanist gave this neighborhood the name Magnolia in the 1850s when he misidentified these trees from a few knots' distance. Madrones are one of our few native broadleaf evergreens, a change from ubiquitous, bristly conifers. The term "madrone" itself, the common name of *Arbutus menziesii*, is exotic, from the Spanish word for the related strawberry tree. This fellow member of the Heath family of trees is known as *madroño* in Spain, and early Spanish *padres* in Mexico and California used this name for the similar Arbutus trees they saw in the New World.

Unfortunately, the trees here on Magnolia are ailing, and no one is quite sure why. It is believed that the stresses of the urban environment have simply become too much for them. Their decline is clearly visible: some branches are bare of leaves, and others' leaves are blotched, their branches turning black. Three different fungi take much of the blame, but there are other threats as well. Some nearby residents would like to see the trees removed to better their views, and vandals have carved thoughtlessly or hacked very purposefully into the madrones in an attempt to kill them. At least eight trees in a particularly beautiful grove of madrones on the bluff were anonymously "ringed" in the 1980s. In this brutal technique, a deep circle is cut into the bark around the trunk of a tree, preventing it from taking in water and nutrients from the soil. All of the vandalized trees, many of them more than one hundred years old, are slowly dying.

The nuts of the one hundred-year-old Spanish chestnut trees along Bigelow Avenue North on Queen Anne Hill are a delicacy among some Asian people. When they fall to the ground in October and November, members of Seattle's Laotian, Vietnamese, and Cambodian communities collect them around the clock; to find them in the dark, they listen for the sound of the nut hitting the earth.

Despite the madrones' struggles, their historic presence here on this hillside means they can and should survive. The bluffs have been logged more than once in their history, but these offspring most likely grew from seedlings of the original madrone population. They are reminders of what this land was like before the city was born. Not only that, they provide the usual arboreal benefits.

They clean the air, and, on this slippery soil, offer some much-needed stability. They drink up water and with their roots create a protective net to help keep soil from shifting. Much of our local wildlife is dependent, at least in part, on mad-

> The Aurora Bridge is a popular perch for the lightning-fast merlin, an aggressive robin-size falcon that catches birds and insects in midair.

rones. Rufous and Anna's hummingbirds feed on their blossom nectar, and their fruits are a feast each fall for such native birds as band-tailed pigeons, varied thrushes, cedar waxwings, and Bewick's wrens. Both northern flickers and crows are known to nest in Magnolia's madrones, and the crows in particular provide food for raptors and some mammals.

Visit in spring, when the madrone is putting out clusters of delicate, honey-scented flowers. Or, for a sensory trip to something like the Mediterranean, bring a picnic and enjoy sunset in late summer, when the warm bark glows and the flowers have been exchanged for orange fruits.

Ailing but still beautiful madrones frame a Puget Sound view on Magnolia Boulevard.

14. Eternal Bloom: Lichens at Mount Pleasant

Where:	North side of Queen Anne, 700 West Raye Street
Phone:	(206) 282-1270
Internet:	NA
Hours:	Summer, 8:00 A.M. to 8:00 P.M.; winter, 8:00 A.M. to 5:00 P.M.
Disabled Access:	Main roads are paved, but gravesites are often surrounded by lawn
Dogs:	Discouraged. If you bring one, be respectful and use a leash and a scoop. Cemetery owners request that visitors do not dispose scoop bags in cemetery garbage cans.
Driving:	Heading north from downtown on Aurora Avenue (S.R. 99), exit just before the Aurora Bridge signed "Queen Anne Next Right." Take an immediate left to loop under the bridge, following signs for Queen Anne U-turn route. At the stop sign, a six-way intersection, stay straight on Queen Anne Drive, which will direct you briefly onto Smith Street. At the next stop sign, turn left onto Queen Anne Avenue. Turn next right onto West McGraw Street. Go three blocks to a stop sign, cross Third Avenue West, and immediately veer right onto West McGraw Place. Stay on this boulevard for several blocks as it veers left and becomes West Raye Street. The cemetery is on your right.
Bus:	2, get off at Seventh Avenue West and West Raye Street on top of Queen Anne Hill

Graveyards, typically associated with the dead and the past, are actually secret gardens bursting with life. In the city, the right cemetery is a naturalist's haven.

First, there are the trees. While a homeowner might stretch the laws of biology to squeeze a 40-foot-tall sugar maple into a 20-square-foot front yard, the acres of lawn and extended timeline available in a cemetery give specimens room to grow to full splendor. The protected acreage also makes cemeteries a favored spot for lichenologists who study those long-lived organisms brightening the wan faces of old gravestones.

> "I rise and fall, and time folds
> Into a long moment;
> And I hear the lichen speak,
> And the ivy advance with its white lizard feet."
> —Theodore Roethke, Seattle poet and University of Washington professor from 1948-1963

Mount Pleasant, one of Seattle's oldest cemeteries, provides nearly forty acres of habitat on the north side of Queen Anne Hill for birds, trees, lichens, and city-weary humans. It is also the final resting place of such notable early pioneers as former Governor John H. McGraw, Asa Mercer, and Daniel and Susannah Bagley.

> Many animals use lichens. Slugs, mountain goats, and black-tailed deer eat them, and birds use them for nests. Manufacturers sometimes put them in perfumes and deodorants for their antibacterial qualities. In Ancient Egypt, mummies were stuffed with lichens to dry them out.

Approaching the grounds you'll walk or drive under linden trees, mostly the rare-to-Seattle Crimean linden, towering above you up to 50 feet. Several other important tree specimens are found within the cemetery, such as variegated sycamore maple and the manna ash. There is a range of conifers, and a brambly hedge thick with viburnums and laurel encircles the grounds. Irish yews punctuate the lawns here and there, erect and divided like upheld hands. The only noise is the buzz of the groundskeepers' power mowers in spring and summer, and the occasional funeral party. Most days this is a great place to quietly stroll the open drives and wide lawns, or rest beneath the shade of a tree. Peek-a-boo views on this north-facing slope stretch from Ballard in the west to the Cascades in the east. Queen Anne birders also know this cemetery as a good birding destination, where nuthatches, varied thrushes, downy woodpeckers, and red-breasted sapsuckers have been spotted, and eagles sometimes pass overhead.

While here, why not discover whether you're cut out to be an amateur lichenologist? Lichens come in a variety of forms, from the delicate green hair that hangs from trees on the Olympic Peninsula, to the mushroom-like bumps on rotting wood. They can live for

> Lake View Cemetery next to Volunteer Park on Capitol Hill is another good place for lichen-spotting.

up to several thousand years, given the opportunity. Most of those found on rock surfaces like gravestones are called crustose lichens, also known as "crusties." These grow flat against rocks or trees—their "substrate." They can be complex, colorful disks, or look more like a powder scattered across the stone. A lichen is actually more of a relationship than a single plant; it's a working alliance between a fungus and an alga and/or a cyanobacteria—the kind of blue-green algae popular with health foodies. No one is quite certain yet if the relationship is actually symbiotic, or if the algae are a sort of victim of the hungry fungus.

This Mount Pleasant Cemetery gravestone's aged, unwashed surface makes an ideal lichen habitat.

One reason a city-dweller might care about lichens is that most are highly sensitive to air pollutants. Their absence in a big city can say a lot about what's mixing with the O_2. There are a couple of reasons for this. First, lichens are without roots. Instead they absorb moisture and nutrients from the atmosphere. They are able to do this better than many plants because they lack a waxy, protective cortex, easily soaking up the moisture—and pollutants—around them. Several European countries, including Italy and Switzerland, now use lichens for air-pollution monitoring. Though these organisms can survive brutally rough conditions, such as frozen expanses of Arctic tundra, they often die when confronted with acid rain or other atmospheric toxins. Many European cities temporarily lost almost all their lichen colonies during the Industrial Revolution—Kew Gardens in London, which now shelters dozens of lichen species, was once reduced to fewer than six. The United States has also created such "lichen deserts," as in parts of the Los Angeles Basin.

Lichenland.com at *http://mgd.nacse.org/hyperSQL/lichenland*, sponsored by Oregon State University, is one of the best lichen sites on the Internet. There you can learn how to identify lichens, as well as find a database (complete with photos!) of Northwest lichens.

You can find pollution-tolerant city lichens on trees, sidewalks, and stone walls that haven't been power-washed. The cemetery provides certain special advantages for lichen study, however. Besides the fact that old gravestones, where lichens grow, are rarely washed or otherwise disturbed, the dates on the stones offer a starting point for determining the age of these long-lived colonies.

At Mount Pleasant, grave areas are broken into sections with numbers or letters painted on the curbs of the driveway. Gravestones as old as the late 1800s are scattered in all areas of this cemetery, but there are a few choice spots worth special attention. Sections 7, 9, and 100F are good for lichen spotting, with a range of very old stones. An especially lichenous site is the raised plot for the Bell family, in section 100F in the northeast part of the cemetery. The graves of Sarah, W. N., and other Bell family members—pioneers after whom Bell Street and Belltown are named—are surrounded by a low stone wall nearly covered over with the circular imprints of lichen colonies in gray, light green, acid yellow, and dusty rose.

Exploring the cemetery with the naked eye you'll see the differences between the colors and patterns of lichens, and make observations such as whether or not they seem to enjoy particular habitats—types of stone or shady or sunny conditions. With a hand lens and a book on lichens, you can find out much more. Countless lichen species are not yet identified. Yours could be one of them!

THE POWWOW TREE

Queen Anne Hill was once home to one of the most revered trees in Northwest history. Picture a trunk so large it would take ten sets of your outstretched arms to encircle it—a cedar tree that was a struggling seedling hundreds of years before George Vancouver ventured into Puget Sound.

The Duwamish tribe knew it as the Powwow Tree, a sacred site reserved for intertribal councils. In the shadow of this silent mediator, local tribal leaders negotiated exchanges and solved disputes. Also an important navigation point for early explorers, it was known as the Landmark Cedar. Seattle sailors called it the Lookout Tree.

In 1891, when Seattle banker Rollin V. Ankeny cut down the 600-year-old cedar to build a home for his daughter, some white settlers joined the Duwamish outcry against the felling of the hallowed tree. Ironically, the home that now stands in its spot is protected as a registered historic landmark. The unassuming Queen Anne-style house at 912 Second Avenue West features a rounded tower, which seems, sadly, to mimic the shape of the former giant's trunk.

OWLS

From the great horned owl, which nests in Discovery Park, to the startlingly white snowy owl, which only rarely flaps down from the Arctic, Seattle is an irregular host to at least eight owl species including western screech, northern sawwhet, barn, and short-eared owls.

If you haven't seen or heard one yet—take heart. Many, such as the long-eared, are secretive or rare and hard to spot. To find owls, Discovery Park naturalists suggest visiting that park in November during the return of winter owl migrants. The owls usually only call prior to nesting season—January and February are good months to listen for their varied range of calls. Late spring evenings are good for spotting barred and barn owls, two species that nest in the park and might be seen flying at twilight.

At Woodland Park, seek out nesting barred owls in late May and June—the babies often perch out in the open and they, like all owl infants, make begging calls that sound like the hissing of a teakettle. It's a lot easier to find an owl by looking down than looking up. Check for "whitewash," poop squirted by owls (and other raptors) onto the ground or the side of a tree beneath a roost. Also piling up here may be owl pellets, well-formed masses coughed up by the raptors, which swallow their prey whole,

Barn Owl

including parts they cannot digest. Pellets range from half an inch to 4 inches long, depending on the species. They contain fur and bones, and dissecting them is a good way to learn what owls eat. Other Seattle parks visited by owls include Camp Long, Seward Park, and Magnuson Park. Discovery Park offers several nature walks with owls on the agenda—call the park visitor center for more information.

Barred Owl

$\mathcal{S}$almon Bay and Beyond:
BALLARD, FREMONT, AND NORTHWEST SEATTLE

Ballard residents have long looked toward the water for commerce and pleasure. On the shores of what is now called Salmon Bay, Native Americans once reaped the harvest of a tidal saltwater estuary where fish and shellfish abounded. Later, shingle mills and fishing opportunities drew a large Scandinavian population to the neighborhood from overseas. Oral histories record memories of codfish drying in backyards in the early 1900s.

Much of Ballard's shoreline is still dominated by maritime activity, such as boat building and repair. The huge Shilshole Marina, on Shilshole Bay on Ballard's western flank, provides slips for sailboats and motorboats. One of Seattle's most popular sand beaches, Golden Gardens Park, is just north of the marina. The bay and beach are ideal for seasonal sea lion viewing and offer a restored wetland walk. Both are described in this chapter.

Visitors to Ballard from out of town are most likely to see the Chittenden Locks, an Army Corps of Engineers project that created a passage for large boats between Lake Union and Puget Sound. Prior to completion of the locks and ship canal, Lake Union drained into Salmon Bay via modest-size Ross Creek, described as just big enough for paddling a canoe. A tour of the Chittenden Locks in this chapter examines how the project transformed the hydrology of nearby freshwater lakes and the area around Salmon Bay. A feature attraction at the locks is the opportunity, in season, to watch salmon swim upstream through the fish ladder.

Away from the shoreline, Ballard has a reputation among city neighborhoods for being short of tree canopy, sparking a movement in the late twentieth century to "re-tree Ballard." One exception to the tree scarcity is Carkeek Park. Located in a Ballard offshoot called Blue Ridge, Carkeek is the largest park in this part of town, with forest, beach, and a salmon stream. Here you can follow a salmon's journey up the beach and along the waters of Piper's

Devoted volunteers have been restoring Carkeek's lovely Piper's Creek since the 1970s. Salmon return here yearly.

Creek. This relatively easy walk can be supplemented with more strenuous hiking in the woods. This chapter gives you the chance to try both options.

15. Carkeek Park Salmon

Where:	Northwest Seattle at 950 NW Carkeek Park Road
Tour Distance:	Under a mile; options for more
Phone:	(206) 684-0877
Internet:	*http://cityofseattle.net/parks*
Hours:	Park, 6:00 A.M. to 4:00 P.M.; environmental center, 10:00 A.M. to 4:00 P.M.
Disabled Access:	Gravel and paved walkways for creek. No beach access.
Dogs:	On leash and scoop. Please don't let dogs run into the creek—it destroys salmon habitat.
Driving:	From northbound I-5, take Exit 173, Northgate/First Avenue NE, turn left onto First Avenue NE. Turn left onto Northgate Way headed west. Cross the intersections of Meridian and Aurora Avenues. Continue westbound to Greenwood Avenue North. Turn right (north) onto Greenwood. Drive two blocks to NW 110th Street and turn left. Cross Third Avenue NW and continue as 110th becomes NW Carkeek Park Road. Descend this road until you reach a sign for Carkeek Park on your left. Turn here. The park's environmental education center is immediately to the right. Stop here for information or continue down this main road until it forks. Go right slightly uphill, and when you see Puget Sound ahead of you, find a parking spot. (If these spots are full, continue on to the next lot.) Walk toward the water to where a pedestrian bridge crosses train tracks.
Bus:	28
Special Note:	Salmon returns begin here around the first week of November, weather-dependent

Begin by crossing the pedestrian bridge to Carkeek's beach (1). From here, walk south about fifty feet to the mouth of Piper's Creek, which flows under the train tracks through three partially submerged culverts. In dry weather the creek here can be reduced to a rivulet crossing the sand, too small to carry even the slimmest of salmon fry to saltwater. This trickle, believe it or not, becomes a waterway with more gusto on a rainy fall day, allowing the chum

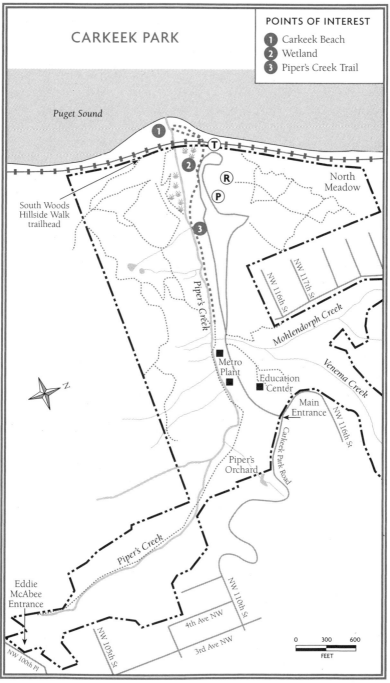

CARKEEK PARK

POINTS OF INTEREST
1 Carkeek Beach
2 Wetland
3 Piper's Creek Trail

Puget Sound

South Woods
Hillside Walk
trailhead

North
Meadow

Piper's Creek

Mohlendorph Creek

Venema Creek

Metro
Plant

Education
Center

Main
Entrance

NW 116th St

NW 116th St

NW 117th St

Piper's
Orchard

Carkeek Park Road

Piper's Creek

Eddie
McAbee
Entrance

NW 110th St

4th Ave NW

3rd Ave NW

NW 105th St

NW 100th Pl

0   300   600
FEET

and coho salmon that return to Piper's Creek to make their entrance. This is the struggling urban creek they left one to five years ago (each species differs in this regard), returning usually by the hundreds to spawn in their natal stream.

They come at different times, but especially during a new or dark moon, after a heavy rain that plumps the stream to optimal fullness, and during high tide. Salmon gather in the Sound near the creek's mouth, and when conditions are right, they begin their upstream migration. A run of coho salmon return here annually around the first week of November, as they have done since they were first re-stocked in the 1970s. They have often finished spawning before returning chum salmon—the only salmon now released into the stream on an annual basis—arrive in the second or third week of November. Chum, which require cooler temperatures than coho, wait for the heavier fall rains to make their passage up from Puget Sound. If you visit at the right time you will spy salmon moving upstream. Look for the wriggling of their bodies as they negotiate the shallowest areas of water along the beach. People often find dead salmon in the pools between sea and stream here during November and December. Salmon may become too weak to reach the creek, or are attacked by raccoons, dogs, or other predators.

Return to the pedestrian bridge and recross the train tracks. On the other side, turn right on the sidewalk at the bottom of the ramp and go past the kiosk to a sign marked "Footpath." Take the path downhill alongside the road. When the path forks, go right downhill (passing a "closed to pets" sign— if you have a dog with you stay on the road until you see the creek and meadow on the right) toward the wetland (2), leaving the roadside path behind. Continue on the trail, keeping the wetland on your right. Stop at any time to contemplate this Seattle Parks and Recreation Department restoration project to correct decades of wetland abuse. Here, and in Carkeek's creeks (the tributaries Venema and Mohlendorph Creeks also run here), are a variety of bugs, amphibians, and fish supported by the ecosystem's improved health. These include not only salmon, but also cutthroat trout and the occasional oddity such as a cast-off goldfish.

Emerging from the wetland area on the path, continue on the crosswalk over the road, and keep walking down the gravel path of the Piper's Creek Trail (3). The creek is on your right behind trees, and a long meadow is on your left. All along this path, from here to where it meets the park's sewage treatment plant, are many good overlooks where you can get a view of Piper's and perhaps salmon.

Coho Alevins

THE HATCHERY DEBATE

The life cycle of salmon is at the heart of a Piper's Creek controversy. Sadly, Piper's had not been a viable spawning ground for salmon for decades before restoration began. Because no wild salmon were returning, stocking the creek with hatchery fish made sense to many stream proponents, who wanted to see Piper's return to its roots. But to some salmon and freshwater creek advocates, stocking was not an ideal solution.

According to the nonprofit organization Washington Trout, there were and are other options for restoring salmon to a stream like Piper's, without introducing hatchery-raised fish. For example, a certain percentage of wild salmon stray from their natal streams and try to colonize other stream systems. If a stream like Piper's is restored and improved, but hatchery fish are not added, it's possible that in five or ten years the creek will be recolonized by straying wild salmon. Adding hatchery fish, which are known to be more aggressive, and releasing them in large quantities—dominating creek resources—makes recolonization much less likely. Not only that, hatchery fish may breed with wild fish, diluting the pure genetic strain. Introducing hatchery fish can mean writing off a stream for wild fish.

It's difficult to understand what makes hatchery fish, originally created from wild salmon stocks, less desirable than colonizing fish, which are also not native to a creek. But hatchery salmon are created with human interference—people decide which salmon will mate to produce the stocks, thus removing the natural selection process. Like a human female, a spider, or a peregrine falcon, a female salmon has its own selection process for a mate. The males wriggling their way toward her have a good chance of being rebuffed unless they have what she decides are the right qualifications. Tinkering with hatchery fish may mean missing out on a stronger genetic strain that a female would ensure with her finicky taste in fathers. Indeed, wild fish are much more likely to survive infancy to adulthood than hatchery-raised fish.

On the other hand, there is a value in hatchery fish as educational tools. When children in local schools raise salmon alevins, they learn about salmon ecology firsthand. And when visitors come to this stream in November, they see for themselves a tangible benefit of creek restoration.

A wild creek, say fish experts, is something quite different than the usual city creek-ditch. Restoring the latter is more an art than a science. There are no predictable coordinates or measurements to follow to create a living system. A ditch, the old model for how to drain excess water out of a city, is intended to move overflow quickly from one place to another using the least area necessary. A stream, designed over time by natural forces, is dynamic and meandering. The artful restoration efforts here at Piper's began in the 1970s, led by the Carkeek Watershed Community Action Project. This volunteer group restored salmon to what had been a neglected waterway. It continues to be the major group advocating for the health of the creek. Volunteers, along with Seattle Public Utilities, make changes to the creek according to what they know about the preferences of fish, and make corrections when they're proved wrong.

Here's what they know: Salmon are weary travelers by the time they've swum from saltwater to freshwater, across a beach, and up this stream to spawn; they like slow water to rest in, deep pools, and shaded hiding places. They do not like a flat, straight stream, where the water moves over gravel and sediment in a choppy, uniform style called a riffle.

Unless you're here during a massive rainfall when the stream is rushing in high volumes, you'll likely notice how Piper's contains some areas with still pools, others with tiny waterfalls, and still others with a slow meandering flow. Before the habitat restoration projects this creek was simply one big riffle. Notice what lines the banks of the creek, and what you see in the water. Artful attempts at making the creek more hospitable to salmon seem to be working. A set of three logs, arranged to look a bit like a K, is called a "K-weir," the backbone of the K form having a hole in it where fish can swim through. This structure creates a deeper, faster moving current of water for fish in areas of shallow, slow water, and scours out a pool like the ones you see here. A "deflector log," like an arm extended out into the water, is also positioned so that water at the edge of the log continually scours out a pool where fish rest and hide. At creek's edge, logs and huge boulders have been placed to prevent erosion—too much floating sediment, a serious problem at this creek located at the bottom of a ravine of unstable soil, can choke fish of oxygen. The planting of native vegetation at stream's edge provides refuge for fish, to protect them from dogs, raccoons, great blue herons, and other hungry or curious souls.

One creek overlook curves out toward the water, backed by a stand of evergreens. The creek is at its prettiest here, winding, protected by overhanging vegetation, dotted with hefty boulders breaking up the flow of water. The pink tags you see hanging in trees over the creek in fall are markers the surveyors for the nonprofit Washington Trout use to note where they've found a salmon nest, known as a redd.

This stream is as vulnerable as it is lovely. It's not a very big or deep waterway, and you can see where people let their dogs run down into the water to play, stirring up sediment and possibly disturbing salmon or fry.

OTHER CARKEEK ATTRACTIONS

Although Piper's Creek and the salmon return are the park's big draw (even the children's playground has a fishy theme), there's much more hidden in this ravine. The following are marked on the Carkeek Park map in this chapter, and worthy of further exploration:

1. Wetland Area. The train tracks cut off what was an estuary here—a mix of salt- and fresh-water where fish and birds thrived—and turned this area into a murky freshwater pond where party-loving park visitors once dumped their trash and only invasive weeds thrived.

Common Horsetail

In the late 1990s the Seattle Parks and Recreation Department dug a deeper pond here and began to replace invasives such as blackberry and purple loosestrife with native plants. The wetland has since regained some hint of its old grace. Flitting over the water, dragonflies indicate the presence of smaller insects they require for their meals. Water striders scramble over the pond surface, and other insects important for salmon suste-nance, called benthic invertebrates, live in the gravel at the bottom. From late spring through the summer you may hear the high-pitched peep of native tree frogs here, or catch sight of a Pacific giant or western salamander. Gawky saplings of cedar, fir, spruce, shore pine, and hem-lock provide shelter for a range of elegant native shrubs and perennials, shoulder to shoulder with clumps of water-loving alder and willow.

Several native plant species are easily recognizable to visitors. Nettle and horsetail, for instance, can be found all over the park lowlands. In past times, local tribes used these plants at the start of the year, the first of the seasonal natives to send out new growth. Visitors can search out four different species of horsetail—a prehistoric plant that was tough enough to survive what dinosaurs couldn't—growing in individual, feathery spikes wherever it can gain a foothold. Most species of horse-tail are partially coated by silicon dioxide, which traditionally made them useful for scouring and light sanding.

2. Piper's Creek Trail. Walk the entire length of the Piper's Creek Trail, about a 1.35-mile walk one-way. Besides getting a sense of park habitat, you'll also come across a historic apple orchard, located on a small slope to

your left as you walk up and away from the creek, past a Metro sewage treatment plant. Planted here by the Piper family in the late nineteenth century, this orchard is slowly being restored. When one specimen dies, it will be replaced by a graft from one of the other trees to ensure genetic continuity.

3. South and North Woods. The South Woods Hillside Walk shouldn't take longer than about thirty minutes, and can be shortened to suit your time and energy. Start by ascending the South Bluff Trail near where the creek goes under the train tracks toward the beach. As you climb the South Bluff Trail you'll overlook the Sound—a good place to catch sunset on a clear evening. At the top of the bluff, turn away from the Sound and into denser woods.

The north meadow is a recommended walk destination in the north woods. Both hike options are on the Carkeek tour map.

Nothing on either slope is old growth except remnant cedar stumps that are no longer "growth," but nevertheless are reminders of the ancient forest, and are being catalogued. The forest contains many alder and maple trees that succeeded the fir, spruce, hemlock, and especially cedar that once dominated these hillsides. The deciduous trees make for a less diverse forest than the evergreen stands they replaced. Work parties since early 2000 have begun to plant trees and remove the choking invasive ivy, holly, and other species that impede the growth of natives, and to improve trails and signage. On the south slope, keep your eyes out for a couple of handsome tall cedars and at least two nurse hemlocks, dead or dying trees that support the growth of a younger tree that is "nursed" on the old wood. Understory plants includes hazelnut, huckleberry, Indian plum, and a variety of ferns. On the ground, many small rodents pass through or live in the park, the most notable being the mountain beaver, a primitive member of the rodent family and not really a beaver at all. You probably won't catch sight of it, but you will see its holes surrounded by piles of dirt. Quite a few bird species can be found in the woods, including pileated woodpeckers, Northern flickers, owls, sparrows, and several species of warblers.

Indian Plum

The shady woods of Carkeek Park are a quiet escape in the midst of the city.

WOODLAND PARK PLEASURES

At the edge of the Phinney Ridge neighborhood, just above Green Lake, the ninety acres of Woodland Park and its zoo and rose garden draw three different, nature-loving crowds. The park, which straddles busy Aurora Avenue, contains woodsy footpaths and places to ride a mountain bike, as well as picnic tables and Frisbee-worthy lawns. Rabbits hopping through the underbrush here may be European wild rabbits, which were brought to Seattle sometime in the middle of the twentieth century from the San Juan Islands, and before that from overseas. These rabbits are at home in the outdoors, away from people, though obviously the park is not their natural habitat. This is also the city's most popular dumping ground for domestic bunnies released by pet owners. Dutch, New Zealand, Holland Lops, and more than thirty other breeds of rabbits struggle to survive in the park, falling prey to diseases and, with their white or other stand-out markings, making easy meals for red-tailed hawks, coyotes, and other local predators. The Washington chapter of the House Rabbit Society (*www.houserabbit.org/*) has rescued domestic rabbits from Woodland Park and offers them for adoption.

The rose garden inside the zoo's entrance at North Fiftieth Street and Fremont Avenue is an official test site for new hybrid rose varieties and a fragrant visit in summer. The award-winning zoo, of course, guarantees sightings of captive animals—but it also happens to be a good wild bird-watching destination. More than 130 species of birds have been seen here, including lazuli buntings and the area's resident bald eagles. The zoo website, *http://zoo.org*, offers a checklist of wild birds seen on the grounds. Walk through the park woods by passing behind the rose garden. For more information, call (206) 684-4075.

Urban streams are extremely hard to keep clean. They're like those dark corners of a basement, where everyone's castoffs collect. Here, what gathers is whatever can be washed downhill from surrounding neighborhoods: the runoff from oil-spotted city streets, the fecal coliform bacteria (one of the biggest sources of urban stream pollution) generated from the use of the outdoors as a bathroom for thousands of city pets, the pesticides and herbicides some gardeners use on lawns and flowerbeds. All of this runs naturally to the low point of the local watershed—the bottom of Carkeek Park. You might not have realized it, but every time you choose not to spray pesticides on your roses, to scoop your dog's poop, or to get your car washed at a place that recycles the wash water, you are making a decision to help save a creek and a fish run.

Examples of personal decisions affecting entire city creeks abound. Here's one from Thornton Creek, a north-end watershed: Neighbors who made daily visits to the creek noticed dead fish floating in the water. When Seattle Public Utilities personnel came to investigate they walked upstream and found a man pressure-washing the concrete outside his house to rid it of moss—after having sprayed it with moss-killing chemicals, which were running down into the creek. With a channel this small, the impact of one person's house-cleaning had a major effect on its quality—one this homeowner, who liked to take his own kids fishing, was remorseful to learn about.

Even with individual awareness, it is very hard to bring this or other urban creeks back to a serious salmon-carrying capacity. The sewage treatment plant at Carkeek overflowed into the waters of Venema Creek as recently as 1999, and ongoing pathology studies of urban salmon show those in some creeks die with high levels of petroleum in their flesh. It may be that only radical changes to how we live in King County would be enough to solve our creek woes. Do human populations want to make the sacrifice to make urban creeks productive again for salmon? It's a question that will become more pressing as Seattle continues to grow.

As the path forks at the end of this area, you may choose to continue on this trail past wooded hillsides and an old apple orchard, return to the wetland, or climb into the nearby woods for some urban hiking.

🦎 16. The Big Dig: Hiram M. Chittenden Locks

Where:	Ballard, at 3015 NW Fifty-fourth Street
Tour Distance:	Under 1 mile
Phone:	(206) 783-7059
Internet:	www.nws.usace.army.mil/
Hours:	Grounds, daily 7:00 A.M. to 9:00 P.M. Visitor center, October 1–April 30, 10:00 A.M. to 4:00 P.M., closed Tuesday and Wednesday; May 1–Sept 30, daily 10:00 A.M. to 6:00 P.M.
Disabled Access:	Yes, except administration building
Dogs:	On leash
Driving:	From downtown Seattle, take S.R. 99 (Aurora Avenue) north to the unsigned, right-hand exit immediately after the Aurora Bridge. Keep to the left lane on the off-ramp. At the stop sign, turn left to go under the overpass on Fremont Way North, and continue to a stoplight at Fremont Avenue North. Cross Fremont Avenue and continue about nine blocks to Leary Way NW. Turn right onto Leary. Go about 1.6 miles to a left turn onto NW Market Street in Ballard. In a little over half a mile, Market becomes NW Fifty-fourth Street. You will see the Lockspot Diner on your left, and the entrance to the locks immediately beyond.
Bus:	17

Entering the gates of the Hiram M. Chittenden Locks (1) you'll notice things are a bit more manicured than at most Seattle parks. Not surprising when you consider that the place is run by the U.S. Army Corps of Engineers, a public organization responsible for the ship-shape maintenance of much larger federal projects such as dams, harbors, and canals. First, you'll pass the enticing Carl S. English Jr. Botanical Garden gracefully sloping up the hill to your right, worth exploring when you've finished this tour. The 1915 administration building is straight ahead of you. Beyond lies one of the Corps' largest projects in Seattle—the locks and the ship canal.

Built in the early 1900s, this enormous undertaking gave the burgeoning city longed-for access to freshwater lakes from salty Puget Sound. The locks (there's a small and a large one, their use dependent on the amount and size of boat traffic) are a pair of chambers used to raise or, in the opposite

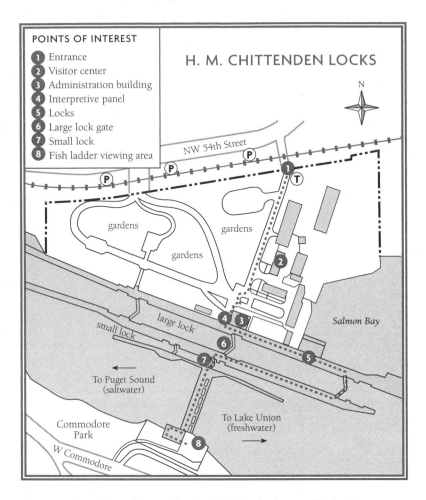

POINTS OF INTEREST
1. Entrance
2. Visitor center
3. Administration building
4. Interpretive panel
5. Locks
6. Large lock gate
7. Small lock
8. Fish ladder viewing area

H. M. CHITTENDEN LOCKS

N

NW 54th Street

gardens

gardens

gardens

large lock

small lock

To Puget Sound (saltwater)

Salmon Bay

Commodore Park

W Commodore

To Lake Union (freshwater)

direction, lower boats from sea level to lake level. The canal links Salmon Bay, just east of here, with Lake Union at the Fremont Cut, and Lake Union with Lake Washington at the Montlake Cut near the University of Washington. The Corps also maintains these locations.

If they're open, the visitor's center (2) and the administration building (3) are excellent starting points. The former is stuffed with locks facts, a hands-on miniature version of the locks, and even a life-size replica of Hiram M. Chittenden, who was the Corps' district engineer in Seattle when the locks were built. Historic photos displayed in the administration building lobby show the site before and during construction. (If the buildings are not open, go to the interpretive panel (4) at the administration building's southwest corner to learn about how the locks operate.)

The project started in 1911, about the same time as its famous larger cousin, the Panama Canal. The main objective locally was to provide passage for Western Washington's abundant natural resources—particularly coal—from the hills to the city and, finally, Puget Sound. In addition, the U.S. Navy and other boating concerns were eager for a freshwater port. One reason was tiny but significant: a wood-boring worm that lived only in saltwater caused serious damage to the wood-hulled boats of an earlier era. Another was that boats would be much easier to load and unload at an inland port free of Puget Sound's dramatic tides.

Although the canal and locks (5) were intended to drive Seattle's economy, you're more likely to spot yachts and other pleasure craft here these days—in 2001 approximately 54,000 vessels were "locked through," but only 10,000 of those were commercial craft, including gravel barges, government research vessels, and fishing boats heading to dry dock on Lake Union. As it turns out,

Cottonwoods frame the Fremont Cut, just east of the Locks. Before 1911, slender Ross Creek flowed here.

the Duwamish Waterway and Harbor Island area in south Seattle became the city's port—an ironic outcome, considering that area rests on tidal flats filled in by dirt removed from a canal project that competed with this one: While the ship canal you see here was still on the drawing board, a Seattle entrepreneur had already dredged thousands of feet of the Duwamish River and hacked and sluiced away at a beleaguered Beacon Hill, hoping to create a canal between the Duwamish and Lake Washington. His project failed when a determined Chittenden was assigned to the Seattle Corps in 1906, and threw his resources behind the north canal project, gaining the backing of the city and the federal government. Most of Seattle came out to celebrate the dedication of the canal and locks on July 4, 1917, as hopeful about its effect on the economy as locals would later be about software and Internet companies.

PARADISE ON WHEELS: THE BURKE-GILMAN TRAIL

It's long and lean and sometimes lovely, a 14-mile paved throughway for cyclists, bladers, and (cautious) pedestrians to travel safely between Ballard and other neighbrhoods in the north end of town, even rounding the north shore of Lake Washington, if they have enough steam. The trail was built in the late 1970s along a railroad right-of-way, and has been a successful alternative to roadways and sidewalks ever since. The city's vegetation management plan considers the trail to have five "classes" of wildlife habitat, but for visitor's purposes, it makes more sense to break the trail up into best uses.

The area from Ballard to the University of Washington area is mostly non-wild, with views of the ship canal, a few fanciful gardens in Fremont, and grassy Gas Works Park in Wallingford—this trail section is there mostly to rescue riders and walkers from the tangle of city traffic. The stretch from Gas Works to the University District is where the best blackberry picking is to be had come late summer. Only the miles of trail north of the university will appeal to those looking for a nature escape—many stretches here remain forested with an overstory of mostly deciduous trees like bigleaf maple, red alder, black cottonwood, and willows that cast a pleasant summer shade. If you're using the trail for the first time, remember to follow a few rules: whether on wheels or foot, keep to the right unless you are passing someone. Use caution at road crossings—cars will sometimes take the right-of-way, even if you don't have a stop sign. Bicyclists must yield to pedestrians and give an audible warning when passing. And—an insider tip for those moving quickly on wheels—watch out for little dogs on long leashes.

This project was an immense undertaking. The outlet from Lake Union before the project was a small creek (known to many as Ross Creek) just upstream from the present locks location, at the Fremont Cut, and only big enough to float a couple of canoes. Where the locks are now was tidelands. And Lake Union and Lake Washington weren't connected.

Now that salt- and freshwater are more forcefully linked, one of the biggest issues is how to keep them from commingling in areas that are traditionally freshwater. As you can imagine, every time a lock opens there's a chance for a "you got your chocolate in my peanut butter" situation with not-so-charming results. Because saltwater is denser than fresh it sinks to the lock's bottom, where it slides in a wedge toward Lake Union and, eventually, Lake Washington, water bodies that are naturally fresh. Saltwater doesn't mix easily with fresh, especially in the sluggish artificial environment here, and thus can cause a damaging stratification or layering of a freshwater ecosystem if it is allowed to intrude. The bottom salt layer lacks oxygen in warm weather, causing problems for salmon and other organisms. In the winter months, constant runoff from the Cascade foothills means saltwater stays put, but in the summer, when flow is low and boat lockages are high, intrusion is a real problem. Lake Union is at slightly less risk because it is small (only about 45 feet deep) and flushed regularly by water drained from Lake Washington. That lake, on the other hand, is our state's second largest natural lake at more than 200 feet deep, and vulnerable to a stratification that could irreversibly damage its ecosystem without preventative measures. Not that the lake's hydrology isn't already topsy-turvy—it was reversed so that the lake drained into Lake Union instead of into the (now largely relict) Black River, which fed into the Duwamish. Underwater sensors along the canal measure the amount of chloride entering Washington's waters in minute portions. Halfway down the gates of the large locks (6) you'll see a rectangular greenish yellow bar—like a gold bar from a cartoon. This block of zinc is placed here to attract the chloride that would otherwise damage the gates—the salt is so damaging the blocks are replaced every three to five years.

Another carefully monitored aspect of this canal is the level of Lake Washington. Lake Union is at the same height it was one hundred years ago, but Lake Washington, in a task that took several months longer than it takes to drain your bathtub, was dropped 9 feet to the level of Lake Union when the two were joined. Maintaining this level is also part of the process of preventing saltwater from migrating upstream—in the winter the Corps holds the lake at about 20 feet, and saltwater stays put in the locks because so much freshwater flushes through. By mid-February they begin raising the level of the lakes again—up to 22 feet—stockpiling water in preparation for the drier summer ahead.

The salt-fresh mix of the locks creates some strange underwater bedfellows. If you come at the right time, you might witness the two weeks of annual maintenance on the small (March) or large (November) locks. The small is shallower and collects fewer species, but according to Corps fish biologists, a long list of fish and sessile, or clinging, sea life make a living in the large lock. From starry flounder and wolf eels, to lamprey and trout, to scallops, blue mussels, and sea urchins, you've got the world's greatest bouillabaisse just waiting for a can of tomatoes. Where else but perhaps an aquarium would herring and small mouth bass bump lips?

Of all the creatures that live here or lock through—many of them do make it through to one side or the other, though it's hard to know how many or what happens to them when they do—no group so influences modern locks operations as the migrating salmon runs. Pass by the small lock (7) and across the dam to the fish ladder viewing area (8), where a large window allows you to see sockeye, chinook, coho, and steelhead as they pass by underwater. As many as four million sockeye smolt outmigrate to saltwater through here, the largest run of its kind in the lower forty-eight states. As you descend the ramps to this area, note the netting covering the water beside you. You are above the fish ladder here, and this barrier keeps salmon, which can leap out of the water 8 or 10 feet into the air, from colliding with concrete. If you're here in late summer or fall you could spot dozens of airborne salmon at a time.

Chittenden foresaw the need for a fish ladder for the locks from the start—unfortunately, ladder technology was not very advanced. According to Corps fish biologists, it is estimated that up until the 1970s, when the ladder was improved, up to 90 percent of the adult salmon were actually using the large lock chamber to get through the system on their lakeward migration. One problem was insufficient "attraction water," the water rushing out of the fish ladder in the opposite direction from the migrating fish, drawing them in the correct direction for migration. The Corps has increased the volume of this water as a solution—because it is flowing continuously, twice as much water is used here daily as at the large lock.

The listing of chinook salmon as a threatened species in Washington in 1996 has required further innovations at the locks, most aimed at increasing the survival rates for juvenile salmon (known as smolts) migrating Soundward. In spring and summer, for instance, look for the white, tubular smolt slides poking out of the dam westward—most juvenile salmon now glide through these to reach saltwater. Before the flumes were in place, studies

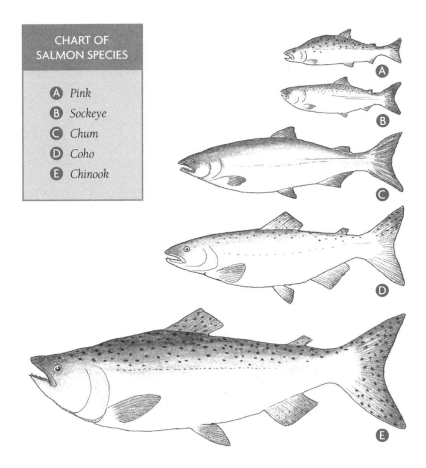

CHART OF
SALMON SPECIES

Ⓐ Pink
Ⓑ Sockeye
Ⓒ Chum
Ⓓ Coho
Ⓔ Chinook

found many juvenile salmon were heading downstream through the locks via concrete underwater conduits. These were lined with barnacles, which wounded and weakened the fish as they scraped against them on the way out. Flashing lights called strobe arrays now installed to deter fish from the conduit entrances have had good results. All these changes have helped—estimates now are that 80 percent of salmon migrating upstream are using the fish ladder and more than 90 percent of juvenile salmon use the flumes. A project like the locks is certainly not environmentally correct by today's standards, but it had the support of settlers at the turn of the last century as a way to turn Seattle into a big, important city. It has changed as environmental awareness has changed. At this point, unlike the water flow of Lake Washington, it isn't really reversible.

17. Shilshole Bay: Sea Lions and Sandy Beaches

Where:	Ballard's Golden Gardens Park
Phone:	(206) 684-7249
Internet:	*http://cityofseattle.net/parks/*
Hours:	24 hours
Disabled Access:	Yes, both docks and beach are wheelchair accessible. Access beach from north end boardwalk near wetlands.
Dogs:	On leash
Driving:	From downtown Seattle, take S.R. 99 (Aurora Avenue) north to the unsigned, right-hand exit immediately after the Aurora Bridge. Keep to the left lane on the off-ramp. At the stop sign, turn left to go under the overpass on Fremont Way North, and continue to a stoplight at Fremont Avenue North. Cross Fremont Avenue and continue about nine blocks to Leary Way NW. Turn right onto Leary. Go about 1.6 miles to a left turn onto NW Market Street in Ballard. Continue on Market as it becomes Seaview Avenue NW, until you pass signs for the Shilshole Bay Marina and the Eddie Vine Boat Ramp on your left. Parking is available at Golden Gardens Park, just beyond the boat ramp. From here you can walk back to the ramp area where sea lions are most likely to be visible.
Bus:	46
Special Note:	Sea lions are most likely to be present from late August through May. To observe them well, be sure to bring binoculars.

Neighbors who move into the Sunset Hill neighborhood above the marina get used to an unusual soundscape—the groans, barks, and grandiose growls of California sea lions, who stop by yearly for an extended visit. You can make the trip here too, to see these giant, gregarious marine mammals in action. At the dock, Puget Sound is before you, its depths teeming with fish. On a clear day the Olympics rise crisply on the horizon. Just north of this spot, the sandy beaches, a rarity in Seattle, of ultra-popular Golden Gardens Park are scattered with beach blankets nearly year-round.

While most female California sea lions remain in the warmer breeding grounds of Mexico and Southern California to nurse their young, many males

California Sea Lions

migrate through Puget Sound in late summer and fall in search of food, which has been depleted in many places farther south. Their numbers peak in April, when more than one thousand sea lions have been counted north of Seattle in Everett, where they like to gather. This is estimated to be about half of all the sea lions living in Washington's inland ocean waters—smaller numbers are also present on the outer coast. More than one hundred sea lions have been counted at Shilshole at one time during peak years. Just outside the rock jetty in front of the marina the sea lions haul out on buoys or a capture platform, their bulk and noise hard to miss.

These agile mammals have sometimes been compared to overgrown puppy dogs, and are cherished at aquariums for their gregarious ways. They are hard to confuse with the other local species, the Steller's (also known as the northern sea lion), which is an endangered species most often seen on Washington's outer coast. Even larger, Steller's have a furry golden coat and only occasionally summon a low roar.

California sea lions are generally unafraid of humans and are easily viewed as they bask or play. They can walk quickly, if awkwardly, on land using their flippers, and take to the water at up to twenty miles an hour. Dark brown to black, they can be picked out at a distance by the large bump on their foreheads (males only).

With all that going for them, you'd think they'd be local darlings. But like all good things, there's a hitch: in this case, a fondness for an endangered run of steelhead.

If you lived in Seattle in the late 1980s or early 1990s you must have heard something about Herschel, a sea lion said to hang out at Chittenden

Locks, just 2 miles from here, gorging himself on the few steelhead passing through. The truth is, there wasn't one Herschel but many, a passel of pesky pinnipeds (a family that includes walruses and seals)—up to forty, at times—being blamed for the dwindling run. One sea lion apparently consumed an average of twelve steelhead over eight hours, a lot when you consider that even twenty years ago the run consisted of only about two thousand fish.

But who can blame the Herschels for doing what comes naturally?

> Sea lions and harbor seals have been known to pass through locks gates and can be occasionally spotted in Lake Washington.

The sea lions, which feed primarily on the much more common Pacific hake, seem to prefer steelhead when they can get them. And the locks, where the steelhead must slow to climb the fish ladder, create a situation akin to shooting fish in a barrel. Since 1989 federal and state agencies have sought to control the mammals and reduce their impact on steelhead runs. Outside the jetty, a haul-out platform was set up as a cage to catch the offenders and relocate them. (It is still used to trap sea lions for tagging and weighing.) But a free trip to Washington's Long Beach Peninsula only made them hungrier when they returned within ten days.

Other deterrent methods such as underwater firecrackers and an inflatable orca suggested by a media-hungry radio announcer apparently weren't convincing enough. The situation came to a head when the National Marine Fisheries Service authorized the Department of Fish and Wildlife to kill the sea lions. Demonstrators rallied, media flocked, and the government backed off until Sea World in Florida offered to take on the marauding mammals. Permanent, 200-decibel underwater noisemakers—the equivalent of a jet engine—were installed at the locks as further deterrent. To hear them, listen for the sound of crickets. Since then, the situation, say officials, is greatly improved—the last time sea lions were seen eating steelhead at the locks was in 1997. Others disagree with the official assessment: Steelhead runs are lower than ever. The state retains the right to use lethal methods on the sea lions if they return, which seems more likely every year. There are signs that some sea lions have become accustomed to the sonic noise used to keep them away, and however cute they are, this time there may not be another aquarium with room for more 800-pound offenders.

From the Eddie Vine Boat Ramp you can walk north and east along the beaches of Golden Gardens to visit another interesting nature attraction, a recently-restored wetland and short loop trail by the park's north beach. The wetlands filter parking lot runoff, and create habitat for ducks such as mallards, wigeons, green-winged teal, northern shovelers, and hooded mergansers.

Pavement was removed to restore Golden Gardens' wetlands. Replanted with native vegetation, the wetlands attract a variety of duck species.

THE OUTSIDERS

Here in Western Washington, a hub of commerce with a busy port, exotic animals and plants are often brought in on ship hulls, nursery plants, or other imported materials. Some non-indigenous species never get a foothold, but some do, in a big way. Non-indigenous species that are vigorous and competitive with natives are called invasive and can wreak havoc on natural resource-based industries and native habitats.

Many plants that have been in the Seattle area for decades have earned this title. The introduced Scotch broom, for instance, a loosely branched shrub up to 10 feet tall, its bright yellow flowers blazing in roadsides and meadows, is a common sight. It forms "monotypic" stands, pushing out other species. Its seeds burst open on hot summer days with an audible "pop," sending its progeny on a flying start. Japanese knotweed is equally noxious. A huge, sturdy perennial 4 to 9 feet tall, it spreads underground by creeping rhizomes, blocks the sun from reaching other plants, and clogs waterways. It can seriously damage lake and riverside habitat.

And any visitor to Green Lake is familiar, whether they know it or not, with Eurasian water milfoil, the feathery aquatic plant that was originally brought in for home aquariums and now chokes at least one hundred water bodies in Washington. For many of these plants, few eradication solutions exist. Around the city volunteer groups work to defeat loosestrife, English ivy, and nonnative clematis vines and replant areas with native species, but invasives are like any other pest—persistent and tough.

Invasive animal species are another category of problem, and one that tends to get more news coverage. The European green crab (*Carcinus maenas*), first seen on the west coast of the United States in San Francisco Bay in 1989, is a small shore crab that moved up the coast and has now been spotted on the outer coast of Washington, but not yet in Puget Sound. This fearsome crab preys on other bivalves (clams, oysters, and mussels), and even crabs its own size, cutting through shells with strong claws. Another anticipated invader is the zebra mussel (*Dreissena polymorpha*), a freshwater species that first gained a foothold in the Great Lakes region of the United States in the 1990s, and has since been spreading westward. It is known to clog intake pipes and take over habitat.

Rules for prevention would be funny if they weren't so serious. Boaters are urged to "stop aquatic hitchhikers" by removing all dirt, mud, plants (including fragments), and animals from their boats, clothing, boots, and other equipment before exiting any water body, and to "eliminate water from all equipment," including the family dog.

The world has long been a place where unruly animals and plants jump ship and try to colonize new territory, and attempts to control species movements are fraught with problems.

Two recent threats are good examples: Only a few gypsy moths had been trapped when the Washington State Department of Agriculture announced in 2002 it would be spraying 16 acres of Ballard, Magnolia, and Salmon Bay to eliminate the "invasion." Gypsy moths can damage and kill trees and shrubs and the females can travel long distances to lay eggs. Ballard's Crown Hill residents organized in protest against the spraying of their yards, fearful of health risks. No gypsy moths have since been found in the area, but the spraying controversy continues. Another tree-damaging pest, the citrus longhorned beetle, was found at a Tukwila tree nursery in 2001, the first to be found out of doors in the United States; the U.S. Department of Agriculture decision to chop and chip all trees potentially infested with its larvae—those within 1/8 mile of the nursery—was not a popular decision with all tree owners.

ARACHNOPHILIA

Seattle is spider heaven. Spiders are prone to drying out, so they thrive in the Pacific Northwest's moist climate. For the squeamish who may not think this is good news, consider that almost no spiders in the Northwest are dangerous to humans. In fact this eight-legged arthropod, unlike your usual household pet, can eat many times its weight in flies, pantry moths, and other bugs that might indeed cause a nuisance. For this, the arachnid asks not for compensation, but simply to be left alone.

Of course, naturalists won't want to leave them alone—these fascinating creatures reward study. Many spiders weave webs, from the familiar flat orb web with radiating spokes, to sheet webs, funnel webs, and other shapes. They have interesting hunting and mating habits, and at least a few species are active and visible at nearly all times of the year.

Late spring is an excellent time to view spiders, when moist conditions allow them to be more active. This is also when native species in particular are courting and reproducing. The backyard, local parks, and your own bathtub are always good places to spot spiders, but a landscape with a variety of habitats, such as forest, meadow and wetland, native vegetation, and unmanicured ground cover is the best place to find a variety of spider species. A top in-city destination is Schmitz Park in West Seattle, where Rod Crawford, an arachnid expert and curator at the Burke Museum has found more than four hundred spider specimens in one day, including some of the city's rarest natives. According to Crawford, around two hundred spider species have been identified within the city. About twenty-five of these species are house spiders, which are rarely seen in the outdoors, and 75 percent are native.

An orb web weaver lays a sticky trap for insects.

Watch for the following arachnids in and around your home:

The most common spiders in Seattle, though not often noted, are the sheet web weavers (Linyphiidae). These spiders, 1 to 3 millimeters long, weave postage-stamp-size webs between the bases of grass blades. In a squishy-moist lawn densities can reach one hundred specimens per square meter.

The native common flower spider (Misumena vatia) lives in flowers and can adapt its color to their petal or pollen color—it can turn white, pale greenish, or yellow.

In spring, watch long grass for the thumbnail-size, black, native wolf spider (Pardosa vancouveri). The name "wolf spider" refers to its method of capturing prey—these spiders hunt down food rather than catching it in a web.

The hobo spider (Tegenaria agrestis), much ballyhooed in the press for its ability to cause health problems in humans, is actually quite rare. A pre-1930 import from Europe, its existence is being challenged by a more recently introduced species, the giant house spider (Tegenaria gigantea), a hobo predator. The giant house spider's venom does not cause illness in humans. The hobo weaves a funnel web with an oval-shaped opening (other, non-harmful spiders weave funnel webs with round openings). Hobo webs tend to be found at the bases of stone or cement walls, in rockeries, or on vacant lots with rubble from old foundations.

The Scarab Society, a Seattle-area group dedicated to spiders and other bugs, welcomes new, active members. They offer field trips, meetings, parties, and a newsletter. Call (206) 543-9853 to get involved.

The rituals of spider courtship are fascinating to watch. Males must draw the attention of females, known as fierce predators. His job is to get her out of predatory mode long enough to mate with her. Courtship styles depend on spider type. Web-weaving males send messages through the web, and a jumping spider, with good eyesight, uses visual cues. Sheet web weavers have a tooth-like projection against which they scrape a file on the side of their jaw, creating enticing vibrations as a cricket would. And spiders with no web or tooth and bad vision rely on touch to get the message across. Watch a female orb web weaver on her web during mating season and you might see a male approach. He will attach a long line to the web, crawl up and begin to pluck the strands. When the female rushes in to capture what she thinks is prey, the male drops to safety. Over and over he does this, sometimes for an hour or more, until she finally gathers he's in the mood for love.

Green Lake Watershed:
GREEN LAKE, RAVENNA, AND THE UNIVERSITY DISTRICT

This area of land is a watershed in theory only these days, ever since the early twentieth century when the lake was lowered and disconnected from freshwater and a drainage route. One look at murky Green Lake confirms that a flow of freshwater would greatly improve conditions. Nevertheless, this is the most popular park in the city, diverse in trees, birds, and human visitors.

This busy lake once drained by way of Ravenna Creek into Union Bay on Lake Washington. At the outlet, before European settlers arrived, a Native American village with five longhouses thrived in an area abundant with fish and overwintering ducks. Ravenna was a rich salmon stream. The creek was diverted into pipe in the early twentieth century to make way for development. It now flows aboveground only in Ravenna Park. Pavement, a shopping mall, and other development stand between the natural creek and its Union Bay outlet. Neighborhood activists have lobbied for years to reconnect the creek with Union Bay. In 2003 this long-awaited project will finally break ground.

Much of Union Bay's western shoreline is now dominated by the University of Washington campus. From here and uphill to the west, the university was built in the late nineteenth and early twentieth centuries on 350 acres of what even then was considered prime real estate, with mountain views and extensive shoreline.

To experience tall trees, wild creatures, and flowing water in the Green Lake, Ravenna, or University neighborhoods today, you'll have to choose your destinations selectively. Start by taking a Green Lake bird tour, a nearly 3-mile walk that introduces you to some of Seattle's visiting and resident bird species. A second tour in this chapter gets you into a canoe on Union Bay, a great vantage point for catching sight of shy birds such as herons, as well as resident frogs and turtles, muskrats and beavers. Ravenna Park is a historic park in a wooded ravine with a creek—it's a place that feels surprisingly remote in such a busy area. The University of Washington campus is a fine place to

Secluded, marshy areas of Union Bay attract green herons, bitterns, frogs, and turtles.

stroll, especially if your walk takes you to such attractions as the medicinal herb garden or the 1895 observatory, the second oldest building on campus. This destination is a stellar place to get a city view of the night sky, stars, and planets under a retracting dome. Finally, though you pass the Union Bay Natural Area on the canoe trip, visiting this unique Seattle habitat by land allows you to explore the open grasslands, marshy areas, and seasonal ponds that make this one of the best birding areas in the city.

18. Swamp Things: Paddling Lake Washington

Where:	University of Washington Waterfront Activities Center
Tour Distance:	About 3 or 4 miles by boat
Phone:	(206) 543-9433
Internet:	http://depts.washington.edu/ima/IMA.wac.html
Hours:	Variable by season. Call for details. Closed November through January.
Disabled Access:	Boat dock is wheelchair accessible. No assistance transferring into boats, but the WAC will store wheelchairs during rental period.
Dogs:	If they like boating! Barking dogs in boat will not allow for birdwatching, however.
Fees:	In 2002, canoe and rowboat rentals were $6.50/hour for the general public, less for UW faculty, alumni, and students. Includes boat, oars, and lifejackets. You must be eighteen or older with a valid identification to rent. Parking at the WAC is free after noon and some days, and rates vary other times. Call for information.
Driving:	From downtown Seattle, take I-5 north about 3 miles to Exit 169 toward NE Forty-fifth Street/NE Fiftieth Street. Take the ramp toward NE Forty-fifth Street and the University of Washington. Turn right onto Forty-fifth. After several blocks turn right at Fifteenth Avenue NE. Turn left onto NE Pacific Street. Get in the turning lane at NE Pacific Place, just across from the University of Washington Medical Center and before the Montlake Bridge. Go left onto NE Pacific Place. Continue straight at the next light, across Montlake Boulevard, and into the parking lot for Husky Stadium. Park in the lot to the right (south) of the stadium. The Waterfront Activities Center is in the building next to the water.

Bus: 43

Special Note: Consider bringing a picnic and pulling ashore in the arboretum for lunch

Union Bay stretches before you as you stand beside your canoe at the Waterfront Activities Center, trying to remember the mechanics of the j-stroke. This part of Lake Washington was deeper and wider before it was lowered in 1916; its waters would once have lapped the stadium and swamped University Village.

Leaving the Activities Center, head north along the dock beside you (1), away from the Montlake Cut. Stay fairly near the shoreline, with Husky Stadium looming on your left. In front of you rafts of vegetation will emerge. Most prominent upon them, especially in summer, are the slowly molting brown flower spikes of our native cattail, *Typha latifolia*. Besides conjuring up sweet memories of lakeside summers experienced or read about in books, cattails are a wonderfully useful plant. They buffer shoreline from erosion-causing

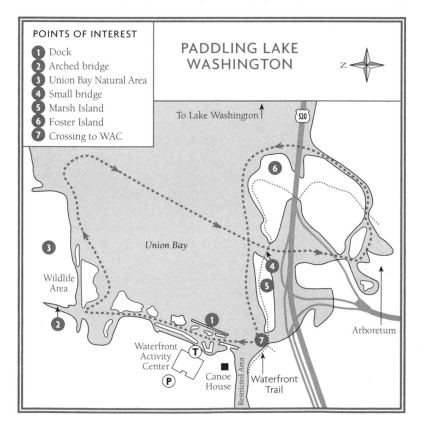

POINTS OF INTEREST
1 Dock
2 Arched bridge
3 Union Bay Natural Area
4 Small bridge
5 Marsh Island
6 Foster Island
7 Crossing to WAC

PADDLING LAKE WASHINGTON

To Lake Washington

Union Bay

Wildlife Area

Arboretum

Waterfront Activity Center

Canoe House

Waterfront Trail

Restricted Area

waves, and are fine habitat for nesting birds. Here you might see red-winged blackbirds or various duck species. Some mammals eat these plants, and some birds use the downy fluff of ripe cattails as nest material. Native American tribes such as the Coast Salish, and intrepid nonnatives, have eaten this plant from root to pollen. The leaves can be harvested for paper or woven mats. The "tail" you see is made up of male flowers on top, which wither soon after flowering, and the longer-lasting female flowers below, that turn brown and blow away as fluff late in summer.

Staying ever west, the way narrows until finally you'll spy a small, arched Japanese bridge (2). The water is usually too high to go under it by boat. Approach this area quietly, as great blue herons often stand here at the edge of the water, so still it's as if they've been placed under a spell. Stay put and watch from a distance, so as not to disturb them. You may see a heron cantilever in ultra-slow-motion over the water, until suddenly it darts its bill into the shallow depths to snatch up a wriggling fish.

The water around here often bubbles, trapped gases from decomposing plant material below. Ravenna Creek, which once refreshed this part of the lake and is now diverted to the Metro sewage treatment plant at Discovery Park, will be reintroduced to this bay and freshen things up in 2003 or 2004. Perhaps a million gallons of water a day will once again flow here, mitigating pollution runoff from University Village and nearby parking lots, and increasing water circulation. It will be interesting to watch how the habitat changes as a result.

To avoid disturbing local wildlife, paddle east of here, but don't pull too close to shoreline or talk too loudly. To the north is the Union Bay Natural Area (3), also known as the Montlake Fill, a former garbage dump on wetlands. You may, if observant, catch sight of one of the smaller herons that hunt here near shore, such as the green heron or the bittern. Once you are across the water from Foster Island, the misshapen pair of lungs on the map, watch carefully for passing boat traffic and make the crossing to the south side of this tour. You are aiming for the small bridge (4) between Marsh Island and Foster Island.

Around thirty different species of fish live in Lake Washington. Those that may be flexing their gills beneath you range from the petite and whiskery catfish to yellow perch, large- and smallmouth bass, five species of salmon, and common carp weighing 40 pounds or more. Any of these scaly specimens, however, would be dwarfed (and probably eaten) by a native species that looms large in Lake Washington fishing mythology, the monstrous, bottom-feeding white sturgeon (*Acipenser transmontanus*). Native to only three West Coast rivers—the Sacramento, Fraser, and Columbia—this behemoth

Non-native white water lilies thrive in Union Bay. They crowd out natives but also provide habitat.

can grow to 14 feet in length and may weigh up to a ton. Although some believe they no longer swim here, tagged specimens suggest these brutes are still stopping by for a snack. Sturgeon can roam freely between salt- and fresh-water, and don't begin to spawn until they are perhaps fifteen years old. Until then, when they head to their homewaters (in this case the Columbia), they can be found in Puget Sound or nearby lakes when not in the ocean feeding. If you're brave enough to look for them, they are elongated, dark gray fish with rows of bony scales on their back and sides, and a flattened snout from which protrude four barbels looking like a really bad moustache. These fish may live to be one hundred years old. Move over, Loch Ness.

As you pass under the small bridge, people in sturdy shoes tromp above you on the arboretum's Waterfront Trail. For more information on what you'll see there, drop in at the arboretum visitor center—probably a separate trip, as it's about a quarter-mile walk on the trail. Underneath the paths, the ground contains peat deposits up to 70 feet deep.

The deeper you get into the marsh ahead of you, the closer you'll get to Seattle's version of a bayou. It's murky and moist, overhung with willows, cottonwoods, alder, and birch trees. Not much is pristine about this place, as it's been channeled, dredged, and filled, and a highway's sonic hiss has been added to the gabble of ducks and croak of frogs. You'll need to bravely paddle beneath this intrusion to reach the marsh's quieter backwaters. Cut west behind Marsh Island (5) if you want to take a little side trip. Otherwise, begin the circuit around Foster Island (6).

When the weather warms, the most noticeable arboretum reptile will emerge from pond-bottom hibernation to bask on logs—our city's turtles, just your typical sun-starved Seattleites. In fact, sunlight is crucial for their biological functioning, aiding, for instance, in digestion and in the formation of eggs in females. A variety of terrapins may be catching rays. Watch for the native painted turtle (*Chrysemys picta*), which has a reddish plastron or lower shell, an olive-gray carapace or top shell, and thin red or yellow stripes on the neck and legs. This species gets irritable when crowded. That's one way to distinguish it from the red-eared slider (*Trachemys scripta elegans*), an introduced species that is so gregarious you might spot several members stacked on top of one another like very thick pancakes. The spiny softshell turtles (*Apalone spinifera*) are softshelled, of course, with a funny pointed nose. They are also recent immigrants to Lake Washington. In fact, the lake is such a popular place for people to release aquatic animal species

Red-Eared Slider

Western Pond Turtle

that it probably hosts as many nonnatives as natives at this point.

One native species you probably won't find here is the western pond turtle, a reptile that is shy of humans, and was once common in Washington. Destruction of habitat, predation by introduced fish and bullfrogs, and diseases perhaps passed along by introduced turtles may be responsible for the decline of this aquatic creature. It is now endangered here. The Washington State Western Pond Turtle Project, in conjunction with the Woodland Park Zoo, has worked since 1990 to restore the turtles, with some success.

In summer you're sure to see white water lilies (*Nymphaea odorata*) all along your tour. These nonnatives reemerge here in late spring after dying back over the winter. They have crowded out other species such as the sunny native spatterdock (*Nuphar luteum* ssp. *polysepalum*) but serve as cover for animals, food for muskrats and beaver (both residents), and nesting habitat for pied-billed grebes. You may spot a female grebe on a nest on the lily pads in summer. Another nonnative, the European iris, echoes the yellow spatterdock color, its erect flower clusters in bunches at the shoreline.

If you're emerging around the other side of Foster Island in the evening, you may become aware of a Hitchcockian influx of crows. They're not here to mob you, they're settling in for the evening. Most of Seattle's crows spend their nights in a communal roost here on Foster Island. This behavior allows them to socialize and to protect themselves from predators such as hawks and owls. In breeding season more crows stay near their own nests scattered throughout the city, so winter is the best time to see this congregation. Stand on a city street at dusk, or look at the sky from your backyard, and you will surely begin to notice corvids (the family name for crow) headed this direction. It is estimated that up to ten thousand crows have roosted in the north end of the arboretum at one time. Crow populations have exploded in Seattle over the years, and many believe these birds bear the blame for the predation of nests of other species such as robins and bushtits. As subjects for the birdwatcher, however, they offer much interest. They are thought to be one of the smartest bird species, with remarkable counting skills and excellent memorization ability. They mate for life, and their nest-building and the fledging of young are relatively easy to observe in city neighborhoods.

If you're ready to flock home to your own roost, complete the circle around Foster Island and make the crossing back to the Activities Center to return your canoe. Watch carefully for boat traffic, especially on weekends. To reduce the amount of time you spend on open water, you may want to cross the lake closer to the opening of the Montlake Cut (7).

🦎 19. Green Lake's Birding Bounty

Where:	North of downtown in the Green Lake neighborhood
Tour Distance:	2.8 miles
Phone:	(206) 684-4075
Internet:	*http://cityofseattle.net/parks*
Hours:	24 hours
Disabled Access:	Yes
Dogs:	On leash, but not conducive to wildlife viewing
Driving:	From downtown Seattle, take I-5 north about 4 miles to Exit 170, Ravenna Boulevard, toward NE Sixty-fifth Street. Take a slight right onto Green Lake Drive North. In a few blocks turn left into the parking lot at the Latona Avenue traffic light.
Bus:	26, 16

Green Lake's motto should be "survival of the fittest." Here, at perhaps the busiest park in the state, everyone competes for breathing room. To keep up, human visitors circling the lake dodge inline skaters and stroller flotillas. The non-human world faces even greater challenges. Ailing cottonwood trees await the city's chainsaw, while the lake's trout struggle for oxygen during seasonal algae blooms. Park birds, in particular, illustrate the savvy required for survival in such a bustling outdoor destination.

Begin in front of the Green Lake Community Center (1) and walk the lake clockwise to the first rounded-off corner where the path forks. In winter look near here (2) for a great blue heron perched out on a piling or diving platform. They hunt—mostly for fish—in the early morning, and in the daytime they sometimes escape the crowds by moving high up in nearby evergreens. A rusty plume of liquid spreading into the lake in this area is the result of soil bacteria breaking down horse manure in the former (1930s) garbage dump in the playfields behind you.

At Green Lake, think twice before you reach for your pocket or purse. It has been reported that several bird species, particularly starlings, have begun to imitate the most popular cell phone rings.

Continue along the path, watching for waterfowl lakeside and admiring maples, birches, and cherry trees on your left. As with many green spaces in Seattle, the Olmsted Brothers developed much of this park's rolling topography and unusual treescape. No one knows exactly which existing trees are Olmsted-selects,

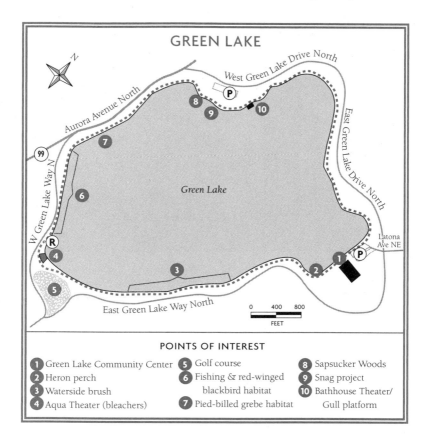

GREEN LAKE

West Green Lake Drive North

Aurora Avenue North

East Green Lake Drive North

W Green Lake Way N

Green Lake

Latona Ave NE

East Green Lake Way North

0 400 800 FEET

POINTS OF INTEREST

1 Green Lake Community Center
2 Heron perch
3 Waterside brush
4 Aqua Theater (bleachers)
5 Golf course
6 Fishing & red-winged blackbird habitat
7 Pied-billed grebe habitat
8 Sapsucker Woods
9 Snag project
10 Bathhouse Theater/ Gull platform

but a brochure available in the Green Lake Community Center gives the species name of nearly every park tree. Information about many of these specimens is also found in *Trees of Green Lake* by Arthur Lee Jacobson.

To understand Green Lake as bird habitat, remember that many birds are only here for one or two seasons of the year. Some migrate according to the weather, while others stay in this general area but search for more breeding space. In the winter when they're not breeding, songbirds and waterfowl can get by in more crowded conditions. As spring and the breeding season approach, however, they need elbowroom. From pied-billed grebes to red-winged blackbirds, they begin to mark out territory, the males often battling for dominance and the right to mate with a female.

A bird walk at Green Lake may yield close to fifteen bird species in summer, while in winter that number can increase to thirty-five or more. Many waterfowl such as wigeons and coots spend the cold season here, then migrate elsewhere for breeding when the weather warms. Although in breeding

Green Lake was lowered in 1911 to make room for this busy park, home to a variety of unusual trees and bird life.

season, which varies by species but is usually in spring or summer, bird numbers are lower, there's much interesting behavior to see, including nest-building, foraging, and the emergence of young. Watch in the waterside brush (3) for bushtit nests, gourd-shaped amalgamations of lichens, mosses, and grasses, fluffy as dryer lint, or the cup-shaped nests of red-winged blackbirds. Remnants of these will be easier to see in winter, when bare branches expose them. Bushtits, described by one birder as "a tiny fuzzball with a long tail," often join a "feeding flock" of perhaps forty or more birds in winter. This protective flocking is abandoned in breeding season when each bird must compete for nesting space. Sometimes a "mixed feeding flock" occurs in which another species, for instance, the black-capped chickadee, joins the bushtits for protection from predators.

Waterfowl seen almost any season here include a variety of duck and goose species (some released by bored bird-owners), and the ever-present plump black American coots, which have short white bills and a red splotch atop a bump on their skull, as if they've all just smacked their heads. Some bird experts might say they act accordingly—although they're clever enough to thrive here at the lake, where they can dive deep and collect plant material for food, they are also known for goofy habits like squabbling with their fellow birds, and pumping their heads emphatically as they swim. They take to the park's lawns regularly, tilting their heads sideways to get the most grass per tug with the length of their pointy, chicken-like bills.

Wigeons are another duck to watch for, either in the water or grazing on the lawns. The male native wigeon is mid-size, with a pinkish breast, brownish sides, a creamy-white forehead, and a green swipe curving from eye to neck. A favorite sport of local birders is picking out the uncommon Eurasian wigeon among the natives. The Eurasians, once rare visitors from across the Pacific, have become rather commonplace in Puget Sound in the last decade. Hybrid Eurasian-American wigeons also show up, indicating that Eurasians are breeding on this continent. The male Eurasian head is reddish, with an orange forehead, pinkish breast, and gray sides. Wigeons and some other birds practice synchronizing behavior you may witness here. One bird pumps its head up and down. This is a signal like a person might offer by waving their arm to urge a friend to move along. It's saying, "Come on! Let's go!" Other birds will join in the gesture until they begin to synchronize, at which point it's time for liftoff.

Pass under large oak trees and reach a set of bleachers on your right, known as the Aqua Theater (4). To your left, across tree-dotted grass meadows, is the park's diminutive public golf course (5), with several unusual tree species, and the largest Douglas fir at the lake.

From here, look southwest with binoculars and you may be able to pick out one of the area's pair of bald eagles, perched high in a tree. In 1999 locals were thrilled to see this species nest at Green Lake, watching as the birds hunted for their two young eaglets. When not perched, they often fly over the water in search of prey. In 2002, eagles built a nest slightly farther away in the elk yard of Woodland Park Zoo. Eagles generally lay eggs, which hatch in April, in the first week of March.

Round the corner past park restrooms to the start of a more exposed section of lake (6). Along this stretch you may see anglers trying their luck with fishing poles. There is also fine bird habitat here among cattails and brush. Green Lake has long been stocked with fish such as carp, trout, and, recently, the predatory tiger muskie. It is hoped this last fish will bring some control to the explosive carp population. Just offshore is a Work Projects Administration-created island that is off-limits to human visitors. Formally known as the Waldo J. Dahl Waterfowl Refuge, it was named for the 1930s parks commissioner who was instrumental in securing funds to build the island. Canada geese nest here, and other birds such as eagles and cormorants use it as a peaceful stopping place.

Brewer's blackbirds can frequently be found in the parking lots of local malls, and they aren't there for the half-yearly sales. Many birds have developed ingenious ways to coexist with the human-made landscape, and this yellow-eyed (the males) glossy bird is one of them. A voracious insect eater, Brewer's blackbirds have learned to dine on bugs caught in the front grilles of cars.

Red-winged blackbird in cattails. The males flash their red-orange shoulders to attract females and intimidate rivals.

Among the blackberries and cattails you'll likely hear the assertive trill ("conk-ca-ree!" is the way bird books describe it) of red-winged blackbirds. In late winter and early spring the males do their best imitation of brave soldiers, puffing up their chests and flashing their red-orange epaulets for the ladies. Sadly, size, not personality, does matter in this blackbird's world. The largest male is especially likely to be allowed breeding access to females. In this species, a number of females nest in a territory that one male defends, maintaining near-exclusive mating rights. He may look like he needs spit-polishing by the time breeding occurs, however. The intense competition for females means he's kept busy fending off other hopeful males. Another interesting behavior of blackbirds and other members of the icterid family is the practice of "gaping." With muscular force, these birds can gape their bills open once they've poked them into the earth, and find food, such as insects and roots, that is unavailable to other species. Old World starlings, which have spread across the country and displaced native species, can also gape, and it is thought that this unusual ability may partially explain their success.

If it's summer, watch for pied-billed grebes at the west side of the lake near Aurora Avenue (7). They create nests on rafts of decaying vegetation offshore, among the water lilies. A particularly affecting sight is the adult grebes carrying their downy, new-hatched young on their backs. Up until they are

Pied-Billed Grebe

about three weeks old, the chicks can get waterlogged and must be carried when not on the nest.

This stand (8) of varied pine species between the tennis courts and bay at the north end of the lake is known informally as Sapsucker Woods, as red-breasted sapsuckers sometimes migrate down here from the mountains after a cold spell. Walk up close to the tree trunks and search for the rows of small holes they drill, like gouges from an errant sewing machine. These birds might be hiding in plain sight on the other side of a tree you're investigating, so be sure to circumambulate each trunk. They have a striking scarlet cap, and when not tap-tapping at wood, are said to have a cat-like meow. Farther along the main Green Lake path from here watch for mulched areas on your right (9) with thick-trunked but dead trees, or "snags," surrounded by an understory of native plantings. A pilot project by Seattle Parks and Recreation, this patch was left here to provide wildlife habitat for birds and other creatures. Fungi and insects live on the decaying wood, encouraging other animals to visit. The project seems to be quite successful. Woodpeckers excavate here winter and spring, nuthatches forage, and black-capped chickadees and downy woodpeckers have nested here.

Soon you will reach the Bathhouse Theater (10) behind which a diving platform draws crowds of gulls. They stand around like Italian countrymen in a village piazza, passing the time. More advanced birders and birding classes come here to pick out the subtle differences between gull types. Also visit on a late summer evening to catch sight of bats taking over the swallows' daytime job of snatching insects in midair.

It's not surprising that many people struggle to pick out the differences between gulls, or even ducks, as our powers of nature observation are generally numbed by a cushioned urban existence. We may struggle to cope with city life, but we no longer need to pay attention to animals in order to find food, protect our young, or learn local secrets. Just along this last leg of the lake is where Green Lake tour leader and bird expert

> Green Lake bird tours are offered in winter every first and third Saturday, starting with the third Saturday in October, ending the third Saturday in March. The tours start at 8:00 A.M. on the east beach steps near the Community Center/Evans Pool. No sign-up, no fee. Dress warmly for standing and watching.

> Why, you may ask, do gulls always stand on one leg? Actually, many bird species use this technique to keep their featherless legs and feet warm, much as humans might draw a hand into the depths of a sleeve on a cold day.

Martin Muller conducted a test on this matter, turning his observant birder's eye toward his fellow humans. He sat under a cottonwood where a bald eagle, fat and white-headed, scanned the lake for fish. Muller counted 485 bladers, joggers, and strollers pass by before at last a couple looked up.

✳ 20. Raising the Dead: Ravenna Park and Creek

Where:	North of the University District at NE Fifty-fifth Street and NE Ravenna Boulevard
Phone:	(206) 684-4075
Internet:	*http://cityofseattle.net/parks; http://home.earthlink.net/ ~ravennacreek/*
Hours:	4:00 A.M. to 11:30 P.M.
Disabled Access:	Yes
Dogs:	On leash
Driving:	From Seattle, drive north on I-5 approximately 4 miles to Exit 170, Ravenna Boulevard. Turn right at the light onto NE Ravenna Boulevard. Continue about a mile to Twentieth Avenue NE, turn left, and turn into the parking lot on your right.
Bus:	71, 72, or 73. Transfer to 74 in the University District

At the turn of the century, weary urbanites considered picturesque Ravenna Park an essential escape from city life. They trolleyed across town to drink from a mineral springs and gawk at one of Seattle's last stands of towering old growth. Even in green Seattle the park was famous for its tall trees, and the realtor who owned the land named his favorites for Theodore Roosevelt and other VIPs of the time. But when the city acquired the land in the early twentieth century, the trees became grist for Henry Yesler's Union Bay sawmill. Later, bucolic Ravenna Creek was put into a pipe near the end of the park to create more land for development.

Despite these losses, the half-mile wooded ravine and its remaining creek are at least as valuable to Seattleites now as they were back then, calming counterpoint to a sprawling city. The beauty of the park and the unfortunate history of its creek have also catalyzed a neighborhood on their behalf.

Ravenna Creek, once a gushing salmon stream flowing from Green Lake all the way to Union Bay, now appears above ground only in the park, where it is fed by hillside springs. Walking through the ravine, watch for skunk cabbage (*Lysichiton americanum*), a vibrant green plant with a bright yellow spadix, or spike, which emerges early in spring, followed by large leaves. If you've ever hiked in the Cascades, you know that this member of the calla lily family only thrives where things are soggy. Find the plant, and you'll find the locations of springs. These are formed by rain percolating into the ground, where it is stymied by the impermeable layers of Lawton Clay that underlie our city. The water runs down the clay and reemerges where the clay approaches the soil surface. The cabbage, by the way, is named for the stink of the plant, particularly the spadix. The smell attracts pollinating insects. The leaves of skunk cabbage, which are waxy, were used by Western Washington tribes for wrapping foods, as cups, and in other ways related to cooking and eating.

In some places the creek meanders back into the woods, and at other times it runs alongside the footpath, where it audibly burbles in the rainier seasons. It is sheltered and cooled by an eclectic sample of native and nonnative species: bigleaf maples, cedars, and alders form the upper canopy, while beneath them grow salal and berry vines and tall tufts of sword ferns. Ravenna provides habitat for at least thirty species of birds and a clutch of cutthroat trout, and is used as an outdoor classroom for biology and entomology students from local schools and universities, who report that the level of bug life in these waters is equivalent to that of a mountain stream.

Since 1948 Ravenna Creek has abruptly ended hundreds of feet before the park boundary, dumped into a sewer grate for a subterranean crosstown commute to the West Point Treatment Plant at Discovery Park. Since 1991 a group called the Ravenna Creek Alliance has drawn maps, held meetings, and pleaded for funding to "daylight" or bring the last mile of this native Seattle stream back to the surface, and to reconnect it to the waters of nearby Union Bay.

In recent years there has been a shift back from the ethos that logged every inch of forest, even in cities, and buried creeks for the sake of convenience. In part this is because people can afford to enjoy nature again, but also because the public seems to better understand the need to restore the city's living systems for the benefit of other animals and plants that rely on them for sustenance. The efforts of the Ravenna Creek Alliance have been rewarded, at last, with a modest success. In 2003 one portion of the waters will be daylighted, up to the edge of the park. From there, an underground pipe will deliver the creek into Union Bay, with creek-inspired art above ground to mark its route. If you follow the ravine west, the path leads you up to Cowen Park, with a play area and lawn.

21. Green Days and Starry Nights: University of Washington Campus

Where:	Northeast of downtown above the Lake Washington shoreline
Phone:	(206) 543-2100
Internet:	http://washington.edu/home
Hours:	Campus grounds, dawn to dusk; observatory, variable (see below)
Disabled Access:	Yes, on campus and in observatory lecture hall, but not for telescope
Dogs:	On leash
Fees:	Parking on campus. Fees vary, call for information.
Driving:	From downtown Seattle, take I-5 north about 3 miles to Exit 169, NE Forty-fifth Street/NE Fiftieth Street and the University of Washington. Turn right onto Forty-fifth Street. Continue east several blocks, crossing Fifteenth Avenue NE, and watch for the campus entrance at the next light, which is Seventeenth Avenue NE. Park on campus or find street parking just north of here.
Bus:	71, 72, 73, and others
Special Note:	The University Observatory is just inside the entrance, across from the Burke Museum. The Medicinal Herb Garden and much of the tree tour is located south of the entrance. The parking kiosk attendant can give you a campus map.

Even when the university moved to the present campus from an expanding downtown in 1894, the gorgeous location along Union Bay was considered a distinct advantage.

"It is confidently asserted that the new site of the University…has not an equal in the world," a writer noted at the time. "Three hundred and fifty acres between two lakes, near an arm of the Pacific Ocean, these acres covered with a luxuriant vegetation and broken by beautiful contours. . . . "

Though much tamed from the days when huge conifers were cleared to make way for buildings, the campus remains justly known for its many trees, a world-class medicinal herb garden, and one of the city's most beautifully framed views of Mount Rainier.

A simple stroll around the grounds will satisfy many visitors, but with a little spare time a tree tour is recommended, as is a historical University Observatory trip. On a sunny summer night observatory visitors can number more than fifty. Everyone takes turns clattering up the narrow stairs to the dome to get a look at Jupiter's four moons, the Orion Nebula, or whatever celestial occurrence has been chosen as that night's feature. The scope is generally trained on one point each viewing night. If it's raining, the dome isn't opened, but you can still tour the building or settle down in an adjoining room for a talk and slide show on that night's theme.

> The University of Washington's Burke Museum has an immense ornithology collection, including the skeletons, skins, and wings of birds. Many are accessible only to scholars, but some are on exhibit in the main galleries. Visit to see up close the miracle of feathers and flight.

THE BROCKMAN MEMORIAL TREE TOUR

The University of Washington has a wealth of trees—more than 450 species and counting. The Brockman Tree Tour was named for a tree enthusiast and UW forestry professor who authored the original campus tree tour. It highlights eighty interesting tree species. The tour, with map and descriptions, can be printed from the Internet at *http://washington.edu/home/treetour/*, or you can pick up a printed copy for $1.50 at the College of Forest Resources.

One highlight is Memorial Way, a colonnade of London plane trees planted in honor of UW alumni, students, and faculty who died in World War I. Memorial Way starts from the campus entrance at Forty-fifth Street, where this destination begins. Another must-stop for many visitors is Rainier Vista, where the already-stunning view of Mount Rainier is celebrated each April with the brilliant pink cancan line of blooming Kwanzan cherry trees just south of Stevens Way. Another spring knockout is the low, wide "Pink Beauty" crab apple between Stevens Way and the Communications Building—it's the only one of its kind known in Seattle. In fall, thirteen red oaks between Smith Hall and the Allen Library don brilliant autumn colors and gather an eager fan club of squirrels scurrying for their abundant acorns. These are located at the west end of the intimate Greek Garden, a favorite on-campus retreat. Throughout the campus are many interesting conifer species, including a large variety of pine trees. Be sure to visit the Sierra or giant redwood, a 106-foot-tall grand dame, towering over the Medicinal Herb Garden on the south end of campus.

You can visit the University of Washington's Herbarium, the largest in the Northwest, and housing more than 560,000 dried specimens of plants, mosses, fungi, and other growing things. Call ahead to find out the schedule at (206) 543-1682.

The herb garden south of Bagley Hall is not on the tree tour but is a great place to linger. Big yellow centaurea, blazing star, Job's tears, gypsy combs, and wild tobacco are a small sampling of plants you'll find in the raised beds. Perhaps the largest of its kind in the Western Hemisphere, the garden grows more than five hundred herbs to sniff and study. Started by the School of Pharmacy in 1911, it continues to be a destination for students of natural healing, as well as gardeners of all kinds. The Friends of the Medicinal Herb Garden has an office on campus, and offers free tours beginning at noon on the second Sunday of each month, May through October. Visit their website at *http://nnlm.gov/pnr/uwmhg/index.html* or give them a call at (206) 543-1126.

UNIVERSITY OBSERVATORY

Once you've left the herb garden, the only other blazing stars you're likely to see can be found through the University Observatory telescope. Entering this building (only open on selected evenings, listed below) is almost like going back to another time, to when the quaint sandstone structure opened as the second building on campus. Not much has changed about it since—the same telescope, a 6-foot-long brass-detailed beauty, tilts skyward. This instrument runs without electricity on mechanical parts, as does the wooden dome, which rolls creakily on three lead balls said to be cannonballs. The building's stone walls smell musty and worn, and there is no heating or cooling system to distort the telescope view. The telescope, with lenses more than a hundred years old, still has better clarity than most backyard models.

The world around the observatory, of course, has been transformed. A century ago the neighborhood would have been surrounded by open fields and a distinct lack of urban light pollution—a modern handicap caused by overuse of artificial lighting that blocks a city dweller's view of the sky. One hundred years ago you would have been able to see the Northern Lights from here, not to mention a glitzy, awe-inspiring Milky Way.

The Seattle Astronomical Society hosts monthly star parties for the public with telescopes and trained volunteers at Green Lake Park and Cromwell Park in Shoreline. For information call (206) 523-2787 or visit *www.seattleastro.org*.

STAR SEARCH

Whether here or with your own telescope at a local park, many celestial events are visible even in this brightly lit city. University of Washington Astronomy Lecturer Ana Larson suggests the following places to point your lens by season.

Winter. Look for the constellation Orion and the Orion Nebula, visible as a fuzzy patch in Orion's sword. For the near future, Jupiter and Saturn continue to be nicely placed in the sky, coming around every year at the beginning of winter and sticking around through early spring. These planets are usually the brightest objects in the sky, and don't twinkle.

Spring. Spring holds nothing so notable. During this time of year, we look toward the Galactic north pole, meaning there are not many nebula (fuzzy white, deep sky objects) to view. We face away from the plane of our galaxy, toward its less crowded regions. By late spring, Alcor and Mizar, the double stars of the handle of the Big Dipper, make a nice target.

Summer. Summer brings the best view of the Milky Way as we peer toward its center. Get away from city lights and see the galaxy shine brightly as a diffuse path across the sky. Two of the best viewing objects for this time of year are the Ring Nebula—a rapidly dying star—and the Hercules cluster—a tight grouping of more than 200,000 very old stars.

Fall. Fall rolls around and the Andromeda Galaxy, at 2.5 million light years away, tops the list. At only four hundred light years away and within our galaxy is the double star Albireo, which shows distinct color differences for two closely placed stars, a hint that not all stars are built the same.

TURN OFF A LIGHT, TURN ON A STAR*

City lights block our view of the night sky, cause dangerous glare for nighttime drivers, can disorient migrating birds, and may even be related to long-term health problems. From a practical standpoint, improper street lighting is an egregious waste of energy.

Few people know yet that it doesn't have to be that way. Much like the issues of water or air pollution in the last century, light pollution is now emerging as the latest opportunity for humans to learn from their excesses. The International Dark Skies Association (IDSA) is pushing for a few practical changes that, collectively, would have a large impact on the problem. First, they'd like to see cities begin replacing old streetlights with new varieties that are shaded to direct light down toward sidewalks and streets.

As it stands, most streetlights are sending 50 percent of their illumination into the sky. The IDSA would also like to see regulations barring excessive lighting in public places.

If we don't tackle this problem, we risk losing not only our health, but what University of Washington astronomy professor Woody Sullivan calls the "culture of the sky," the stars, planets, and other night companions referenced by writers and artists from Shakespeare to Cat Stevens. "You know what Oscar Wilde said?" Sullivan asks. "That 'we may be in the gutter, but at least we are looking at the stars?' Well, these days if you're in the gutter, you can't even see the stars!"

For more information, visit the local chapter of the IDSA, Northwest Dark Skies, on the web at *www.scn.org/darksky/*.

*Motto of the Dark Skies Association.

22. Reclaiming Paradise: Union Bay Natural Area

Where:	Northeast of Downtown
Phone:	(206) 543-8616
Internet:	*www.depts.washington.edu/urbhort/*
Hours:	Dawn to dusk
Disabled Access:	Horticulture center has sidewalks and paved paths. The natural area is unpaved.
Dogs:	On leash. Not conducive to bird watching.
Driving:	From downtown Seattle, take I-5 north about 3 miles to Exit 169, NE Forty-fifth Street/NE Fiftieth Street and the University of Washington. Go right onto Forty-fifth Street and follow it east through the University District, past the UW campus, down the hill (viaduct), and past University Village. At the next major intersection, a five-way stop with a light, turn right (south) onto Mary Gates Memorial Drive. Continue for the equivalent of two blocks to the corner of NE Forty-first Street. The Center for Urban Horticulture is on your right at the bend where Mary Gates Memorial Drive becomes NE Forty-first Street.
Bus:	Routes 25 and 30 stop at NE Forty-fifth and Mary Gates Memorial Drive

It's the city's most exquisite garbage dump—well, former dump. The grass-lands, ponds, and Lake Washington shoreline of the Union Bay Natural Area

(UBNA), or "the fill" as it is known by regular visitors, is a sanctuary for birds, a place to see painted turtles sunning themselves, and spy great blue herons sneaking up on their fishy prey. Known by long-term locals as "garbage bay," this once-glorious wetland area was used as a waste site by the city of Seattle and the University of Washington. The dump was filled and capped in 1966, the first step toward restoring a rank trash heap back into something spectacular.

Here, on a warm late summer day, goldfinches and warblers flit from thistle to fescue, towering cottonwoods cast a welcome shade, and the irksomely invasive but oh-so-pretty purple loosestrife spills at the edges of ponds in lavender pools.

The fill is considered a preeminent birding spot in Seattle. Different habitats including a large lake, small permanent ponds, seasonal ponds, woods, prairie, and marshland attract a huge diversity of birds. More than 150 species have been spotted here, including unusual-to-Seattle birds such as Harris' sparrow, Lapland longspur, yellow-headed blackbird, clay-colored sparrow, and Say's phoebe.

Part of the UBNA's appeal for birds (and humans) is that it is one of the few spaces in the city with both freshwater ponds and open fields. Owned by the UW and managed by the Center for Urban Horticulture, it is an outdoor laboratory for the university, where classes come to learn about birds and ecosystems. They and several volunteer groups also participate in restoration projects here. In recent years they have worked on removing invasive species, such as loosestrife, which drives out native plant species, and planting North-

Union Bay Natural Area's varied habitat, including wetland and meadow, is rare in Seattle. Wildflowers and grasses thrive.

While all herons are carnivorous, only a few of them, including the green heron occasionally seen at the fill, are known as "bait-fishing" types. These herons are known to place insects, flowers, twigs, or other small floating objects on the water's surface to attract fish. Thus do bait-fishing herons join humans as some of the world's few known tool-using animals.

west native trees and plants, such as red alder, Pacific madrone, red osier dogwood, sedges, and rushes—further habitat for local and migrating birds.

Although the fill is frequented by birding pros, it is an excellent place for beginners, too. Borrow or buy a pair of binoculars and a bird identification guidebook, try to get here first thing in the morning, and you are bound to spot a few "lifers" (birder lingo for first-time sightings of a species) before breakfast.

Start at the center, and walk the grounds, then follow the main path, Wahkiakum Lane, west into the natural area. Within the area you will find four different ponds, perhaps more in winter. Different bird populations are here at every season. Migrating shorebirds come in late summer–early fall, waterfowl in late fall–early spring. Here are a few excellent spots for potential sightings:

Lawns and landscaping around the Center for Urban Horticulture: Warblers, hummingbirds, waxwings, and sparrows.

The grove of cottonwoods west of the horticulture building: Downy woodpeckers, red-eyed vireos, spotted towhees, Lincoln's sparrows, and western tanagers.

Ponds: A variety of ducks and shorebirds.

FOR THE BIRDS

It is easy for city dwellers stuck in offices or enduring stressful commutes to find their senses dulled to seasonal change. The arrival of spring or the waning of summer in Seattle can be a subtle affair, marked mostly by the opening and closing of umbrellas. For birdwatchers in our city, however, this yearly cycle is always punctuated by exciting entrances and exits. A rufous hummingbird buzzing into the yard is a better indication of spring's arrival than the emergence of any groundhog, and even without snow, birders see winter coming when rafts of waterfowl dot the Sound and local lakes. Seattle is fortunate to have a mild climate and abundant shoreline, which means there isn't a season here when birdwatching isn't interesting.

One easy way to get introduced to the avian year is to welcome it at home. Local nurseries can suggest bird-enticing plants to add to your backyard or apartment balcony, particularly Northwest natives that produce seeds, berries, or nectar flowers, and provide plenty of cover.

Your lush landscape may draw a crowd but could also make birds harder to spot. Many people rely on feeders to draw birds out. Any good nature store can advise you on the various models and requirements. Certain species will require certain feeds: goldfinches and pine siskins, for instance, will want thistle, while hummingbirds, of course, love sugar water (no need to dye it red). Black-oil sunflower seeds, typically recommended for "starter" feeders, entice a variety of species such as chickadees, grosbeaks, nuthatches, and juncos. Suet cakes, made from animal fat, are clearly not a natural snack for wild birds, but they are nutrient-rich and a draw for many including flickers and bushtits. A variety of feeders will probably net you the widest range of birds.

You will certainly get frequent visitors or residents of Seattle, such as those mentioned, but you may also lure a rarity, a bird experts consider to be outside its usual range. An example of this took place in late winter 2002, when a tropically bright male painted bunting, defying guidebooks that place its home squarely in the warm southeast, drew crowds to a feeder on Capitol Hill.

Feeders do require diligent maintenance. They should be disinfected frequently to avoid transferring diseases between birds, which can spread through droppings. (A bleach solution is often recommended for this but less-toxic solutions are being developed—ask for advice when you buy your feeder.) To foil cats, position feeders in inaccessible places, either above thorny shrubs, high in a tree, or perhaps outside second story windows.

One other concern involves the plague of rodents a messy, neglected feeder will bring you. Squirrels and rats may converge on either feeders or seed piles collecting under them. If this is a problem, choose models that thwart interlopers, and have a bottom tray to keep seeds from falling. Some people enjoy watching squirrels feed and put out special peanut feeders for this purpose. Birds also need places to bathe and drink, and your efforts will be enhanced by furnishing a bath or dripper, which slowly releases water from its tip.

One thing you don't have to worry about is whether or not these devices make birds too dependent on humans. Only a small portion of a bird's food requirements is provided by even the most generous feeders.

If feeder-watching becomes as compelling to you as a suet cake to a woodpecker, you might even take the pastime to its outer limits—introducing a feeder outside your workplace.

The southeast corner of the fill, beyond the cottonwoods on the main trail: In this marshy area with cattails watch for green herons, great blue herons, and marsh wrens, as well as turtles. Moving south toward the more open waters of Union Bay expect various duck species, including wood ducks, ruddy ducks, common goldeneyes, common mergansers, and wigeons.

Green Heron

Also watch tall trees for such raptors as peregrine falcons, merlins, and short-eared owls. Along the slough, dead trees or "snags" provide good nest sites for woodpeckers.

If you've still got the energy after a morning's birdwatching, drop in at the Center for Urban Horticulture. Here, adjacent to the natural area, wander through a variety of ornamental garden beds made up of mostly nonnatives, part of the center's experiments with different gardening methods and species. The Marylou Goodfellow Grove behind the center buildings on the way to the UBNA features native Northwest plants, including trees in spectacular bloom in early summer. Inside, the center offers a variety of resources for learning about plants in general and urban gardening in particular, including classes and a renowned horticultural library.

> The American goldfinch is the Washington state bird. Watch for this small yellow songbird darting among the thistles, whose seeds are its preferred food.

SHE'S A GRAND OLD LAKE

Green Lake was formed by the Puget Lobe, an ice sheet that covered the area some thirteen thousand years ago. Originally, the north end's Haller and Bitter Lakes drained into this body of water, which itself flowed into what is now Ravenna Creek, and finally to Union Bay. After the glacier receded and trees, mostly deciduous, reemerged here, sediment filled in the lake bottom. In addition, the process of revegetation brought birds and fish, adding more "waste" to the mix. If you are here in the summer, you'll smell the swamp funk of decomposing algae. A lake as old and well used as this one goes through a process much like forest succession. Green Lake, in other words, should eventually become Green Meadow.

Cutting off the flow of water to and from the lake and lowering it, as was done in 1911 to create the park, substantially accelerated this process. To maintain the lake in its current state requires a variety of strategies, from the voracious milfoil harvester you see chomping through algae beds, to doses of algae-thwarting chemicals that are like a face-lift on an aging visage—merely postponing the inevitable.

EXPERT TIPS FOR BEGINNING BIRDERS

Author of *Rare Encounters with Ordinary Birds: Notes From a Northwest Year*, Seattle writer and seasoned birder Lyanda Lynn Haupt has a wealth of good suggestions for turning the baffled bird lover into a budding ornithologist. The following are some of our favorites:

1. Don't forget that birds have wings. This means you can't approach their identification in the same way you would a flower or a mushroom. If you're paging through your field guide, trying to match a picture to a bird, the bird will inevitably fly off and leave you wondering whether it had one wing bar or two. Instead, bring a pen and paper, and leave the field guide aside until you've had a good long look at your subject. Observe as many details about it as you can, take notes, and make a rough sketch. Then you can turn to your field guide with a good foundation for making a solid identification.

2. Don't obsess over color. The first thing people often report about a bird is the color of its feathers, but many species have a similar basic color, and it takes more subtle details about the bird's plumage pattern, shape, behavior, voice, and habitat to make a good identification. Observe all you can!

3. Expect UFOs. Even the best birders can't accurately identify every bird that flits across their path. It's better to admit that you don't know what a particular bird is, than to make an incorrect guess. This inevitable layer of mystery is one of the things that keeps birding fun.

4. Give birds their space. As observers, our first responsibility is to the well-being of the birds we are watching. If you get so close that they begin to look nervous, or actually fly away, you could be interrupting important migratory, breeding, or nesting activities, possibly even endangering the birds or their young. A respectful distance will ensure that the birds behave naturally and comfortably, and will ultimately allow you to see more of them.

5. Engage in journeys of discovery. With so many bird alert hotlines and websites, it becomes easy to get caught up in seeking rare, exciting birds, and to be distracted from the honest joy of exploring a place, and seeing what birds occur there, common or not. Any place and any bird can be seen with new eyes when you take a simple walk with nothing but your binoculars and notebook.

SUNDIALS

Until the 1800s, people around the world relied on the sun to tell not only the time, but also where they stood in the yearly cycle of light and darkness. A watch may give you split-second accuracy, but it also separates you from an understanding of the year's passing. The sundial, an instrument that has been used to tell time since at least 1500 B.C., is an excellent way to reconnect with the real meaning of time in the natural world—the lengthening and shortening of shadows over the course of a year (and day) is a reminder that we live on a rotating globe.

Surprisingly, cloudy Seattle is home to a large and varied collection of sundials for public viewing. A tour of some of them is available at *www.sundials.co.uk/~seattle.htm*. If you only have time to see three or four, the following choices are particularly recommended for a sunny day outing:

1. University of Washington Physics/Astronomy Building sundial (Pacific and Fifteenth, facing the Burke-Gilman Trail). This streamlined metal wall dial has an explanatory plaque showing you how to determine the time and the day of the year. Because of its position on a southwest-facing wall, it works mostly in the afternoons.

2. Gasworks Park (North Northlake Way at Meridian Ave North). This gorgeous mosaic dial capping the big hill in the park was made by artists in the 1970s. It uses your own shadow to determine the time.

3. Sam Hill Mansion (814 Highland Drive on Capitol Hill). This vertical dial is on a historic private residence, but is easily visible from the street. It dates from 1909.

4. Pacific Science Center (Seattle Center). This 1994 dial is located in the middle of a pond.

*D*own to Earth:
SOUTH SEATTLE

South Seattle and West Seattle should hold a contest for our city's "Faraway so Close" award. They are not particularly hard to get to, but often overlooked by non-residents; there are Seattleites who live their whole lives knowing there's a Seward Park and a Kubota Garden, but never actually getting there. That's all the better for those wise to the natural wonders of the area, who watch cedar waxwings flitting over a quiet pond in a magical Japanese garden, or stand among trillium blossoms in the shadow of Seattle's oldest tree. From butterflies and eagles to mountain beavers, here you will meet some non-human residents who depend on the health of our city's green spaces.

To Native Americans, South Seattle was not remote at all. What's now Seward Park on the shores of Lake Washington was a hub of tribal life. Looking south from Seward Park's Bailey Peninsula to Mount Rainier in the distance, one can imagine smoky camps pungent with drying fish and cedar baskets brimming with berries of all shapes and sizes. At one time up to six longhouses dominated the shoreline from Seward to Pritchard Beach 2 miles to the south, each probably boasting the better view of Tahoma. In the summer, other tribes would travel from as far away as the Puyallup and Skagit Rivers for kokanee, Lake Washington's prized non-migrating sockeye, which still thrive here. Although hunting and gathering is now done in grocery store aisles, Lake Washington's beauty is still a major attraction.

Inland from the lake, in verdant oases hidden in the midst of development, salamanders scuffle under leaves and fat salmonberries ripen in cool ravines. You can begin your exploration by taking a wild plant tour along Taylor Creek in the depths of Dead Horse Canyon. A second tour provides an enlightening contrast, exploring the Japanese-American philosophy behind the carefully tended landscape of Kubota Garden. One destination takes you through Seward Park in search of nesting eagles. This park's nature center draws on the diverse offerings of the Bailey Peninsula, hosting classes from wild plants and the geology of the area, to owl and bat walks. A satellite office of Seattle's Audubon Society is slated to open here. A second

View butterflies and the city from Bradner Gardens.

destination shows you where to look for butterflies in Bradner Gardens Park, one of Seattle's first pesticide-free parks. Bradner's exemplary gardens provide solutions to problems peculiar to city gardeners. Finally, students at Dearborn Park Elementary School have turned their neighboring forest and wetland into outdoor classrooms, as well as a destination for those seeking knowledge about native plants.

❋ 23. Dead Horse Canyon: Wild Plant Walk

Where:	South of the Rainier Beach neighborhood
Tour Distance:	0.5 mile loop
Phone:	(206) 684-4075
Internet:	NA
Hours:	Dawn to dusk
Disabled Access:	No
Dogs:	On leash
Driving:	From downtown Seattle, take I-5 south to Exit 161, Swift/Albro. Head east and take Swift Avenue South to South Myrtle Street. Myrtle will turn into Othello Street. Follow this about 0.75 mile to Rainier Avenue South. Turn right onto Rainier. Continue south on Rainier about 2.5 miles to Sixty-eighth Avenue South. Turn right onto Sixty-eighth and follow about 0.5 mile to the trailhead.
Bus:	106
Special Note:	If you're new to plant identification, use a field guide with photos, or find someone who knows plants to walk with you. Do not taste plants unless you are absolutely sure of their identification.

Near the southern end of Lake Washington, the now clean waters of Taylor Creek splash through what has been called the finest urban forest in Seattle. A trash dump and drug-use area until 1996 when neighbors decided to reclaim it, the 50-foot tree canopy of Dead Horse Canyon protects osprey, pileated woodpeckers, red-tailed hawks, cutthroat trout, raccoons, opossum, coyote, and the occasional deer. This clandestine ravine is also home to a plethora of native plants with medicinal and other practical uses.

Plants became a major focus of the canyon restoration effort after neighbors, with the help of Seattle Parks and Recreation, Seattle Public Utilities, Big Brothers and Big Sisters, and Renton High School students, hauled out tons of trash including everything from refrigerators to beer kegs. Volunteers

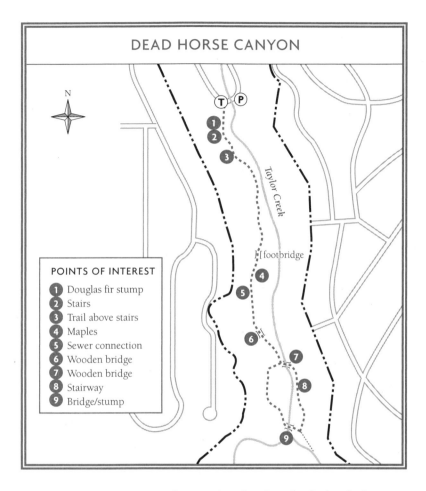

DEAD HORSE CANYON

N

Taylor Creek

footbridge

POINTS OF INTEREST
1. Douglas fir stump
2. Stairs
3. Trail above stairs
4. Maples
5. Sewer connection
6. Wooden bridge
7. Wooden bridge
8. Stairway
9. Bridge/stump

continue to remove invasive plants and replant Douglas fir, hemlock, Western red cedar, vine maple, Indian plum, hazelnut, fern, salal, huckleberry, salmonberry, and red osier dogwood. The goal is to return the twenty-nine–acre canyon to its pre-logged state. So far more than five thousand new trees and plants have contributed to this goal.

Another aspect of the restoration effort involves reintroducing indigenous salmon to Taylor Creek. As the area was developed in the second half of the twentieth century, a number of barriers cut off salmon access to spawning grounds. Seattle Public Utilities is in the process of adapting culverts and restoring the creek bed to allow salmon to return.

Standing at the Dead Horse trailhead facing the canyon, you could be on Mount Rainier's Wonderland Trail. The last time it looked this unspoiled was in the late 1800s, before the Taylor family built a sawmill where the creek meets Lake Washington, about a half mile to the east. The property was logged at least twice, and the mill closed in 1916.

Urbanites are often surprised to learn how much food is growing around them all the time. Did you know dandelion leaves are a great source of iron and an excellent immune booster? Or that nettles are chock full of vitamins and minerals and tastier than spinach—once you learn to harvest them without getting stung? Dead Horse Canyon is home to a variety of edible and medicinal species.

As you pass the bulletin board at the start of the trail and before you get to the first set of stairs, look for a large, rotting Douglas fir stump (1) up the hill to your right. At the base of the hill below this stump, you'll find the broad, hand-like leaves of palmate coltsfoot (*Petasites frigidus* var. *palmatus*). Named for an eastern plant that has the same medicinal applications and, unlike this plant, really does look like a pony's hoof print, coltsfoot is unusual in the plant world because its flowers appear before its leaves in early spring, rising like a clump of pale pink dandelions on a single stalk.

Coltsfoot is used by herbalists to help "dry" the lungs and improve breathing. Because it's so wet here, the Northwest has a lot of drying plants—plants that are antiviral, antibacterial, and astringent. Herbalists harvest coltsfoot leaves when they are salad-plate–size or smaller and dry them. Campers appreciate them raw for a fresh, salty taste to spice up a soup or other dish. Coltsfoot likes to keep its "feet" wet and is usually found in moist forested settings. These wet spots are especially vulnerable to trampling, so stay on the trail and avoid crushing unseen roots.

Palmate Coltsfoot

Another "equine" plant can be seen in this same wet patch. Horsetail or *Equisetum arvense* is a non-flowering prehistoric plant so tenacious it was the first to sprout in the aftermath of Mount Saint Helen's 1980 eruption. Once the dominant plant of this region, it soared to heights matching those of the tallest trees in the canyon today. One ancient horsetail fossil is so large that when placed on its side it occupies two rooms in a Denver museum. Medicinally used for its ability to heal urinary tract infections, once you remove its spiky "leaves," the tender stalk can be chewed (and spit out, or not) for its juice—a good thirst quencher for hikers. When it first comes up in the spring, the rhizome sends up a tender, asparagus-like shoot that can be eaten raw or steamed. This plant is packed full of minerals including boron, which helps build flexible bones. If you're fighting this plant in the garden, it's good to know that it grows on long underground stems called rhizomes, so pulling up one section will not remove the whole plant. Step back from the Lilliputian forest of *equisetum* and try to imagine them towering above you in massive pre-ice age swamps.

As you walk along the trail and begin to ascend the first set of stairs (2), look to the right to see another ancient plant that's ubiquitous in Dead Horse, the sword fern (*Polystichum munitum*). Non-flowering, the sword fern reproduces by way of spores, which are found in clusters called sporangia. These "spore houses" are grouped in bunches called "sori" on the underside of each frond. The spores are carried off by the wind and, when the right conditions prevail (they need water to reproduce), a spore will grow into a miniscule heart-shaped plant called a prothallium. This short-lived hermaphrodite produces from the union of its own egg and sperm what we know as the fern, which can live for hundreds of years. Fern spores have antibacterial properties, and the fronds were used by Northwest Coast peoples to protect food when cooking or drying, and as bedding and flooring material.

Just above the stairs to the right you'll see the piggy-back plant (*Tolmiea menziesii*) (3), sometimes called "youth-on-age" because small buds on the leaves produce baby plants. The new plants weigh down the "mother plant," which develops rootlets ensuring continued propagation. Look under larger leaves with established "children" to find these roots. Known as a "woundwort" to herbalists, this plant is astringent, so it will dry a wet wound, kill germs, and help pull cut skin tissue back together.

In the canyon along the creek to your left, up the hill to your right, and dotted along the trail, you'll see many specimens of *Acer macrophyllum*, the bigleaf maple. In the fall, its sometimes serving-platter–size leaves turn brown to golden yellow. Like their eastern relatives, the sap from these maples can be used to make syrup, but it takes 48 ounces of sap to make just 1 ounce of a cotton-candy tasting syrup. Its leaves are edible in early spring, and so are the green samaras, the Latin word for elm seed; the elm shares winged, one-seededness with the maple. Kids know the seeds as "helicopters."

Along this stretch of the trail (4) there are some beautiful old maples and firs in the canyon to your left. Look to the right of the trail to see a red cedar with telltale lines of holes drilled by a hungry sapsucker.

As you move along the trail, you'll see a large cement sewer connection on your right (5). Directly across the ravine from this marker is a bigleaf

Snags like this natural one in Dead Horse Canyon are being used in restoration projects around the city because they provide important habitat.

maple sporting several layers of fern fringe. These delicate fronds belong to the licorice fern (*Polypodium glycyrrhiza*), which is a common epiphyte (a plant growing on another plant) on this species of tree. As its name indicates, this fern's rhizome tastes like black licorice. It's soothing medicine for sore throats and is used by herbalists to treat inflammatory problems and allergic reactions.

To the right of the first long wooden bridge (6) you'll see an impressive Western red cedar (*Thuja plicata*), a survivor of this canyon's original forest. Looking over the bridge and down its 200-year-old trunk you can see an ancient cut mark, but for some reason loggers left this tree as a testament to the past.

According to a Coast Salish myth, cedar was created in honor of a man who was always helping others, and red cedar certainly fulfilled that mission in Northwest Native cultures—for both spiritual and pragmatic reasons. This tree was used for food, clothing, shelter, fuel, and blankets. Its antifungal and antibacterial properties prevent rotting, so it was used for canoes, houses, totem poles, and many other daily tools.

Keep left as you come to a fork in the trail (the path on the right heads up hill), and you will come to a second long wooden bridge (7). Standing on the bridge facing downstream, look for the white-gray smooth bark of another useful "red" tree with antibiotic properties. Like red cedars, alders were highly prized by Native Americans. Alder was known as the best fuel for smoking salmon, it was used for red and orange dye, and medicinally alder's inner bark was known to cure respiratory ailments. Red alder (*Alnus rubra*), named for the bright orange-red of the cut wood, is cooling to our systems. Herbalists use alder to take the heat out of inflamed areas. If you want a treat for tired feet, pack some of these cooling leaves around your socks, then pull on

Used as medicine for colds and sore throats, local Native Americans also chewed the licorice fern's rhizome for its sweet, black-licorice flavor.

your boots. One of the first trees to come back in clear-cut areas or other disturbed sites, alder's fast growth rate (5 to 6 feet a year) and ability to fix nitrogen improves disturbed soils. Alders are old at fifty.

As you leave the bridge, look to both sides of the trail to find the yellow-flowered large-leaved avens (*Geum macrophyllum*). A sign of environmental health in the canyon, geum won't flourish in unclean areas. Avens is an astringent plant and is another of the

Red Huckleberry

herbalist's woundworts. Its hairy stalk can grow 3 feet tall. Look for buttercup-like flowers or the many hooked fruit that will cling to your socks if you get too close.

The next stairway (8) winds around the exposed roots of a fallen Douglas fir tree. This nurse log is growing several new trees along her "spine." These baby hemlocks and cedars will take their nutrients from the bark and, if left undisturbed, will grow in a telltale line that speaks unmistakably of their origin.

This could be the kind of log that gave Dead Horse its name. In logging nomenclature, when trees are felled in places where they can't be removed, or if they're not deemed worthy of being hauled out, they're called "dead horses."

The trail will fork; stay on the main branch to the right. (A narrow path continues straight ahead.) You will soon come to a final wooden bridge. In the creek to the left of the bridge is an old stump sporting a small hemlock tree and the feathery greenery of the red huckleberry (*Vaccinium parvifolium*) (9). This bush's tart orange-red berries are a great source of vitamin C, which is most helpful to the body when eaten fresh. The vitamin C in plants is actually a compound including riboflavin, ascorbic, and citric acids; a whole vitamin complex, not the elemental vitamins you buy bottled. The body more readily absorbs vitamins and minerals from plants.

Continue across the bridge and the trail will loop back to just before the second large bridge. Along the way you will pass some sizable old-growth cedar trees with fire damage. As you leave the canyon, listen for flickers, chickadees, or the cock-a-doodle-doo of a backyard rooster reminding you you're still in the city, or listen to Taylor Creek and forget.

HERBAL MEDICINE

Perhaps as old as Taylor Creek, herbal medicine, the use of plants to heal human ailments, has been used by every known past and current culture on earth. With a growing interest in natural foods and medicines in the United States over the past few decades, many herbs such as echinacea, ginseng, and gingko biloba have become household words. In this country, herbal medicine is usually defined as a medicine practice using European or North American plants. Traditional Chinese medicine uses the flora of China or Asia, and Ayurvedic herbal medicine uses plants native to India. It's common for herbalists to use plants from all over the world, including those that fall outside the definition of herb (a seed plant with a stem that dies back annually). Medicine can come from a mushroom, seed, tree bark, or anything else in the world of flora. The goal of many modern herbalists is to bring back ancient knowledge lost since the proliferation of synthetic drugs.

24. Kubota Garden: Idealized Nature

Where:	In the Rainier Beach neighborhood at 9600 Renton Avenue South at Fifty-fifth Avenue South
Tour Distance:	About 1 mile
Phone:	(206) 684-4584
Internet:	www.kubota.org
Hours:	Daylight hours, admission free
Disabled Access:	Mostly gravel pathways, call in advance to have the gate opened at an easy-access side entrance
Dogs:	On leash
Driving:	From downtown Seattle, take I-5 south to Exit 158, Pacific Highway South/East Marginal Way. Turn left toward Martin Luther King Jr. Way and continue up the hill about three-quarters of a mile on Ryan Way. Turn left onto Fifty-first Avenue South and continue one-half mile. Turn right onto Renton Avenue South. Drive a short distance farther and turn right into the entrance to the garden at Fifty-fifth Avenue South.
Bus:	106

It's hard to believe that twenty lush acres could remain so well hidden in the city, but on a winter weekday you're likely to find yourself alone in Kubota Garden. Like the concept of *kumade* in Japanese garden design where a space

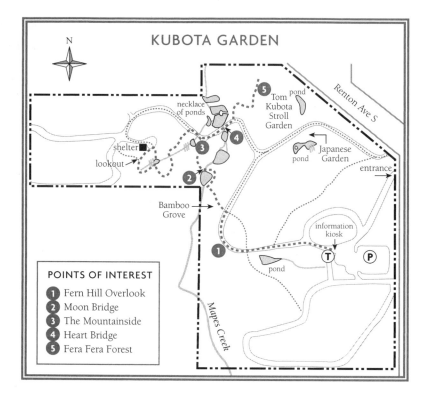

KUBOTA GARDEN

N

Tom Kubota Stroll Garden

necklace of ponds

shelter

lookout

Japanese Garden

pond

entrance

Bamboo Grove

information kiosk

T   P

pond

Renton Ave S

Mapes Creek

POINTS OF INTEREST

1 Fern Hill Overlook
2 Moon Bridge
3 The Mountainside
4 Heart Bridge
5 Fera Fera Forest

is teasingly, playfully, only partially exposed to the viewer, you could easily miss the entrance. Just as Kubota's interior kumade appeal to birds like pileated woodpeckers, barred owls, and cedar waxwings, the garden as a whole serves as refuge for the street-worn senses of Seattle's two-legged mammals.

In 1906, at the age of twenty-five, Fujitaro Kubota gave up the status and inheritance he would receive as the first-born son of a rice farmer and village leader, left the island of Shikoku in Japan, and moved to the United States. He established his own Seattle landscaping business in 1923 and was renowned as a pioneer of Japanese gardening in the Northwest. Kubota designed many private and public gardens in the area, including Japanese gardens at Seattle University and the Bloedel Reserve on Bainbridge Island.

In 1927, Kubota was drawn to five acres of land in the Rainier Beach neighborhood. Though swampy and dotted with old-growth stumps, the land was home to a year-round creek. Little by little, as money would allow, he purchased all of the twenty acres that comprise Kubota Garden today. This was also the location of the family's home and nursery business. Kubota had always hoped the garden would one day be open to the public, and this dream was realized in 1987 when the Kubota family sold the gardens to the Seattle Parks and Recreation Department.

Kubota employed traditional Japanese gardening concepts with American twists, showing a creative spirit and sense of humor that shocked some traditionalists. One example of this is the "drive-thru garden"—the Kubota Garden of the 1930s was designed to accommodate America's love affair with the big automobile. Although Kubota Garden is now strictly for pedestrians, you can still see some of the curbs from the former vehicle-friendly design.

The traditional Japanese gardener seeks a perfected or idealized nature. By using "passive attitude and dynamic action," first he or she spends time listening to the land to help guide the shape of the garden, then begins a design based on the spirit of the place. There is usually no master plan, and a Japanese garden develops over time.

Perhaps the best example of idealized nature here is Kubota's rerouting of Mapes Creek, the life force of the garden that feeds all of its ponds and waterways. You can view the unaltered headwaters of the creek from the Fern Hill Overlook next to the ravine (1). From these waters the rest of Kubota's garden vision sprang to life. Except for the replanting of native conifers and removal of invasive plants like blackberry and ivy, this is the only unsculpted area in Kubota Garden.

The garden and creek have benefited from each other over the years. It's likely that the still-visible portions of Mapes Creek would be pipe-bound had Kubota not chosen to channel the water through his garden. And when Kubota Garden was abandoned during World War II when Kubota and his wife were interned for four years, the creek's water-retaining clay soils kept the plantings from withering in the summer drought months.

As a result of the wartime neglect, silt clogged the ponds, a 4-foot wall of weeds replaced well-tended lawns, and Kubota's proudly pruned signature red and black pines grew to unmanageable proportions. Serendipity or garden "design by chance" is also a theme in Japan, where wartime neglect has also occurred intermittently over the centuries. In this time of "growing free" the garden came into its own, with the line between gardened and wild becoming less distinct.

After the war, determined to reclaim his lifework, Kubota and his sons reestablished the family landscape business, and expanded the plantings into undeveloped areas. The price of war included paying back taxes on their land.

Return to the main trail walking past a bamboo grove to the bright-red Moon Bridge (2). Based on bridges built in China 2500 years ago, if you look at the span's reflection in the pond, you can see a full moon shape. Next to the bridge is a giant horsetail fossil imbedded in basalt. Found in an Issaquah quarry, this plant grew wild forty to forty-five million years ago when our region enjoyed tropical weather. Japanese gardens are noted for their use of stones, and Kubota was known for being the first Seattle-area gardener to integrate large stones into gardens.

In the ancient Japanese religion of Shinto, nature was not only alive in breathing things, but also in rocks, trees, mountains, and rivers, which possessed gods or spirits called *kami*. These mostly friendly spirits protected humans in return for their respect and care. Called a heavenly barrier or heavenly seat, a place surrounded by rocks was believed inhabited by gods. Similarly, a cluster of trees was known as a divine hedge, and moats and streams were thought to demark sacred ground.

When you come upon a rock grouping in the garden, notice that no placement is random. Each rock is meant to evoke a human characteristic or emotion. Standing stones like the fossil represent strength and authority, while stones with flat tops represent a feeling of peaceful calm.

Following the path to the left will bring you to the base of the literal and figurative pinnacle of Kubota's career. The Mountainside (3) was completed in 1962 when he was eighty-three years old. Designated a Seattle Historical Landmark, it was shaped from more than 450 tons of rock collected near Mount Si east of Seattle, and is landscaped to mimic a mountain in the Cascades.

Looking up the mountainside and beyond to the swaying Douglas firs and hemlocks at its peak, it's easy to see why more than eighty different kinds of bird species have been counted here over the past decade. More than fifteen species choose to nest in the garden, including Anna's hummingbirds, Cooper's hawks, and downy woodpeckers. The various habitat niches within the garden combined with the wild attributes of the ravine woods and the powerline green space to the southwest provide a wildlife corridor for birds and other animals. Although a formal survey has not been done, raccoons, deer, bats, and foxes have been seen here, as well as frogs and salamanders.

Traditional Japanese gardens avoid colorful conifers or flowering plants, but Kubota was known to be "exuberant" in his planting choices. Many provide nectar and berries for birds and other animals, including dogwood, honeysuckle, holly, cornelian cherries, yews, juniper, cotoneasters, and pyracantha. People flock here in the spring for blossoming rhododendrons, dogwoods, and azaleas, and in the fall for colorful displays of maples, dogwoods, and dwarf sasa bamboo plants.

Japanese kumade create small sheltered spots attractive to animals, and another more obvious draw to wildlife is the abundant water supply. Unlike gardens in Japan and a boon to animals and birds, Kubota Garden is large. Katsura, one of the most revered gardens in Kyoto, is considered big at a mere 4.5 acres. An unseen benefit to fauna is the fact that the garden manager makes building healthy soil a gardening practice. The staff uses no insecticides or fungicides, and a very small amount of weed killer on pathways each year.

The waterfall adds to Kubota's goal of making a hike up the mountainside akin to a walk in the Cascades; on a clear day the mountain range can be seen in the distance.

Follow the narrow winding trail upward, over and past a zigzagging Mapes Creek as it makes its most dramatic appearance plummeting 100 feet. At the top, a shelter frames the Cascade Mountains in the distance; in the Japanese concept of "borrowed scenery," a distant view acts as an extension of the garden.

After you've explored the mountainside, follow the path to the Heart Bridge (4), named for its position at the center of the garden. One of the land's original trees, a red cedar, is located next to the bridge. "Reuse" is not a new concept created by city recycling promoters, but an ancient Japanese gardening element. The lower footbridge across the pond is made of second-hand granite steps placed askew because in traditional lore, evil spirits can only walk in a straight line. This is especially appropriate since these steps originally led to the doors of the King County Courthouse.

More recycling takes place in the nearby Tom Kubota Stroll Garden, where rocks and some of the trees came from the grounds of a Boeing office building before it was torn down. In the Japanese Garden section built in the 1930s, the stones are glacial remnants gathered from farm fields in Rainier Beach. Located near the top of the mountainside is a concrete bench salvaged from Capitol Hill's old Broadway High School. Even trees have been reused here, with one of the most striking examples being the Camperdown elm—a favorite with kids because of it's tent-like hanging branches—which was relocated to the stroll garden from a Seattle backyard.

Next to the stroll garden is the Fera Fera Forest (5), a dark, peaceful hideaway formed by a group of evenly spaced gold threadleaf cypress. Fera Fera is shorthand for this tree's botanical tongue twister: *Chamaecyparis pisifera filifera aurea*. The result of nursery stock that grew tall before it was sold, these trees serve as reminders that this was not just a display garden, but a

The Heart Bridge stretches over one "bead" on the garden's necklace of ponds, the result of digging and rechanneling all-season Mapes Creek.

business. Look for examples of other nursery stock "forests" in the garden, including a birch grove, a stand of pyramidalis conifers known as the "sentries," and the "spruce sea," a collection of dwarf spruce and weeping blue atlas cedars.

> Plantings in Kubota Garden aren't marked. Fujitaro Kubota chose plants based on their forms and the emotional responses they evoked. When Kubota was asked the name of a tree or shrub he would answer, "*Wakarimasen*," Japanese for "I don't know," which visitors often took to be the name of the plant in question.

In Kubota Garden there are many pathways to choose from. Wander to find your own kumade and consider how Kubota crafted his perfected Northwest nature with the guiding spirit of his homeland, and how that essence is continually shaped by the nature of his adopted home.

25. Bradner Gardens Park: Waiting for Butterflies

Where:	In the Mount Baker neighborhood at Twenty-ninth Avenue South and South Grand Street
Phone:	(206) 684-4075
Internet:	*www.seattletilth.org; www.cityofseattle.net/parks/ parkspaces/gardens.htm*
Hours:	4:30 A.M. to 11:30 P.M.
Disabled Access:	Yes
Dogs:	On leash
Driving:	From downtown Seattle, take I-5 south to Exit 164, Dearborn/Fourth Avenue South/Airport Way. Take the Dearborn off-ramp and head east on Dearborn about one-half mile to Rainier Avenue South. Turn right onto Rainier and travel a little under a half mile. Turn left at the light onto South Massachusetts Street. Go east about eight blocks uphill to Twenty-ninth Avenue South and turn right. The gardens are on your right and the butterfly garden is in the southeast corner.
Bus:	14

From a 75-foot garden-theme tile mosaic and ornate hose bibs, to a carved bench decorated with the salmon lifecycle, to wire fence panels adorned with recycled farm implements, art's as much a constant in Bradner Gardens Park as photosynthesis. In the first coalition of its kind, neighborhood activists joined with King County Master Gardeners, the P-Patch Program, and Seattle

Tilth to develop the park as a center for gardening education focused on issues unique to city dwellers.

As one of Seattle's first pesticide-free parks, Bradner presents the clean bill of health necessary for butterflies to thrive. Their sensitivity to these poisons makes them indicator insects, "canaries in a coal mine" that tell us when the system is getting out of balance.

This is just one reason butterflies are so much more than "flying flowers." In addition to the caterpillar's marvel of metamorphosis, butterflies compound eyes can see ultraviolet colors invisible to us, their transparent wings are covered in hundreds of thousands of colorful scales, their hearts run the length of their bodies, and their taste sensors are in their feet. Despite these exceptional traits, these creatures need the warmth of the sun to fly. If the weather's not in her favor, a butterfly can spend the better part of a two-to-four-week average lifespan waiting out the rain under a leaf umbrella.

BUTTERFLY WATCHING TIPS FOR BRADNER GARDENS PARK

1. Visit the garden in summer in early to mid-afternoon, the warmest time of the day.
2. Sit quietly for a while on the steps leading into the garden, watch and wait. You also may be treated to the aerial acrobatics of Anna's hummingbirds.
3. If you see a butterfly on a plant, approach slowly from behind it to get a closer look. Make sure your shadow does not pass over and startle it.
4. Use an inexpensive hand lens to view the wing scales and compound eyes.
5. Butterflies like the salt in your sweat and if you quietly approach with your hand outstretched, one might land on you, uncoil its proboscis—a sucking tube that can be as long as the butterfly's entire body—and take a taste. Butterflies don't chew their food, but suck it in through these built-in straws.

For local butterfly events, contact the Washington Butterfly Association at *wabutterflyassoc@earthlink.net*. This group sponsors field trips and classes in the Seattle area. The North American Butterfly Association can be found at *www.naba.org*.

Although they can be found here year-round, summer is the most prolific butterfly season, and the top of the rock-slab steps in the butterfly garden at Bradner Gardens is a good viewpoint. Butterflies prefer good-size open spaces offering a range of colors and a variety of their favorite plant species. Good caterpillar habitat is nearby in a wooded stand to the southwest. (If you plant a butterfly garden, don't forget to provide caterpillar host plants.)

Butterflies are members of the order of insects called Lepidoptera, meaning "scale wings." This defining feature separates moths and butterflies from all other flying insects. If you look at their wings through a magnifying glass you can see tiny scales overlapping like shingles. The scales help absorb sunlight, are thought to provide a slippery defense against predators, and, in some males, produce scents used to attract females.

Bradner Gardens' "mascot" is the parks department's only working windmill. This early twentieth century Aermoter is used to recirculate pond water to deter stagnation and the accompanying mosquitoes.

In one lifetime, lepidoptera have four incarnations. They begin as an egg—usually attached to a leaf. In three to twelve days the egg will hatch into a voracious larva, a caterpillar that eats until it grows to 27,000 times its hatchling size! After four to six moltings, the caterpillar becomes a legless pupa, which hardens into a protective chrysalis to await the final and most renowned transformation.

What happens inside the chrysalis is described as a complete meltdown. Butterfly body parts are sparked into growth at the pupa stage when the caterpillar stops releasing juvenile hormones. Inside its safe enclosure, the caterpillar dissolves into a cellular stew that transforms into the emerging butterfly. Some over-winter inside the chrysalis, while others emerge as adult butterflies in just seven to ten days.

Here are some summertime species common at Bradner:

Woodland skipper (*Ochlodes sylvanoides*). Skippers are named for their bouncing flight pattern. When not in flight, they hold their wings at a unique angle, in a posture reminiscent of a paper airplane. The tops of this skipper's wings are orange with jagged brown borders and the lower wing has a large reddish spot. Its underside varies from yellow to rufous to brown. Skippers like to sip from asters and lavender, and some species have been clocked at 30 miles per hour.

Red admirables (*Vanessa atalanta*). Also known as red admirals, admirables are strong, fast flyers that dart around the garden. Look for distinctive orange-red bands against a dark brown-black wing, and a few white spots gracing the outer wings. They like butterfly bush, asters, sedums, and rotten fruit. The males are very territorial and will follow if you enter their space.

Lorquin's admirals (*Limenitis lorquini*). Recognized by their sailing flight pattern, Lorquin's have a brown-black back marked with a wide, white V, and rusty orange wingtips. Gutsy and territorial, the males have even known to chase away gulls. You may see them perching on a branch, then darting out to investigate passersby.

Lorquin's Admiral

In winter, if you see a half-eaten leaf still attached to an apple or cherry tree, it may be protecting a Lorquin's admiral caterpillar. They roll themselves into a leaf with protective silk, wait out the winter in this self-woven sleeping bag, and crawl out in spring to eat the tree's fresh leaves.

Western tiger swallowtail (*Papilio rutulus*). Seen mainly in June and July, the swallowtail is the Northwest's showiest butterfly. Often confused with the well-known monarch (which prefers warmer climates and needs milkweed to thrive), on close examination swallowtails look quite different. They are larger and yellow (as opposed to the orange monarch) with black vertical striping, and blue and red markings on the lower wings.

MOTHS: UNSUNG HEROES

The oft-ignored wallflower cousins of butterflies, moths are quietly important pollinators and essential food for spiders, birds, and bats. In Washington there are ten times as many moth species as butterflies. Although some moths are day fliers, they differ from butterflies in that they are mostly nocturnal, usually duller in coloration, have threadlike or feathery antennae, and for many species, their pupa is wrapped in a silky cocoon. Moths and butterflies sip from many of the same plants including mock orange, jasmine, honeysuckle, and bee balm, though moths prefer night bloomers. Like butterflies, moths unroll a long proboscis to suck up flower nectar.

The human need to light up the night plays havoc with a moth's navigation system. Many scientists believe moths use the moon and stars as reference points for flying—by keeping the same angle to these celestial bodies, they keep on course. Moths are fooled by our artificial moons.

If you go moth watching on a summer evening, you will have much better luck in a dark area, as the proliferation of urban night lighting has caused a huge decrease in moths. If you're lucky, you could see the hummingbird-like hover of an eyed sphinx moth (look for the striking blue and black "eyes" below pinky red swaths on the lower wings), or the amazing 4-inch wingspan of the polyphemus moth (only one, in 2002 in Discovery Park, has been reported in Seattle over the past decade). The yellow underwing (*Noctua comes*) is less showy and more common. A flashlight covered with red cellophane or fabric (as with many nocturnal creatures, moths cannot see red) allows you to observe moths without disturbing them.

✻ 26. Seward Park Natural History: From Bedrock to Eagles

Where:	On the south end of Lake Washington on Lake Washington Boulevard South
Phone:	(206) 684-4396
Internet:	*www.sewardpark.net*
Hours:	Park, 4:00 A.M. to 11:30 P.M.; Seward Park Nature Center, 9:00 A.M. to 6:00 P.M., Tuesday through Saturday
Disabled Access:	Yes, on Trail 1
Dogs:	On leash, not conducive to eagle viewing
Driving:	From downtown Seattle, take I-5 south to Exit 163A, West Seattle Bridge/Columbian Way. Keep left at the fork in the ramp and merge onto South Columbian Way. Keep right toward Fifteenth Avenue South. Follow the arterial a little more than 1 mile to Beacon Avenue South. Turn right onto Beacon and continue about a half mile to South Orcas Street. Follow Orcas about 2 miles into Seward Park and go to the parking lot on the right. The nature center is the brick building next to the playground.
Bus:	39

If you'd like a crash course in Seattle's natural history, Seward Park is an outdoor classroom well suited to your studies. Pick up a trail map at the nature center and venture beyond the perimeter loop trail into the lesser-known heart of the park. Here in springtime trilliums stretch for light among towering old-growth firs, screech owls vie with hairy woodpeckers for nest sites, and mountain beavers dig their secret tunnels.

Geologically, you're standing on a drumlinoid ridge, an elongated stretch of rocks piled in the wake of a retreating glacier. Many of these rocks were dragged all the way from British Columbia. Called the Bailey Peninsula, the ridge reaches 169 feet at its high point, but the steep terrain is largely disguised by forest when approaching the park. This is one of only three places in Seattle with exposed bedrock. Ancient marine mollusk fossils embedded in the rock have been dated to the Oligocene epoch some 26 to 37 million years ago when the Puget Lowland was part of the continental shelf. The Seattle Fault runs parallel to the I-90 bridge just north of here, and scientists believe these rocks were pushed above ground when the earth south of the fault line was lifted 20 feet during a major earthquake eleven hundred years ago.

At up to 7.5 feet, an eagle's wingspan makes an impressive silhouette against the sky, known as a "flying plank." They rarely flap their wings as they soar, riding updrafts to conserve energy.

The park's 270 acres boast the largest stand of old-growth Douglas firs, cedars, and bigleaf maples in the city, as well as healthy stands of hemlock and madrone. Make a point to visit the oldest Douglas fir in Seattle located on Trail 1. Seward is also home to hundreds of wild native plants, including one of the city's only patches of poison oak, which has been erroneously attributed with "itching away" the axes of early loggers. Long before people imagined the new city of Seattle would one day reach the lakeshore, this peninsula was earmarked for parkland in 1892. This, combined with the fact that its two principal owners didn't live in Seattle, kept the forest relatively intact.

Bats, beavers, and salmon can be found here, as well as an abundant array of woodland and water-loving birds, including Seattle's only flock of parrots thought by some to be scarlet-fronted parakeets. More commonly found in the Andes Mountains from Venezuela to Peru, it's theorized that two or more pet birds were released or lost more than a decade ago, and their numbers have since increased to sixteen and counting. These birds' harsh cries and bright feathers, brilliant in contrast to the evergreens, make for many a head-scratching visitor. They enjoy eating bigleaf maple flowers and visit bird feeders for sunflower seeds. During winter they are more often seen in the Maple Leaf neighborhood of northeast Seattle.

The park's nesting bald eagles warrant special attention. Once a rare sight in the city, it wasn't until the early 1990s that urban eagles became commonplace. A DDT casualty, eagles were an endangered species until 1996, when they were downlisted to "threatened." After DDT was banned in 1972, the birds gradually began to recover. In 1977, the first pair of bald eagles to nest in Seattle in recent history chose a tree in Seward Park to call home. Two eagle pairs now nest on the peninsula, including the oldest "couple" in the city, which are believed to be the "grandparents" of all of the other Seattle eagles. In 2002 there were two active nests in the park.

Myth: "That must be the female warming the eggs on the nest." Both female and male bald eagles share egg-warming duties—the division of labor varies with each pair.

These raptors keep the same territories for years, so if you know the location of a nest, you're likely to see them. Due to their size and predictable whereabouts, eagles are a great starter bird for students of natural history. Many live in Seattle year-round due to the abundant food supply, with an increase in the population during winter when eagles that nest farther north travel to our unfrozen waterways in search of food.

Throughout the nesting period they add materials to carefully constructed nests made of branches, twigs, and grasses, which can weigh up to 1000 pounds. Lined with layer upon layer of leftover fish bones, animal fragments, and excrement, an eagle nest is a smelly, though sturdy home. Just as they begin to bring food—and the accompanying bacteria—to the baby eaglets in April, the parents start incorporating evergreen branches into the nest, an ingenious choice because of these trees' natural antiseptic properties.

Though fledging varies from year to year, July is usually when the young eagles are learning to fly—a good time to visit for a chance to view first flights. The young birds work themselves into a frenzy preparing for takeoff, but once airborne, they make it look easy. Landing is another tricky maneuver with a steep learning curve, and eaglets can end up on the ground instead of on the branch they were aiming for. It's dangerous to approach a downed bird, which could be frightened enough to use its 1-inch-long talons. Report such sightings to the park nature center or the State Department of Fish and Wildlife.

In Washington, these raptors have established many more territories (each territory consists of one nesting pair that may defend several nest sites) than outlined in the initial recovery plan. Four hundred was the target number, and there are currently more than 1000 nesting pairs. Due to its urban character, King County's target was zero, but we now boast more than thirty territories. The population is so abundant that some healthy adult birds that could nest do not, and active nests are closer in proximity than the birds normally prefer.

Sign up for a free eagle-watching class for a chance to view the birds through a spotting scope with a naturalist. You can also ask someone at the nature center for help in locating a nest.

HOW TO PRESERVE EAGLE HABITAT

1. Advocate leaving dead trees (snags) and large trees located near the water that bald eagles need for nesting.
2. Lobby to stop development on steep slopes. The resulting erosion ruins water quality and disrupts tree roots.
3. Find alternatives to using pesticides and other poisons. Remember that whatever you spill on the road or pour on your lawn ends up in surface water and eventually inside fish, an eagle's primary food source.

LIFE BEFORE SEATTLE: NATIVE VILLAGES

Although Europeans settled in the Seward Park area surprisingly early in Seattle's history—in April 1852, just five months after the Denny party arrived at Alki—Native Americans had called it home for centuries. Prior to the pioneer era, there had been four to six longhouses between the Bailey Peninsula and Pritchard Beach to the south. This area was probably popular for hunting deer, netting ducks, fishing, and gathering berries and wapato, an aquatic plant prized for its starchy tubers, which were baked and eaten. Abundant cattail leaves were likely collected here to be woven into mats to insulate longhouse walls and to make summerhouses. The plant's fuzzy seed down was used as diapers, for dressing wounds, and filling pillows.

According to historian David Buerge, who has written extensively on the Duwamish tribe, the beach stretching north from Seward Park was a popular place for fishing, as well as hunting muskrats and birds. An area near the peninsula isthmus is said to have been a "native garden of sorts."

Thomas Talbot Waterman, an ethnography pioneer who interviewed Puget Sound elders in the early twentieth century, collected thousands of regional Native American place names, including these for the Seward Park area:

Brighton Beach (south of Seward Park): *Xaxao'Ltc*, "taboo" or "forbidden." A supernatural monster purportedly lived at this point.

The isthmus connecting Bailey Peninsula with the mainland: *Cka'lapsEb*, "the upper part of one's neck." This word is employed regularly for "isthmus."

Bailey Peninsula, especially its northern end: *SkEba'kst*, "nose" (*bE'ksid*, "nostril").

BEAVERS, TRUE AND FALSE

Two "beavers" are found at Seward Park, but only one of them is a true beaver. The imposter is the oldest living rodent species, the mountain beaver *(Aplodontia rufa)*, a sort of living fossil.

Named by California miners because of the species' inclination to gnaw bark and bite through limbs like true beavers, the misnomer may have been promoted by trappers to increase the value of the pelts. Mountain beavers look somewhat like large hamsters, and are also known as "boomers" for their vocalizations, which include whistles and moans. Because this furtive, nocturnal creature spends most of its life underground and rarely ventures more than a few yards from its den, you're more likely to see the opening to its burrow than the mountain beaver itself. Look for a small hole 4 to 6 inches in diameter surrounded by clipped vegetation (they find sword fern, salal, and nettles tasty). You can also look for small "haystacks" of dried plants near their burrows, which are thought to be used for food storage and to line their nests. Mountain beavers also live at Camp Long, Discovery Park, and Carkeek Park.

With a lodge a short swim away along the western shore of Lake Washington, American beavers (*Castor canadensis*), the true beavers, frequent the Bailey Peninsula to harvest trees for food and building material. Look at the poplars along the western shore for evidence of their gnawing. Most active at dawn and dusk, North America's largest rodent makes quite an impression, when "standing" nearly 3 feet tall at the edge of the lake (although that's nothing compared to its 700-pound relative from the Pleistocene!). Hunted almost to extinction in the mid-1800s for its luxurious pelt, beavers are now common in the Northwest. Known for a paddle-like tail, a beaver will slap the water loudly to frighten an intruder and warn its family of danger. Excellent swimmers with suitably webbed feet, these animals can be spotted traversing the lake with their heads above the water trailing large wakes. Second only to humans in their ability to alter their environment, by contrast they create places of great diversity attractive to a host of other animals.

Common muskrats (*Ondatra zibethicus*) also frequent the park's edges. These water-dwellers have partially webbed feet and are much smaller than beavers. They move their scaly, vertically flattened tails side-to-side as opposed to the beaver tail's up-and-down motion. Another good swimmer, the northern river otter (*Lutra canadensis*) can sometimes be seen playing along the park's southern shores. A member of the weasel family, an adult male's sleek body can reach 4 feet from head to tail.

Mountain Beaver

27. Dearborn Park Elementary School: A Forest (and Wetland) of Learning

Where:	On South Orcas Street between Beacon Hill and Rainier Valley
Phone:	(206) 252-6930
Internet:	*www.seattleschools.org/schools/dearbornpark/*
Hours:	Call for a tour, or visit after school or on a weekend
Disabled Access:	Limited
Dogs:	On leash
Driving:	From downtown Seattle, take I-5 south to Exit 163A, West Seattle Bridge/Columbian Way. Keep left at the fork in the ramp and merge onto South Columbian Way. Keep right toward Fifteenth Avenue South. Follow the arterial a little more than 1 mile to Beacon Avenue South. Turn right onto Beacon and continue about a half mile to South Orcas Street. Turn left. In a short distance, the school driveway is on the left. On weekends, park outside the gate even if it is open.
Bus:	36 (stops at Beacon and Orcas)

There isn't much open space between Beacon Hill and the Rainier Valley, so Dearborn Park Elementary School's outdoor "classrooms" offer refreshing alternatives to pavement for students and visitors alike. The Dearborn Park Children's Forest and Alder Wetland began as science projects and now provide community access to two inviting habitats.

For many years, "Don't kick the ball into the woods!" was all Dearborn Park students knew of the largely deciduous forest on the school property's north side. In 1995, an innovative science curriculum that focuses on hands-on environmental education was the impetus for students to start investigating the woods rather than avoiding them. Soon children were seeing the forest for the trees. After hours of removing invasive plants and plotting and planting their own "baby forests," students now regard the woodland with fondness and a protective sense of pride.

In an area populated with post-logging deciduous opportunists, students broke trail in 1997 with the help of the Washington Forest Protection Association, EarthCorps, Starflower Foundation, and the U.S. Forest Service, powered by several city grants. Soon every grade was involved in some way with

Students helped craft this maple-leaf adorned gate that marks the entrance to the Dearborn Park Children's Forest.

stewardship and restoration, from studying soil to removing invasive plants. Almost every teacher found a reason to bring at least part of their studies outside: In math, students calculated tree heights, art students drew native plants, and for poetry class the woodland offered inspiration.

The Children's Forest trailhead is just north of the school parking lot. Pass through the metalwork maple leaf gateway (fashioned by Dearborn students with the help of area high schoolers) to meander through 2.6 acres thick with bigleaf maple, alder, and cottonwood trees. The trail seems longer than its actual length in feet, as the circuitous pathway leads over a bridge traversing a seasonal stream. Diverse undergrowth includes Oregon grape, salmonberry, snowberry, red elderberry, salal, and vine maple.

Each year, a fifth grade class is in charge of stewardship. Children work with naturalists to learn the inner-workings of the forest and earn badges that recognize them as forest guides responsible for providing tours to the public. They work together in teams to identify and remove invasive plants, tag native plants, then design and plant their own small plots of nascent forest, including trees, shrubs, wildflowers, and ground covers. Look for these newly planted areas next to the trail where they are roped off to prevent trampling. The long-term goal is to plant a mixed conifer and deciduous forest that will slowly replace aging trees.

The fifth-grade guides are well versed in the land's history and their forest's ethnobotany, introducing visitors to native plants and invasive species. Pointing to thimbleberry, they'll invite you to feel the feathery soft texture of the leaves, earning this plant the nickname, "toilet paper of the woods." Breaking off a sword fern leaf, they'll demonstrate a local Native American game called "pala-pala" in which each player counts how many leaflets she can break off in a single breath. You'll learn that hazelnut twigs are so pliable they were used as twist-ties, and nettle stems so strong they were twined into rope by area tribes. Did you know that flies pollinate Indian plum because the flowers smell like rotting meat?

In the year 2000, the school's second outdoor education project began slowly emerging beneath ivy and blackberry brambles. The Alder Wetland, which provides an entirely different ecosystem where students can expand their environmental studies, is down the hill on the opposite side of the school. Enter the gate and follow a short trail to a viewing platform. Punctuated with substantial stands of skunk cabbage (this perennial plant can live for seventy years and clearly some of these specimens must be grandmothers), the quarter-acre wetland trickles down the adjacent ravine. Students will continue to reforest the wetland edges and investigate the source of these springs. Large logs fashioned into impressive benches for outdoor learning were carved from a Seward Park old-growth Douglas fir storm victim.

Visit in the fall when the maples are in their golden glory, or spring when every leaf celebrates with its own ebullient shade of green. Both the wetland and forest are open to the public. Call ahead for a guided tour by a fifth-grade naturalist, or visit on your own after school hours.

*G*reen Peninsula:
WEST SEATTLE AND THE DUWAMISH RIVER

"As wild a spot as any on earth," was Arthur Denny's assessment of Seattle's first ill-chosen, weather-beaten town site near the tip of Alki Point. The landscape has been drastically altered since Denny, eleven other adults, and twelve children waved farewell to their schooner, the *Exact*, on that rainy November morning in 1851. But the fact remains that some of Seattle's wildest corners survive here on the Duwamish Peninsula, serenaded by Puget Sound on her western flank, buffeted by Elliott Bay to the north, and swept by the Duwamish River to the east.

Far from uninhabited when Denny and his clan disembarked on what had long been used as a Duwamish burial site, archeological evidence dates human inhabitation of the peninsula to 300 B.C. There were at least seventeen native villages in today's Seattle area when the Denny party set foot on what is known as *Me-Kwa-Mooks* in the Nisqually tongue, meaning "shaped like a bear's head." Looking at a map you can see two distinct ears, and it's interesting to speculate how people without the benefit of this bird's-eye perspective extrapolated the bear. Shell middens—the accumulated debris of thousands of shellfish suppers—found along these shores are evidence of the abundant estuarine environment of the rivermouth. At low tide one can still see what Native Americans call a "spirit boulder" south of the Fauntleroy ferry dock. A tour in this chapter outlines some of the geology of the area, making it easier to understand the significance of this rock called *Psai-Yah-hus*, the dormant horn-headed serpent responsible for landslides and earthquakes.

Sadly, the people who welcomed Denny's party and kept them from starving in those first winter months still struggle for federal recognition as a tribe. The Duwamish are working to raise funds to rebuild a longhouse at a former village site on the river to serve as the cultural heart of their people.

Though many equate West Seattle with the blading/volleyball set along Alki Beach, it is home to some of the most diverse nature experiences in the

A young beachcomber reaches into another world at a West Seattle tide pool.

city. From the highest point in Seattle, 512 feet above sea level at the base of the High Point watertower at Thirty-fifth Avenue SW and Myrtle Street, to scuba diving below sea level, and everything in between, there is much to explore. You can golf with red foxes on the West Seattle Golf Course—and the Camp Long Nature Center staff offers bat-watching hayrides through the golf course grounds on summer evenings. Practice your conifer identification using the towering trees of Schmitz Park Preserve as guides while listening for the fluting call of the Swainson's thrush, or seek out octopuses during April's

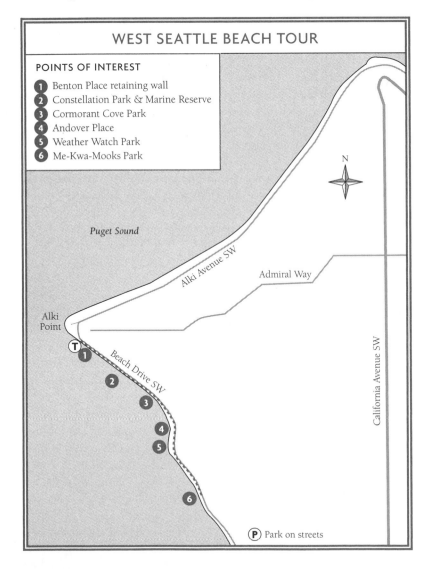

low tides at Me-Kwa-Mooks Park. West Seattle is also home to the Longfellow Creek Legacy project, an effort to create a 3-mile-long corridor of connected pedestrian pathways along this urban waterway.

Take a geological tour of Alki and visit some innovative seashore parks that mix art and nature. Another tour takes bicyclists nearby the path of young salmon heading out to sea, along a series of revolutionary habitat restoration sites along the Duwamish River. Three destinations take you into the interior of the peninsula to one of Seattle's two remaining old-growth forests, the city's only bog restoration project at the headwaters of Longfellow Creek, and to Camp Long, home of one of Seattle's most creative nature education programs, for an introduction to mushroom identification.

28. West Seattle Beach Chronicles: From Broken Earth to Storied Sky

Where:	Just south of Alki Point on Beach Drive SW and Alki Avenue SW
Tour Distance:	2 miles
Phone:	(206) 684-4075
Internet:	*www.cityofseattle.net/parks/*
Hours:	Daylight hours
Disabled Access:	Sidewalk above beach affords views of the fault evidence
Dogs:	On leash
Driving:	From downtown Seattle, take I-5 south to Exit 163A, West Seattle Bridge/Columbian Way. Keep right at the fork in the ramp following the sign for the West Seattle Bridge and Spokane Street. Go over the West Seattle Bridge to Fauntleroy Way SW. Continue straight for several lights, then turn right onto SW Alaska Street. Turn left onto Forty-ninth Avenue SW. Turn right onto SW Hudson Street. Hudson becomes SW Jacobsen Road. Turn right onto Beach Drive SW. Instead of following the arterial right onto Sixty-third Avenue SW, stay left on Beach Drive and continue to the intersection with Alki Avenue SW. Park on the road.
Bus:	37
Special Note:	To see the geological formations and experience prime tide pooling, visit during a minus-1 tide or lower

Alki Point is well known as the ill-chosen stormy campsite of the first Seattle settlers and less known as an ancient Duwamish tribal burial ground. Perhaps least known of all is that this jutting triangle of land was undersea eleven hundred years ago until a major earthquake drastically rearranged the landscape. This tour introduces you to striking evidence of the Seattle Fault, three community parks focused on natural history, and exceptional birding and tide pooling spots along the way.

Start the tour at Beach Drive SW and Alki Avenue SW, where a cement ramp leads to the beach. Before you head to shore, look out over the beach to see the exposed rib-like ridges of bedrock that were lifted 20 feet during what today's newscasters would certainly proclaim "Quake 900 A.D."

A fault is a place where there is a break in the earth's crust, usually, as in this case, far beneath the surface. During an earthquake, the two rock masses on either side of the split begin to move. The Seattle Fault is actually a "fault zone," where there are many small fractures. Most scientists believe that during quakes, the Seattle Fault creates an up and down motion. To picture this, place your hands palms together and move them slightly, one up and the other down.

Scientists believe this major earthquake lasted approximately 40 seconds and would have hit 7.5 on the Richter Scale. In 1992, several pieces of evidence converged to solidify the Seattle Fault hypothesis. An imaginary line from the exposed bedrock points northwest to Restoration Point on Bainbridge Island, where geologic studies related to the fault began. This sand-colored point of land was lifted 20 feet just as Alki was, while points north dropped as much as 5 feet. A giant tsunami is believed to have followed the tremor, washing tons of sand onto land. In addition, the shaking upended forests and made beaches of high ground. An ancient Douglas fir mummified in sand and mud at West Point in Magnolia was carbon-dated to the year of the quake. The Seattle Fault also solved the mystery of three submerged forests in Lake Washington, which slid into the lake the same year. The fault is known to stretch from Bainbridge Island to East Lake Sammamish, and runs nearby almost directly beneath the Seattle-to-Bainbridge ferry route.

The westward curve of the rocky ribs here is one expression of the force of moving pieces of the earth's crust. Like a stack of cards rammed against a wall (in this case, the fault is the wall), these layers of Seattle's "history" were shuffled violently and repeatedly, during many separate earthquakes along the Seattle Fault over many millions of years.

Geologists can only speculate why the Seattle Fault exists, but these types of fissures develop at pressure points far beneath the earth's surface. Fueled by radioactivity within the mantle (the layer of earth between the crust and core), heat creates convection currents that cause earth's crustal plates to move.

Seattle sits at the intersection of two major underground forces: The Juan de Fuca Plate is essentially dragging the western edge of North America north at the rate of 4 centimeters per year. At the same time, the Juan de Fuca is diving slowly beneath the North American plate, the "subduction zone" responsible for activity in our Cascade volcanoes, including Mount Saint Helen's explosive statement in 1980. Also, the Pacific Plate is sliding north along the San Andreas Fault, and the friction across this fault is helping to drag the adjacent part of North America to the north–northwest. In combination, these forces are causing Oregon to slowly push Western Washington into British Columbia at a rate of about 4 millimeters per year. All this pressure needs to be released somehow—enter the Seattle Fault.

Walk down to the beach to stand on the telltale ridges. Centuries of wave action delineate sand-grain–size differences between layers of the exposed bedrock. These variations tell ancient stories of big storms, calm weather periods, floods, or landslides—each resulting in slightly different sedimentary structures. About 30 million years old, these sleepy sandstone layers hide their shaky past under seaweed, barnacles, and sea anemones.

Walk back up the ramp and continue your tour south. Just below the cement retaining wall opposite Benton Place SW (1), look for more exposed bedrock. As you head south on the sidewalk, you are walking down Seattle's own Avenue of Stars, a collection of twenty-seven constellations arranged by season. Set in bronze and labeled with the names of prominent stars, these constellations can be seen from here during the appropriate season. One of three Beach Drive Shoreline Parks on this tour designed by artist Lezlie

Jane, Constellation Park and Marine Reserve (2), promotes education and conservation by bringing the cosmos and underwater world together. After visiting Gemini, Orion, and Taurus, stop at the mock tide pool complete with bronze octopus, sea stars, and moon snails. This pool is meant to lure visitors down the ramp to the beach, where they can

A life-size giant Pacific octopus beckons visitors onto the beach at Constellation Park and Marine Reserve.

Osprey

search for living sea creatures at low tide. A mural depicting various players in "The Intertidal World" divulges how green sea urchins move, who eats beach hoppers, and how sand dollars get a meal. Future installations at this site will include a night sky map, a moon dial—which will tell the time of the night one week before and after the full moon—and a life-size sculpture of the mythological character Andromeda, who will emerge from the deep only at low tide.

In summer, this is one place you might witness the osprey's impressive fishing maneuver. When seen from below, this raptor has a light-colored body and upper wing, with darker outer wings that can reach 5 feet from tip to tip. It will hover like a helicopter before rapidly and dramatically plunging head and feet first into the water after fish prey. The pads of an osprey's feet are barbed to grip the slippery meal, which might be carried home to a nest in nearby Schmitz Park Preserve.

Head south one-tenth of a mile to Cormorant Cove Park (3), another community initiative honoring seabirds that frequent this area. A tiled mural explains the connection between healthy near-shore habitat and a thriving salmon population. Organizers formed a beach cove where only rubble existed before, naming it after the flocks of double-crested cormorants regularly seen resting on the rock jetty that stretches out into the water north of here.

Tons of landfill was removed to restore the buried shoreline at Cormorant Cove Park where winter birders regularly see harlequin ducks and common loons.

You can learn a lot from local birders, who like to come here in the winter and early spring. Twelve kinds of waterfowl typically seen here are pictured on mural bricks, including the Barrow's goldeneye (known for swallowing whole shellfish), brant goose, common loon, northern shoveler, and harlequin duck (named for its spectacular markings). This small park has a picnic-perfect sandy driftwood beach and hand-launch boat access.

After the last Ice Age ended 13,500 years ago, fossils indicate that horses, bison, caribou, woolly mammoths, and mastodons roamed where Seattle's urban bipeds throng today. Washington's state fossil is the Columbian mammoth, which died out about 10,000 years ago. This member of the elephant family arrived in North America from Asia via the Bering Strait, snacking on grasses as it moved southward. Fossils of this mammoth have been found on the Olympic Peninsula.

A little farther south is a Seattle Parks sign for Andover Place (4), a small public access pathway to the beach. Just south of here is the easily missed Weather Watch Park (5), marking the former site of a ferry dock that served Alki neighbors in the early 1900s. Like an opened time capsule, a column topped by a Brant geese weathervane is inset with photos and stories of local Native American history, white settlement, early Alki beach memories, and weather and cloud information. Did you know that raindrops aren't normally tear-shaped? One weather fact here proclaims that if you could see them in slow motion, their shapes might mimic a jellybean, pancake, peanut, hotdog, football, or human foot. Olympic Mountain lovers will appreciate a bronze relief map set into a bench that lists the names and altitude of the peaks visible from here. This park also offers beach access.

Continuing another half mile south, you'll come to Me-Kwa-Mooks Park (6), a well-known tide pooling area, where naturalists from Camp Long

Columbian Mammoth

For helpful identification details and photos of sea creatures and seaweed found on Seattle beaches, visit the Seattle Aquarium's guide at www.seattleaquarium.org/conservation/Beachguide.htm.

bring visitors to hunt for octopuses at low tide. Few tide poolers realize they are searching for mossy chitons on top of another piece of Seattle Fault evidence. From the Emma Schmitz Memorial Overlook above the beach, at low tide you will see curving raised patterns on the beach. These are the exposed peat layers of a 25,000-year-old former bog—a wetland pre-dating the glacier that shaped our Seattle landscape about 15,000 years ago. Geologists speculate that compression of the earth's crust along the Seattle Fault zone, which extends south from Alki Point to Lincoln Park, may have warped these peat beds from their original horizontal layers into a series of gently undulating hills. Centuries of wave action wore off the tops of these hills to form these convex and concave shapes.

A large boulder sits in the middle of a related phenomenon of note. Surrounded by a "racetrack" of peat, this bowl shape was created when the north/south compression was apparently compounded by east/west movement, by forces or processes unknown. The resulting cupped shape is what those in the geology biz call a "doubly plunging syncline."

Me-Kwa-Mooks is revered by tide poolers for its variety of habitats, from sandy and cobbled beaches to large boulders where nudibranches like to hide—a.k.a. sea slugs, some of these fancily clad creatures glow like neon signs. Shy red and baby giant octopuses like to curl up in silt burrows below the peat ridges—you have to look carefully to spy a stray tentacle. The sandy areas host dense beds of eccentric sand dollars. Unlike the whitewashed shells prized by beachcombers, live dollars are purple and velvety, and filter feed from a vertical position, moving diatoms into their mouths with tiny hairs. Also found here are California sea cucumbers. Looking like big, reddish spiny pickles, these incredibly soft creatures move like inchworms. The largest chiton in the world, the giant or gum boot chiton can reach 10 inches in length and can live for twenty years—their brick-red leathery bodies are shaped like a raised oval. Gum boot plates are commonly found in native shell middens. Eight overlapping plates are the distinguishing feature of all chitons, and those of smaller species are the turquoise-hued, butterfly-shaped shells collected by beachcombers.

As the tide comes in over these ancient bogs, return to where you started, or continue a couple of miles south to Lincoln Park. Situated on land that appears to be uplifted by Seattle Fault quakes in the same manner as Alki, this park is a good place for a walk through the woods or a swim in Colman Pool, Seattle's only heated saltwater swimming pool (open summers).

✳ 29. Duwamish River Restoration Bike Tour: Industrial Evolution

Where:	King County's Cecil Moses Memorial Park in Tukwila, bordering southwest Seattle
Tour Distance:	4.5 miles
Phone:	(206) 382-7007
Internet:	*www.pugetsound.org*
Hours:	Daylight hours
Disabled Access:	Cecil Moses Memorial Park and Herring's House are most accessible
Dogs:	On leash, but not conducive to wildlife viewing
Driving:	From downtown Seattle, take I-5 south to Exit 158, Boeing Access Road/East Marginal Way. At the end of the ramp, turn right. At the next large intersection, turn left onto Tukwila International Boulevard (formerly Pacific Highway South). Travel one block and turn right onto South 112th Street. There is parking at the street end. You will see a pedestrian/bike bridge across the Duwamish River here. This is the north end of the Green River Trail, which heads south along the Duwamish and Green Rivers to Kent. Cross the pedestrian bridge to Cecil Moses Memorial Park and the North Wind's Weir restoration site (T).
Bus:	174, get off at South Norfolk Street and walk across the river on the pedestrian bridge to Cecil Moses Memorial Park
Special Note:	This tour follows two bike trails to connect two areas of the Duwamish River. To get from one area of the river to the other it is necessary to bike through a busy mix of commercial, industrial, and residential areas. See map for bike route instructions.

It's easy to feel hopeless when you read news coverage of the Superfund-listed Duwamish River. Over the past one hundred years, Seattle's great river has been dredged, filled in, paved over, and polluted, so that only 2 percent of its original 5300-acre wetland habitat remains. Yet osprey and people live and fish here, seals and river otters swim here, and millions of juvenile salmon

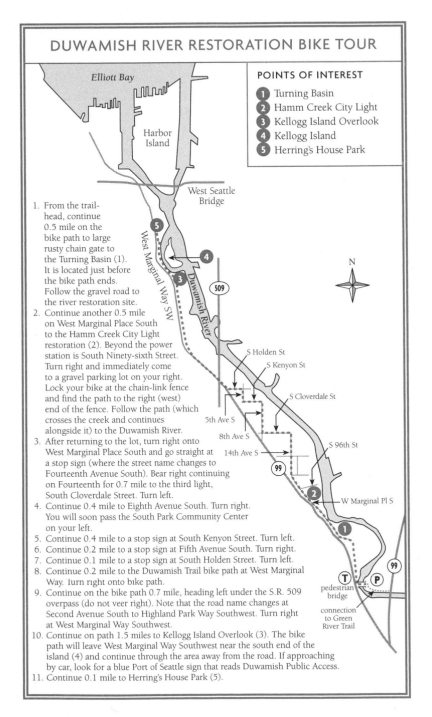

DUWAMISH RIVER RESTORATION BIKE TOUR

Elliott Bay

Harbor Island

POINTS OF INTEREST

1 Turning Basin
2 Hamm Creek City Light
3 Kellogg Island Overlook
4 Kellogg Island
5 Herring's House Park

West Seattle Bridge

West Marginal Way SW

Duwamish River

509

N

S Holden St
S Kenyon St
S Cloverdale St
5th Ave S
8th Ave S
14th Ave S
99
S 96th St
W Marginal Pl S

T P
pedestrian bridge

connection to Green River Trail

99

1. From the trailhead, continue 0.5 mile on the bike path to large rusty chain gate to the Turning Basin (1). It is located just before the bike path ends. Follow the gravel road to the river restoration site.
2. Continue another 0.5 mile on West Marginal Place South to the Hamm Creek City Light restoration (2). Beyond the power station is South Ninety-sixth Street. Turn right and immediately come to a gravel parking lot on your right. Lock your bike at the chain-link fence and find the path to the right (west) end of the fence. Follow the path (which crosses the creek and continues alongside it) to the Duwamish River.
3. After returning to the lot, turn right onto West Marginal Place South and go straight at a stop sign (where the street name changes to Fourteenth Avenue South). Bear right continuing on Fourteenth for 0.7 mile to the third light, South Cloverdale Street. Turn left.
4. Continue 0.4 mile to Eighth Avenue South. Turn right. You will soon pass the South Park Community Center on your left.
5. Continue 0.4 mile to a stop sign at South Kenyon Street. Turn left.
6. Continue 0.2 mile to a stop sign at Fifth Avenue South. Turn right.
7. Continue 0.1 mile to a stop sign at South Holden Street. Turn left.
8. Continue 0.2 mile to the Duwamish Trail bike path at West Marginal Way. Turn right onto bike path.
9. Continue on the bike path 0.7 mile, heading left under the S.R. 509 overpass (do not veer right). Note that the road name changes at Second Avenue South to Highland Park Way Southwest. Turn right at West Marginal Way Southwest.
10. Continue on path 1.5 miles to Kellogg Island Overlook (3). The bike path will leave West Marginal Way Southwest near the south end of the island (4) and continue through the area away from the road. If approaching by car, look for a blue Port of Seattle sign that reads Duwamish Public Access.
11. Continue 0.1 mile to Herring's House Park (5).

rely on this waterway as a protective channel where they can slowly prepare for life in saltwater—and, years later, find respite on the last leg of the journey home. Since the early 1990s, restoration efforts dotting these banks have engendered a sense of hope, and early indications show that these endeavors are working.

In an effort to create a corridor of precious estuarine habitats, representatives from federal, state, and local agencies, tribal governments, and citizen's conservation groups with the help of untold volunteers have muddied their boots at more than a dozen restoration sites. The Duwamish is a tidally influenced waterway, meaning its levels vary greatly at high and low tide. This tour includes multiple stops, all with pathways to views overlooking the river, many with benches and small parks.

Picture the original waterway, fanning out in a wide delta similar to the Nisqually River south of Tacoma. Her salt marshes and mudflats once stretched from the foot of Beacon Hill to below Duwamish Head in West Seattle, and tidal surges carved ever-changing pathways to her mouth. The Duwamish Tribe lived here when Egyptians were building pyramids. For them, this is where the world begins. At least six tribal villages, with cedar longhouses up to 300 feet in length, dotted the river delta when settlers began pounding together homes here in the mid-1800s.

Begin your tour at the Cecil Moses Memorial Park (T). The dredging and straightening projects of the early 1900s began just downstream from here, so this is the only place on the tour where you can see the original meander of the river. Go to the park's riverbank to visit the North Wind's Weir estuary restoration site. Started in December 2002, it is named for a Native American legend about the origin of the seasons. During a war, North Wind constructed a weir—a fence to retain and catch fish commonly used by the Duwamish—across the river to keep the salmon from migrating upstream. From the pedestrian bridge over the river, looking north at low tide you can see the exposed rocks said to be the remains of the mythical weir.

Though far fewer than before, the fish return each year—wild-spawning and hatchery chum, coho, steelhead, and cutthroat, as well as two endangered-list species, the Puget Sound chinook and bull trout. The Muckleshoot and Suquamish Tribes catch more than 35,000 salmon here each fall. The Duwamish River hosts five of the seven species of Pacific salmon, and all of these fish need wetlands.

At this bend in the river young salmon begin the chemical transformation necessary to move from fresh- into saltwater. These "anadromous" fish rely on sheltered rest stops where they can wait out the physiological changes that allow them to progress into increasingly saline water. Here they can rest,

Healthy stands of cattails are one part of restoration efforts at the Turning Basin site on the Duwamish River.

feed, and find protective hiding places in water that is generally too shallow for larger predators. The more time they can spend feeding in places like these, the bigger they will be by the time they reach Puget Sound and the greater their chances for survival. Providing a connected corridor of these estuarine habitats is one of the major goals of Duwamish River restoration.

Typically, young salmon cling to the shoreline as they move downstream, following the shape of the bank and going where it leads them. The North Wind's Weir site on the west bank was chosen because the land shape creates a calm outlet away from the main flow of the river.

This is the youngest restoration project on the tour and like most fledglings, it looks a little rough around the edges with straggling baby trees and shrubs above the tide line. Marsh plants including native sedges are protected by what looks like a maze of miniature clotheslines—wire fencing to discourage Canada geese from pulling up young plants. At low tide, logs and other habitat structures are revealed along the shore.

Providing a good contrast is the Turning Basin (1), the oldest restoration site on the river, circa 1994. Head down river along West Marginal Place South about 0.5 mile to the wide spot in the river originally enlarged so ships could turn around safely. This site was chosen because young fish were consistently found resting out of the river current in the little bay to the north. Walk past a rusty chain-link gate—remnants of an abandoned ferry boat removed to make way for the marsh—along the gravel road. A sign details the ABCs of restoring fish habitat from mudflat to riparian buffer (the small forest of trees and shrubs). Volunteers worked with agencies to form a sloping beach so that different elevations are exposed at rising and falling tides creating a variety of intertidal habitats—breeding grounds for the small organisms salmon eat.

> Puget Sound tribes preserved clams by drying them on strips of tanned cedar bark. Strings of the dried meat were an important trade item, and Native Americans from east of the mountains coveted these clam "necklaces," which they snacked on as they journeyed home.

The treed area is more than just a natural "fence" between road and river, it provides a home for another essential fish food. Called "drift insects," spiders, aphids, and wasps are blown into the water where they make up an important part of salmon diet. Some scientists believe they are so crucial that the best use of any open space on the river is planting native trees. Studies show this restoration work is successful because young salmon are eating the food produced at these sites.

Continuing another half-mile down river, you'll reach the Hamm Creek City Light restoration project (2) at South Ninety-sixth Street. The first part of the trail parallels West Marginal Place and leads to a culvert where Hamm Creek pours out of a wide pipe. Follow the creek approximately 0.3 mile along one of the largest undeveloped parcels of land on the industrial Duwamish to the restored estuary at the river. Despite the drone of S.R. 99 in the background, you're likely to encounter a heron or kingfisher, and in the fall, waterfowl such as buffleheads, mergansers, and gadwalls. This surreal walk defines urban nature. The carefully planned creekscape is a wild splash against a backdrop of enormous rusty ship hulls and stacks of industrial objects.

The portion of Hamm Creek you see here would still be underground if it weren't for the passionate volunteer commitment of neighborhood activist John Beal. Beal nursed Hamm Creek back to health beginning in 1978—playing any role necessary along the way, from watchdog to wildlife caregiver to field scientist. When he started hauling garbage out of the creek it was completely devoid of life, but by stopping pollution at the source and working to rebuild the ecosystem, the waterway slowly resuscitated. Beal swears the water is now clean enough to drink. One person's devotion has had immeasurable positive impact on this area, and many claim his tenacity and success gave others hope and laid the foundation for all Duwamish restoration.

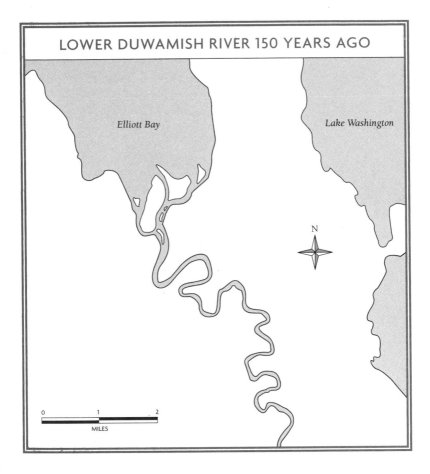

LOWER DUWAMISH RIVER 150 YEARS AGO

Elliott Bay

Lake Washington

N

0   1   2
MILES

In the fall, this is a good place to look for mature salmon jumping out of the water as they migrate up the creek. River otters, seals, sea lions, and dozens of birds have also been spotted here. In the birdwatching community, the Duwamish is a noteworthy place to visit, with one Audubon volunteer likening it to the popular Montlake Fill area near the University of Washington.

FROM SERPENTINE TO STRAIGHTWAY: THE DUWAMISH PAST AND PRESENT

The Duwamish Watershed once spanned more than 1600 miles—a drainage basin that included the Cedar, Black, Green, and White Rivers, as well as Lake Sammamish and Lake Washington. Then came the Europeans, their ships, and economic desires. A deeper, straighter, wider waterway was

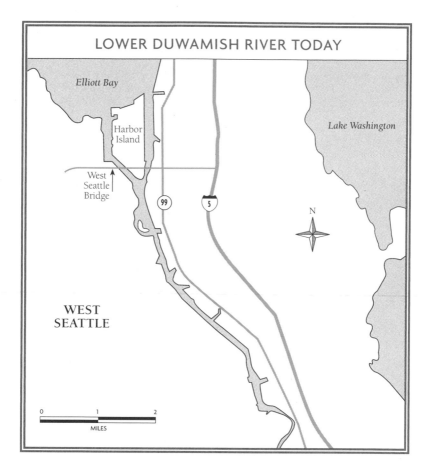

necessary to allow access to the sawmills, lumberyards, breweries, and rendering and slaughtering houses planned for the land along reengineered riverbanks.

By 1917, 20 million cubic yards of mud and sand—enough muck to reach about a mile high if piled onto Safeco Field—was removed, transforming 10 miles of the lower river into a canal 4.5 miles long. The marshes and mudflats were filled in and Harbor Island grew from mounds of Seattle's displaced earth. At the same time, two-thirds of the Duwamish tributaries were diverted or lost. To stop frequent flooding, the White River was channeled to Tacoma and the Cedar to Lake Washington. The Black River disappeared altogether when construction of the Lake Washington Ship Canal lowered the lake's water level by 9 feet.

Continue on your longest leg of the journey (about 5 miles) to the Kellogg Island Overlook (3), marked with a Port of Seattle sign. The estuary here would be Puget Creek's natural outlet, but instead its water is shunted through a storm-water pipe and sent underground to an outlet 400 feet north. The creek marks the historic location of a native village, and the Duwamish Tribe one day hopes to bring it out of the pipe. Across Marginal Way, a sign indicates the future site of a cedar longhouse—a place the tribe hopes will help preserve their cultural heritage and bring awareness to river issues.

In addition to fish, the Duwamish people relied on the abundant shellfish that once thrived here. At low tide, clams, oysters, mussels, and cockles overflowed their cedar baskets. This place was known as *Yil-eq'-qud* or "Where There are Horse Clams," and *Hah-ah-poos*, for the basket caps favored by villagers.

TOURING THE RIVER BY WATER

Frequent paddlers on the Duwamish River say their favorite thing about urban kayaking is that you never know what you'll find next: From baseball-size gems (washed glass buried in the riverbank behind a glass factory) excavated from Seattle's "emerald mines" to city stalactites caused by calcium carbonate leaching out of concrete beneath overpasses, to the dark, cave-like recesses under Harbor Island docks. Two of the easiest public access sites for hand-carried boats are on Diagonal Avenue South off Marginal Way South on the river's east bank (follow Marginal Way to the end), and Duwamish Waterway Park in South Park on the west bank. Both are best used at high tide.

Pacific Water Sports, (206) 246-9385, rents canoes and kayaks, teaches classes, offer tours, and has tips for other launch sites along the Duwamish.

Kellogg Island (4) is the remaining half of a natural island. The opposite side was scooped away to widen the main shipping lane. Between the island and the mainland is the only existing natural curve of the original lower waterway. Osprey hunt here in summer (look for their nest on a light pole to the north) and rufous hummingbirds sip from flowering red currant blossoms in early spring. The nest boxes seen on pilings just north of the island are part of a program to encourage purple martins (large swallows, the male noted for his blue-black color) to nest here. Once numbering in the hundreds in this area, martin populations have dwindled due to habitat loss and competition with starlings and house sparrows.

Immediately to the north (5), the Herring's House Park wetland project, marked with a City of Seattle sign, is the largest on the river. Built on a former shell midden, the name comes from early oral histories that indicate this place was renowned for herring and salmon. To catch the abundant fish, the

Duwamish people used stationary weirs and sharpened hooks or spears made of bone. Archeological findings near here date human inhabitation to 300 B.C. Red-winged blackbirds sing from cattail stalks and eagles soar overhead. In springtime bald eagles can be seen aerial fighting with the neighboring ospreys. Before trees leaf out, an eagle's nest is visible to the north in the forested West Duwamish Greenbelt across West Marginal Way.

Herring's House is the former home of the Seaboard Lumber Mill, one of the first and biggest mills in Seattle, which left a legacy of contaminated ground both on- and offshore. This was removed and replaced by clean soil as a first step in the restoration of eleven acres of tidelands.

Walk along the path to the river overlook—a good vantage for imagining the wide reach of the former river delta, where you can now see the restored tidal basin. Snags are one of the most prominent features of the Herring's House landscape. These dead trees provide critical habitat in mature forests, and they have been imported here as one piece of the environmental puzzle.

From here, you can keep on the bike trail heading toward the beaches of Alki, or head back upriver the way you came.

SHORELINE STREET ENDS

If you're looking for a quick waterfront getaway, there may be one hiding at the end of your street. Seattle's early planners envisioned street ends with visual or physical access to Seattle's waterways as tiny public areas, but over the years, many of these secret assets have been neglected, overgrown, or swallowed up by adjacent property owners. In the year 2000, the City of Seattle revised its permit guidelines and the city council adopted a policy for use of shoreline street ends, making public access a priority.

There are 149 of these gems in the city, many of which are undergoing brilliant transformations by Friends of Street Ends and community groups. Some of the highlights are Twenty-eighth

Whether for picnicking, reading, or fishing, street-end parks are Seattleites's collectively held waterfront real estate.

Avenue NW in Ballard, East Martin Street in Eastlake (called Good Turn Park), East Roanoke Street on Portage Bay, and a group called the "string of pearls" in Leschi and Mount Baker. For a map that lists them all, call the city at (206) 684-5147 to request *A Seattle Guide Map to Shoreline Street Ends*.

30. Mushrooming at Camp Long

Where:	West Seattle at 5200 Thirty-fifth Avenue SW
Phone:	(206) 684-7434
Internet:	*www.camplong.org*
Hours:	Tuesday through Sunday, 8:30 A.M. to 5:00 P.M.
Disabled Access:	Some paths are accessible
Dogs:	On leash
Driving:	From downtown Seattle, take I-5 south to Exit 163A, West Seattle Bridge/Columbian Way. Keep right at the fork in the ramp following the sign for West Seattle Bridge and Spokane Street. Go over the West Seattle Bridge to Fauntleroy Way SW. At the first light, turn left onto Thirty-fifth Avenue SW. Continue south about 0.6 mile up the hill (look for a Camp Long sign) and turn left onto Dawson Street to enter the park.
Bus:	21
Caution:	Don't eat a wild mushroom unless you are sure of its identity. Harvest from herbicide-free areas. Take only what you will use.

Wildly abundant Camp Long is a forager's paradise because it provides a variety of habitats suitable for mushrooms. The park's sixty-eight acres are part of the Longfellow Creek Greenbelt—an expansive wildlife corridor. A former scout camp, Camp Long offers year-round nature classes on everything from mushroom identification and flying squirrels to making seaweed stationery and stargazing. This is the only city park where you can rent a log cabin for the night ($35 year-round). If you sleep over, you'll be ready to start out early the next day, mushroom book in hand.

Their bizarre looks match their funny-sounding names: puffballs and stinkhorns, cow's noses and turkey tails, yellow parasols and shaggy manes. Colorful additions to the forest landscape, many mushrooms can turn an ordinary dinner into an extraordinary meal. Even the non-edible ones are interesting to learn about.

Mushrooms are the fruit of meandering fibrous bodies called mycelia, which remain largely hidden from view in their vast underground networks. You may have encountered a mycelium's white, hair-like tendrils under an old log or while digging in the garden. Certain kinds of mycelia and certain trees have developed relationships that help mushroom hunters with identification—they come to expect specific mushrooms under their corresponding trees. To protect the mycelia, mushroom hunters should stay on established trails. It's best to remove a mushroom with a kitchen knife (to help preserve the stem to aid identification), and replace your divot. Because the mycelia assures the mushroom will sprout again after the appropriate rainfall, picking mushrooms is the equivalent of picking berries.

Harvesting a mushroom is essential to positive identification, as many of its characteristics are best observed by cutting it in half or scraping back the gills or top layer of the cap. Another excellent identification tool is a spore print. Spore color is a very helpful way to identify gilled mushrooms because the microscopic reproductive cells retain their color, unlike other parts of the mushroom, which can change as it ages. To make a spore print, take a mushroom cap and place it gills down on a sheet of half dark and half white paper (so both light or dark spores will show up). Cover it with a glass bowl and wait. It can take several hours or overnight for enough spores to fall onto the paper for a good print.

Each fall, hundreds of freshly harvested regional mushrooms are on display in Seattle at the Puget Sound Mycological Society's exceptional Wild Mushroom Show. Sniff fungi that smell like licorice, coconuts, and maraschino cherries; sample taste treats at the cooking demonstrations; or make mushroom spore prints. For information, call (206) 522-6031.

In October or November, your foraging could be rewarded just outside the front doors of Camp Long's 1930s-era lodge, assembled from discarded ship ballasts and historic diorite bricks salvaged from original Seattle streets. Hiding below a birch tree's peeling white bark among the camouflaging leaves of fall, you might find two mushrooms that have developed relationships with the birch.

Paxillus involutus (a.k.a inrolled pax or poison pax) is one of the most abundant fruiting mushrooms in Seattle. This mushroom is not tasty and can be poisonous. Its cap can be flat, but is often funnel-shaped—and might be holding water from recent rains like a cup, looking somewhat like a partying gnome's lost goblet. The blades on the gills run way down the stalk and peel off easily, like a jacket covering the interior part of the stem. It has brown spores.

Leccinum scaberum (a.k.a. birch bolete) is a tasty edible mushroom identifiable by its tan, brown, or gray cap; white flesh; spongy pore layer under the cap; and white stalk with small brown or black scales. It has brown spores.

Wandering down the path away from the lodge and into the park, the slope on your right is a good place to look for mushrooms associated with the Douglas fir tree.

Gomphidius subroseus (a.k.a. cow's nose) is an edible mushroom with a crunchy texture despite its exterior; you peel off the slippery top before cooking it. Cow's nose has white or gray gills that run down the stalk, which is yellowish near the base. It has dark gray or black spores.

Suillus caerulescens (a.k.a. fat jack or Douglas fir suillus) is the mushroom most associated with Douglas fir. Fat jack is medium to large in size and edible. It has a slightly orange or yellow, yellow-brown or tan cap with a spongy yellow underside. The stalk is solid and, when cut or rubbed, will slowly take on a blue hue. Although the young caps are rounded, they widen and flatten as they mature. This mushroom's pores have an angled shape and are brown or cinnamon colored.

Not all mushrooms fruit in the traditional umbrella shape. Saprophytic fungi, which derive their nutrients from dead organic material, act as the forest's maintenance team, decomposing dead plant matter. Without them, you couldn't see the forest for the debris. These fungi are both commonly found on decaying conifers, and can be seen along Camp Long's nature paths:

Pleurocybella porrigens (or angel wings) are clusters of white, fan-shaped, thin fungi, which grow like sprouting shelves on rotting conifers. Easily confused with oyster mushrooms, they're more delicate and not as tasty, though still good to eat.

Fomitopsis pinicola (red-belted conk) is key to the decay of dead conifers. A member of the polypore family (tough shelf-like fungi that share a voracious appetite for dead wood), this conk has a reddish or reddish black upper cap with a white or pale yellow underside (which will not stain brown when cut or scratched). It has no stalk and is found on dead wood. Conks are considered too tough to eat.

As the number-one decayer of dead conifers, the red-belted conk is an essential but silent partner in the success of a forest ecosystem.

These are but six of the hundreds of mushrooms found at Camp Long and throughout the Seattle area. Novices can easily become frustrated by the sheer variety of fungi, but first-timers can take heart in one of the biggest misconceptions about mushrooming: that expert foragers know them all.

FROM THE CAMP LONG NATURE LOGS

Camp Long naturalists encourage visitors to describe what they experience during their visits in phenology notebooks—records of changes in flora and fauna through the seasons and through the years. One way to improve your own powers of observation or to encourage a young naturalist is to begin a nature notebook at home. When do maple tree "helicopters" fall? Blackberries ripen? Crows collect twigs for nests? Here is a sampling excerpted from Camp Long's collections of natural phenomena:

Jan. 18: Shrew mole seen under log by trail to golf course shed.

Jan. 29: A barred owl flew in and sat in the trees right over our heads and watched us for 20 minutes!

Feb. 7: Nettles now at 4 feet high, perfect for first harvest.

March 2: First banana slug of the season seen at night.

March 16: Two baseball-size egg masses of Northwest salamander in southern pond.

March 18: Bushtits mating in ocean spray and building nest in same shrub. East of picnic tables outside lodge kitchen.

March 20: Trillium on Glacier/Longfellow Creek Trail.

March 31: Crows snapping twigs for nests.

April 10: Garter snake sunning on trail.

May 10: Pacific tree frog in rushes by west side of south pond.

June 11: Heard and saw red fox near east picnic shelter.

July 6: First 10-lined June bug (beetle) of season flew into library in lodge—hissing when picked up.

Aug. 25: A pileated woodpecker took flight not 5 feet from me and clung to the side of a nearby tree.

Sept. 15: California tortoiseshell butterfly seen in forest by trail near cabin 8.

Sept. 28: Bat seen at golf course entrance from fox-watching hayride. Three foxes on course.

Oct. 6: Peregrine falcon flying east over lodge.

Nov. 10: Pouring rain! Thousands of robins are singing—it's like a giant birdbath.

Nov. 18: Very cold, lots of fallen leaves. Clear skies and meteor showers.

Dec. 16: Townsend's warbler foraging for bugs, varied thrush in Douglas fir.

SALAMANDERS AMONG US

Viewing their small size and meek appearance, it's hard to believe that salamanders are among the most significant predators in the forest. From the time they hatch out of translucent, shell-less eggs, through their larval stage, and on into adulthood, these voracious amphibians eat all that wriggles before them—a diet dominated by insects and other invertebrates such as slugs, snails, and sowbugs. In healthy forests, the collective weight of salamanders may be equal to that of deer, which means they comprise a commanding pest-control squad.

For information on how you can get involved in wetland protection, call WETNET, the Washington State Wetlands Network, at (206) 652-2444. WETNET is a program of Audubon Washington.

Even though they can be abundant, salamanders are rarely encountered by people. These creatures are mostly nocturnal, often live underground in burrows or in thick surface debris, and hide in cool and dark places to keep their sensitive skin from drying out. And unlike frogs, salamanders have no voices to sing us a reminder of their presence. Mistakenly associated solely with ponds and lakes, such waters are only "gene exchange pools" for pond-breeding salamanders, which visit for one month each spring. In urban areas, these waterways are commonly stormwater ponds, because other breeding areas have been filled in. Salamanders rely on healthy forests and—crucial for the pond breeders—green corridors that connect woodlands to pollution-free breeding ponds.

The most common salamander in Seattle is the long-toed salamander, which sports a yellow or green stripe down its back and is named for the long fourth toes on its hind feet. Known as "mole salamanders," the long-toed and another Seattle resident, the Northwestern salamander, mostly remain underground or hidden aboveground under moist duff and other organic matter. They both lay their eggs in ponds where the larvae hatch out and live an underwater existence like tadpoles until they mature, develop limbs, then head back to the woods. Both species spend much of their time below ground using existing mammal tunnels as well as hollow chambers formed by roots that rotted away.

The Northwestern salamander is dark chocolate-brown, shiny, and smooth-skinned with a swollen gland area behind the eye. It defends itself by secreting a white substance from its cheek and tail glands that looks and acts like Elmer's Glue—immobilizing or hampering predators by gluing them into submission. The Northwestern prefers to stay underground during winter and summer weather extremes, and emerges mainly at night during spring and fall, hunting for food on the surface under woody debris. Although seldom seen, when disturbed, this salamander communicates by making a clicking noise that can be readily heard by humans.

Another salamander found here is the stouter-bodied ensatina, which is able to "lose" its tail when grabbed from behind. The self-amputated appendage dances around to occupy the attacker (possibly a shrew or snake), while the salamander makes a crawl for it. The ensatina's coloration can be red, orange, brown, or tan. Its tail narrows near the base and can look worm-like. Ensatinas have no aquatic larval stage and their young hatch out of cream-colored eggs as miniature 1-inch-long adults.

Western red-backed salamanders live in the woods year-round, preferring coniferous forests. Eggs are laid in underground nests where the female broods them until they hatch in late summer or early fall. The young surface when it begins raining in earnest. The misleading name refers to a stripe that runs the length of its body, which can be orange, green, yellow, brown, gray, or black—but not necessarily red.

Research collected in Seattle-area wetlands suggests that many salamander species have gone extinct locally or are in decline for many reasons. The number one killer of eggs and larvae is habitat destruction, particularly changes in wetland hydrology—alterations to the depth, duration, and frequency of wetland water flows. Hydrology problems result when runoff from roofs, roads, and other impervious surfaces is channeled into sewer drains rather than into wetlands, thereby cutting off water flow and causing these areas to dry out earlier in the year. If this rerouted water reaches wetlands, it causes major fluctuations in water levels, leaving eggs dangerously exposed after the water recedes. Another major factor in habitat destruction is that development leaves little cool, damp forested habitat that isn't influenced by heat, dryness, and wind from adjacent streets and buildings. Development also isolates wetlands, so when salamanders die out in one location there is no opportunity for recolonization, thereby permanently wiping out populations.

The most common and wide-ranging Western woodland salamander is the Western red-backed salamander.

The salamanders described here live in the forests and wetlands of Camp Long. The park's nature center classes allow you to meet and learn about these essential amphibians and their kin. For details, call (206) 684-7434 or visit *http://camplong.org*.

FOXES AT THE NINTH HOLE:
GREENER GREENS CARE HAS UNEXPECTED OUTCOMES

In recent years, the West Seattle Golf Course has made changes to improve the lives of non-golfing guests. Adjacent to Camp Long, the course is home to a variety of wild animals including quail, beaver, raccoons, squirrels, and at least one family of red foxes. Use of herbicides and pesticides has been decreased, with a corresponding increase in wildlife activity. Foxes, which eat berries, insects, squirrels, birds, mice, and other small rodents, may even be helping to control some unwanted four-legged visitors.

Although pest-control products may be targeted at a particular nuisance species—an insect, rodent, or plant—very often the chemicals affect non-target organisms, such as predators or scavengers that eat the poisoned animal. Every little bit of a chemical released into the environment may have a much larger effect than people realize. Some chemicals build up in fat stores, and each subsequent animal to ingest the poison passes it up the food chain. Other pesticides mimic hormones that can disrupt an animal's reproductive cycle or cause defects in fetal development. Chemicals used to kill rodents and insects are especially dangerous for foxes.

In an effort to preserve habitat, the golf course maintains undisturbed brushy areas along the greens where foxes often decide to den. Known as "cat-like canines," foxes love to pounce, and cubs sometimes surprise golfers when they "capture" and run off with errant golf balls. These playful mammals have become an integral symbol here, where an illustration of a fox graces the golf course's logo.

Red Fox

31. Roxhill Bog: Headwaters of a Legacy

Where:	Across from Westwood Village at Twenty-ninth Avenue SW and Southwest Barton Street
Phone:	(206) 233-2046
Internet:	*www.ci.seattle.wa.us/parks/proparks/projects/ RoxhillPark.htm*
Hours:	6:00 A.M. to 10:00 P.M.
Disabled Access:	Yes
Dogs:	On leash, but not conducive to wildlife viewing
Driving:	From downtown Seattle, take I-5 south to Exit 163A, West Seattle Bridge/Columbian Way. Keep right at the fork in the ramp following the sign for West Seattle Bridge and Spokane Street. Go over the West Seattle Bridge to Fauntleroy Way SW. At the first light, turn left onto Thirty-fifth Avenue SW. Continue south about three miles to SW Barton Street, then turn left. Look for the Roxhill Park sign at Twenty-ninth Avenue SW. Turn right and park in the lot next to the playground.
Bus:	21, 54

Bogs get a bad rap. Typecast as boot-enveloping muck factories suitable for mosquitoes and little else, the expression "bogged down" does little to improve this reputation. But bogs and fens (close cousins) fill a unique biological niche. They are uncommon in King County, and rarer still in the city, where wet areas are generally filled in for development. As one of the last remaining significant peatlands in the city, you could say Roxhill Bog deserves old growth status.

Like other wetlands, bogs can help prevent flooding, cleanse polluted water, and provide habitat for birds and animals. What sets them apart is that bogs are comprised of peat, organic soil that develops where plants grow more quickly than they can decay. Year after year, dead plants pile up, compressed by the weight of decades of growth—these partially or incompletely decomposed plants form peat. Bogs take thousands of years to form, and one wetland biologist estimated that Roxhill's 6 to 10 feet of peat took 10,000 years to accumulate.

Peat is a popular soil amendment and agricultural peat mining frequently destroys bogs. High-carbon peat is used for fuel in some European countries, notably Ireland and Finland.

Peat bogs help prevent global warming by storing massive amounts of carbon. As plants grow, they remove carbon from the atmosphere (helping to counter the effects of burning fossil fuels). The centuries of plants layered in peatlands are estimated to make up more than 10 percent of the carbon stored on land, compared to 25 percent stored in northern temperate forests.

Roxhill restoration efforts began in the year 2000, when city engineers and volunteers liberated a peat bog that had been buried for thirty years. This corner of the park was reputedly so wet that groundskeepers would sink when they tried to mow it. The Roxhill project offers a glimpse back in time to a former wetland that stretched as far as the eye could see, encompassing the school grounds to the south and the shopping center to the north. To keep these Westwood Village stores "afloat" when that site was developed in the 1960s, it was necessary to drive more than a thousand support beams up to 40 feet deep! Now, instead of avoiding a soggy

Centuries-old peat has been uncovered at Roxhill Bog, making a home for unexpected plants and wetland-loving animals.

patch of grass, neighbors stop on the pathways and bridges to look for mallard duck and killdeer hatchlings, point out the bog laurel's pink blossoms, or watch dragonflies and violet-green swallows catching breakfast.

Undisturbed wild bogs have developed intricate relationships over hundreds of years. Organizers knew they couldn't recreate this overnight, but they believed that wild plants in a restored wetland would enrich their local park. The Roxhill project has become a community focal point, drawing hundreds of volunteers, where neighbors now meet and discuss curiosities of the bog rather than just pass each other by.

Volunteers added more than 35,000 native plants to water edges and surrounding areas, including bog rosemary, bog birch, yellow marsh-marigold, Labrador tea, and bog cranberry. Many of the plants you see at Roxhill are Ice Age remnants, which rode south from the Arctic on the backs of glaciers— their transport eventually melting, leaving them behind. Unique to bogs, many of these plants have learned to thrive in an environment that can be as acidic as orange juice. Despite wet conditions, this acidity makes it hard for plants to absorb water. Labrador tea has a leathery upper leaf and fuzzy underside which helps prevent water loss. Bog rosemary and bog laurel have thick, waxy leaves to help retain water.

Roxhill's peat is comprised mostly of sedge, a grass-like wetland plant with tough-looking leathery leaves. Several types of sedge have been planted around the bog as part of the restoration effort. As you walk the perimeter trail, look for slough sedge, which can be identified by its drooping spiked flower heads. This sedge continues to be the basket-weaving material preferred by the Makah tribe.

Peat is rich with plant nutrients, but the acidity of the bog water results in chemical sleight-of-hand that makes these essential "foods" unavailable to plants. A carnivorous plant called round-leaved sundew has adapted to living in this soil by adding nitrogen-rich insects to its diet. An insect eater like the Venus flytrap, the sundew snares mosquitoes, midges, and gnats (plus the occasional

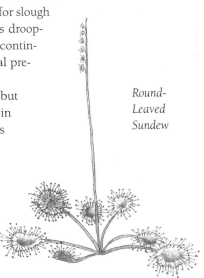

Round-Leaved Sundew

hapless dragonfly) on the dewdrop-like sticky tips of its leaf blades.

As the drainage basin for sixty surrounding acres, Roxhill Bog collects sediments and pollutants from rain and storm water runoff. Plants absorb some pollutants while the spongy peat soil helps filter sediments. At the headwaters of Longfellow Creek, this wetland acts as an essential water filter for a 3.5-mile-long waterway that's home to coho salmon, ensatina salamanders, and red foxes feeding downstream.

Not wishing to artificially introduce wildlife to the bog, volunteers are encouraged by the results of their "if we plant it, they will come," philosophy. Roxhill has drawn an impressive array of birdlife, including American wigeons, belted kingfishers, red-winged blackbirds, and Cooper's hawks. Although there is something to see at any time of year, early spring and summer offer the color and charisma of blooms and bird broods.

The second phase of the Roxhill project involves unearthing three more peat areas to the north with a viewing platform at bog level. Volunteers are adding 42,000 plants including a maple forest on the eastern border. The excavated fill will become the foundation for a new ball field, while pathways and bridges will connect the new wetlands with the existing loop trail.

LONGFELLOW CREEK LEGACY TRAIL

Roxhill Bog is one stop on the Longfellow Creek Legacy Trail. This community-based project involves creating a 3-mile pathway along the creek, from the headwaters at Roxhill winding through the Delridge Valley to Yancy Street. From here, the water continues via pipe under a steel plant to where it joins the Duwamish River west of Harbor Island.

The creek drains a 2000-acre watershed and is one of the few year-round free-flowing creeks in Seattle. In addition to Roxhill Bog, several spots along Longfellow have already been restored and provide access to this renewed urban waterway. In early November, visitors can see salmon spawning at Yancy Street, where restoration efforts have contributed to improved fish habitat. The creek is also home to cutthrout trout. Known by locals as a wild oasis, the Longfellow Creek Natural Area comes alive with color in fall. Check out the wooded area adjacent to Greg Davis Park, which commemorates a Delridge resident whose dedication and hard work are legendary in the community. Every plant you see at the park is native except for the Chinese chestnut, Davis's favorite tree.

Take an urban creek hike for a glimpse of the legacy in the making: Wind your way through the woods at Camp Long (1), down to Southwest Brandon Street to explore the loop trails in the Longfellow Creek Natural

Area (2) and Greg Davis Park (3). Continue through the residential neighborhood to the green space spanning from Southwest Genesee to Southwest Yancy Streets (4), where artwork honors nature via the striking Salmon Bone Bridge and Dragonfly Pavilion. For more information, go to *www.longfellowcreek.org* or call (206) 233-2046.

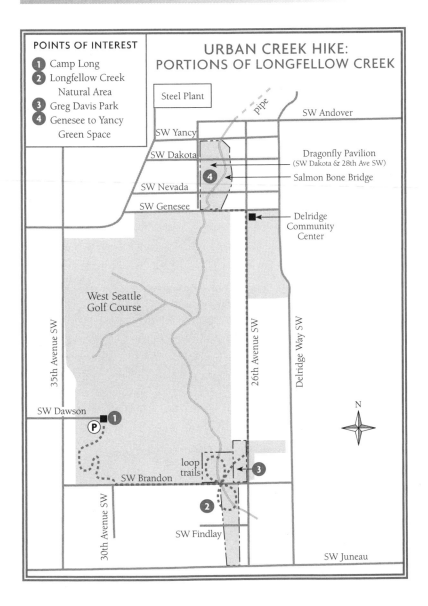

POINTS OF INTEREST

1. Camp Long
2. Longfellow Creek Natural Area
3. Greg Davis Park
4. Genesee to Yancy Green Space

**URBAN CREEK HIKE:
PORTIONS OF LONGFELLOW CREEK**

Steel Plant

Pipe

SW Andover

SW Yancy

SW Dakota

Dragonfly Pavilion
(SW Dakota & 28th Ave SW)

4

Salmon Bone Bridge

SW Nevada

SW Genesee

Delridge Community Center

West Seattle Golf Course

35th Avenue SW

26th Avenue SW

Delridge Way SW

N

SW Dawson

P 1

loop trails

3

30th Avenue SW

SW Brandon

2

SW Findlay

SW Juneau

❋ 32. Schmitz Park Preserve: Seattle's Forest Past

Where:	West Seattle at 5551 SW Admiral Way
Phone:	(206) 684-4075
Internet:	*www.cityofseattle.net/parks/parkspaces/Schmitz.htm*
Hours:	4:00 A.M. to 11:30 P.M.
Disabled Access:	Partial access is available by taking the paved pedestrian road connecting to the park at Alki Community Center, 5817 SW Stevens Street, (206) 684-7430
Dogs:	On leash
Driving:	From downtown Seattle, take I-5 south to Exit 163A, West Seattle Bridge/Columbian Way. Keep right at the fork in the ramp following the sign for West Seattle Bridge and Spokane Street. Go over the West Seattle Bridge to the Admiral Way exit. Follow SW Admiral Way about 2 miles until you reach the park entrance. In summer 2002 the parking lot was removed to daylight the stream. Park on Admiral Way on the bridge just west of the park entrance.
Bus:	56

The roots of a mammoth Douglas fir reach across the forest floor in Schmitz Park Preserve.

Follow any path into Schmitz Park Preserve and it's hard not to be wowed by the wildness of it. Just fifty-three acres in size (three blocks long by two blocks wide), it offers a walk into our forested past like no other natural area in the city. Starting in 1908 several parcels were donated to the city as parkland, the largest by Ferdinand Schmitz, a German immigrant who served on the parks commission and astutely anticipated the need to protect some of what was left of the city's great conifer forests. Although the biggest, straightest trees were logged, and more than one hundred trees fell during a major storm in 1992, considerable old growth remains. Caretakers of the park have tried to keep the experience of walking here as close to a hike in the Cascades as possible.

Enter via the former parking lot access road, and come to a clearing with several walking trails heading south. Although there is a primary loop trail, Friends of Schmitz Park Preserve encourage visitors to go into the forest without a map, believing this contributes to a feeling of discovery—they measure the trail system in hours, saying it takes approximately three to sample every option. Several narrow dirt tracks lead from the main trails to mammoth log bridges over the stream, dead ends, or street-ends. Volunteers even promote respectful exploration of off-trail areas (try not to trample baby plants), especially for those who are looking for a quiet place to meditate or observe birds—more than twenty-five species have been counted here including the winter wren and Swainson's thrush, two birds not often heard in the city and known for their captivating songs. If you feel lost, follow a streamside trail downhill. Visit in spring for trillium and skunk cabbage flowers, or summer for a cool respite from the hot street. Some neighbors say it's most enchanting just after a snow.

A LITTLE HELP FROM YOUR FRIENDS

The Friends of Schmitz Park Preserve originated after a severe winter storm in 1992 brought down more than one hundred of the park's old trees. Concerned for the long-term health of their neighborhood refuge, volunteers have since planted thousands of trees and plants, and can't bring themselves to leave the park without pockets full of garbage. If you would like more information about a "friends" group in your area, or how to start such a group, please call the Seattle Parks volunteer coordinator at (206) 684-4557.

As the faint swish of traffic noise from Admiral Way fades into the background, your ears become attuned to forest sounds—the hush of wind in tree

needles, the determined hammering of a pileated woodpecker, the movement of water over stones. At night, you can hear owls calling to each other, or catch a moonlit glimpse of the resident red fox as she hunts.

Schmitz Preserve is the best place in the city to see the characteristics of an old-growth forest. Unlike second-growth forests where most trees are the same age, here you have trees of varying ages, from seedlings to 450-year-olds and much in-between. Openings in the canopy cleared by fallen trees allow sunlight to reach a diverse understory of shrubs, herbaceous plants, and new generations of trees. Bring your identification book because the preserve is packed with native plants—from vine maple and thimbleberry to fringecup and foamflower. Old snags tower next to living trees—cedar snags can stand for one hundred years or more—providing a vertical safety zone for uncountable critters, from raccoons and chickadees to carpenter ants and fungi. Downed trees become "nurse logs" for seedlings and myriad organisms, the majority of them invisible to us. Check out the great mama of a Douglas fir "nurse stump" where the main trails intersect at the stream—it's colossal, well hidden, and topped by a soaring bigleaf maple.

Although most visitors understandably gape at the grand old trees—a Western red cedar that would take four or five people with outstretched arms to encircle, and impressive specimens of Douglas fir and Western hemlock—one of the little known secrets of old-growth forests is that there's more life in the snags, fallen logs, and rotting stumps than in the living trees. In his book, *The Hidden Forest*, Jon Luoma explains that "for all the decay, life abounds here." Pacific Northwest forests hold a greater mass of living cell matter per acre than tropical rain forests—some five hundred tons of living tissue per acre!

It turns out that Seattle's oldest recycling venture doesn't have anything to do with sorting your garbage into colorful bins. In a diverse forest ecosystem like that of Schmitz, uncountable microscopic organisms along with their larger conspirators (mites, pill bugs, millipedes, fungi, and banana slugs) perform the most important and perhaps least understood recycling of all—turning organic matter into the energy that fuels an old-growth forest. In such an ecosystem, within the measure of your footprints teem 32,000 invertebrates. Tree and plant roots cannot absorb the majority of nutrients until they have been "processed" by one of these countless soil dwellers—it's estimated that only one in thirty invertebrates is known to science. Just something more to marvel at when you have gotten your fill of towering cedars, birdsong, and salmonberries.

This downed tree has a second life as a natural (and slippery) bridge across the creek in Schmitz Park.

MEET THE DECOMPOSERS

Turn over a small piece of rotting log (please gently turn it back over when you're through) along a Schmitz pathway and you're likely to encounter some of the leading actors in the old-growth drama.

✻ Here's a reason to like slugs: the banana slug (*Ariolimax columbianus*) plays an important role in breaking down decaying plant matter, fertilizing the soil, and distributing seeds and spores. The second-largest slug in the world, these land mollusks have been recorded at 10 inches in length and weighing up to a quarter pound. They can range from white to black, but yellow and greenish tan are common, often with black blotches. Why the slime? It plays a role in mobility, traction, defense (actually gluing shut the mouths of some would-be predators), navigation, and helps the slug absorb water.

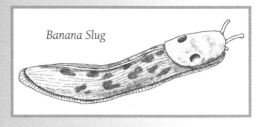
Banana Slug

✻ The millipede *Harpaphe haydenian* is one of the keystones of forest recycling. Ranging from black to brown in color with yellow spots, its body is made up of dozens of segments sporting two legs, though they don't add up to one thousand as the name implies. Its hallmark is grinding detritus into bite-size chunks that will be used by thousands of smaller arthropods (from mites to springtails), to make soil. It is said that every single leaf, both deciduous and coniferous, that falls on the ground in a Northwest forest goes through the gut of this one species of millipede before it enters the soil ecosystem. Pick up a millipede and it will likely curl into a defensive posture and respond with "chemical warfare" by emitting a harmless (to humans) amount of cyanide, which smells like almond extract.

Millipede

✻ The white, thread-like tendrils you see under rotten wood and elsewhere in the forest are likely to be networks of mycorrhizae, or "fungus root." The word describes the mutually beneficial relationship between plant roots and fungi, an existence so intertwined they act as one organism. A recently accepted theory among botanists and ecologists asserts that plants rely on mycorrhizae to provide them with sustaining nutrients from the soil and to assist with water uptake. In turn, because they

Because slug slime absorbs water, it's very difficult to wash off. To "de-slime," rub your hands with a towel before washing with water, or rub your hands together until the slime collects into a blob that can be brushed off.

do not create their own food, fungi rely on plants for the sugars created through photosynthesis. Creating a giant "nutrient net," mycorrhizae can spread over hundreds of square feet of forest floor, vastly increasing the reach of the tree's root system. It is also theorized that mycorrhizae play an essential role in the breakdown of organic matter, infusing the soil with an enzyme that helps free nutrients that are some of the most difficult to break down.

ID THE BIG THREE

Douglas fir, Western red cedar, and Western hemlock are the conifers that put the "emerald" in our city. The following tips will help you tell them apart. You can see good examples of these at Schmitz Park Preserve, which is home to an assortment of trees native to the area including grand fir, Pacific Yew, red alder, bigleaf maple, vine maple, cascara, Pacific dogwood, and Pacific madrone.

Douglas fir (*Pseudotsuga menziesii*). The Tree That Built Seattle is renowned for its thick bark (that of 2000-year-old specimens grows to 20 inches thick), which makes it resistant to fire. A popular story used by naturalists makes it easy to identify Douglas fir cones: Once there was a huge fire and the animals of the forest headed for cover. The mice ran from one tree to the next asking for protection, but they were repeatedly turned away until they came to the Douglas fir, who offered them a hiding place in her cones. If you look at the cones, you can still

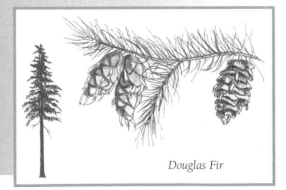

Douglas Fir

see the tails and back legs of the mice scampering inside.

On young trees the bark is smooth and often has resin blisters. As the tree ages, its reddish-brown bark becomes chunky with deep, irregular cracks. The inch-long, blunt needles are scattered singly over the twig. They are green above with two white bands underneath.

Western red cedar (*Thuja plicata*). Known as the "cornerstone of Northwest Coast Indian culture," cedar wood was used to build everything from cradles to canoe bailers to longhouses. This tree is so powerful, Native Americans believe it strengthens those who stand with their backs to its trunk.

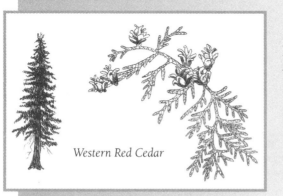

Western Red Cedar

If you crush its leaves in your hands, you can learn to identify it by smell alone. The deeply fragrant, bright green foliage has a pattern that looks like a flattened braid. The leaves are shed after three to four years.

The cedar's small, woody cones grow upright and are shaped like rose buds. Unmistakable, the thin, reddish brown bark is stringy and soft to the touch.

Western hemlock (*Tsuga heterophylla*). One of the easiest ways to identify Washington's state tree is to look for its distinctive drooping top and graceful skirt-like branches. Its short needles (generally less than 1 inch long) are arranged in flat rows and are feathery soft. Its woody, egg-shaped cones are usually only about 1 inch long.

It's a welcoming tree, as *Trees of Seattle* author Arthur Lee Jacobson writes, "No native tree of Seattle is as pleasant to meditate under: something about its soft carpet of needles and sturdy bole proves peaceful, comforting, and strengthening, as if it were an arboreal embodiment of the very spirit of Mother Earth."

Western Hemlock

*N*ortheast Seattle:
LAKES, PONDS, SPRINGS, AND WETLANDS

If you try to navigate this neighborhood with the popular Fast Map, a laminated card found in many local glove compartments, you'll be at a loss. The mapmakers chose the upper right-hand corner of their document as the least obstructing location for their logo, casually covering up most of northeast Seattle in the process. Could it be that this area is of no interest to outsiders?

Certainly, the neighborhoods here are almost like city suburbs, with few monuments or other visitor attractions. And where nature is concerned, only the ancient Wedgwood Boulder was unyielding enough to be preserved here in its natural state. The city set aside no Green Lake, Golden Gardens, Alki, or Lincoln Park for the area—Magnuson Park was only acquired after the military abandoned the site—just a few playgrounds and playfields.

But slowly, over the last forty years or so, the area has been gathering green steam. Abundant once in wetlands, springs, and streams that were gathering places for local Native American groups, northeast Seattle is also home to the city's largest watershed: Thornton Creek. No other creek in the city can boast three separate nonprofit groups named after it—these organizations and others have cleaned up adjacent wetlands, educated the public about stream health, and rallied to bring more of the creek to daylight.

The shores of Lake Washington here are also important in both native and nonnative history, and the transformation of Sand Point Magnuson Park from military base to grand scale city park in the 1980s and 1990s means a prime stretch of this waterfront is finally accessible to the public.

Near the end of the twentieth century a burst of environmental activism in the area got quite a few projects started—most in some way connected to Thornton Creek, which drains 11.6 square miles of northeast Seattle. Meadowbrook wetland and the Meadowbrook Detention Pond cover two such spaces in the heart of the northeast. This chapter's walk visits a winding, pond-laced

The Thornton Creek Watershed is Seattle's largest, home to fish, birds, amphibians, insects, beaver, coyote, and over 200,000 people.

wetland trail behind a community center, and, across the street, a Seattle Public Utilities detention pond that is a refuge for area wildlife. A second tour leads you through Sand Point Magnuson Park, whose four hundred acres, formerly flattened by military airstrips, are slowly being reclaimed. There are waterfront vistas, and wide stretches of meadow alive with birds. Magnuson Park fans are in conflict over the best use of this huge but unruly resource, and the tour addresses this issue as well. One area destination, Paramount Park, is far north, just outside city limits but easily accessed by I-5. It's worth the trip to hear the "kree-eeks" of native Pacific tree frogs, and witness the restoration of a wetland by volunteers. The other destination, the North Seattle Community College campus wetland, was once a bog, and is now a small but semi-wild area for wandering, where waterfowl gather in winter and frogs sing in summer, when plums, blackberries, and apples are ripe for the picking.

33. Wide Open Spaces: Sand Point Magnuson Park

Where:	On Lake Washington northeast of the University District
Tour Distance:	3 miles
Phone:	Park, (206) 684-4946; Magnuson Environmental Stewardship Alliance, (206) 524-8713
Internet:	*http://cityofseattle.net/parks*
Hours:	May 1–Labor Day, 4:00 A.M. to 11:30 P.M. day after Labor Day–April 30, 4:00 A.M. to 10:00 P.M.
Disabled Access:	Yes, on boardwalk and many other paved areas
Dogs:	On leash, but the city's largest off-leash dog area is in this park
Driving:	From downtown Seattle, take I-5 north about 3.5 miles to the NE Sixty-fifth Street exit. Head east approximately 4 miles on Sixty-fifth until you cross Sand Point Way NE into the NE Sixty-fifth Street entrance to the park.
Bus:	71,72, or 73, switch to 74 or 75 in University District
Special Note:	This huge park's natural areas are divided by parking lots and pavement. For a quicker tour, bring a bicycle or roller blades to carry you on the flat paths from one site to the next. Also, the meadow areas here can be quite wet and muddy in winter and spring—wear boots if you want to explore. Additionally, security restrictions at the adjacent Western Regional Center of the Department of Commerce affect a small corner of this tour. Carry photo identification to access that area.

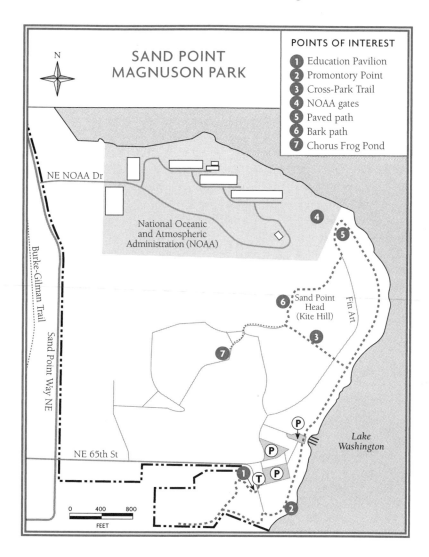

SAND POINT MAGNUSON PARK

N

POINTS OF INTEREST

1. Education Pavilion
2. Promontory Point
3. Cross-Park Trail
4. NOAA gates
5. Paved path
6. Bark path
7. Chorus Frog Pond

NE NOAA Dr

National Oceanic and Atmospheric Administration (NOAA)

Burke-Gilman Trail

Sand Point Way NE

Sand Point Head (Kite Hill)

Fin Art

NE 65th St

Lake Washington

0 400 800
FEET

There's no such thing as a pristine city park, but few Seattle green spaces have been demolished and renovated, abused and fussed over like Sand Point Magnuson Park.

If, like many people, you only come here to launch a boat or take a cooling swim in summer, you're missing quite a bit. More than four hundred acres, in fact. Seattle's second-largest park after Discovery, Sand Point ranges from the crumbling bluffs of Promontory Point to small stands of remnant forest. It spreads across the squishy meadows of midpark, and along the 1-mile-long expanse of shoreline. Unlike Discovery Park, with its guided walks, woodland trails, and protected beach, Sand Point is not primarily managed for nature and wildlife. Not yet, anyway. Certainly, the next decade will decide much about what kind of park this enormous waterfront green space will become. Walk here for long, and you'll form your own opinions about the best use for this prime waterfront real estate.

The area was swampland when modern settlers arrived, and Native Americans made camp here by Mud Lake, a spring-fed lake that drained into a short salmon creek that spilled into Lake Washington. In 1917, the creation of the ship canal that connected Lake Washington to Lake Union lowered these shores by 9 feet, drying up the creek but leaving a shrunken Mud Lake, the site of Seattle's first children's camp in the 1920s. The entire area passed into Navy hands soon after, and much of it was paved for runways. The miniature Main Street at the park's north end was created to serve the new Navy airfield. Mud Lake was filled and the terrain, once undulating, was leveled. World War II pilots were trained here, and Bill Boeing is said to have launched his first round-the-world flight from these grounds. When the City of Seattle and the National Oceanic and Atmospheric Administration (NOAA) received a portion of the park in 1981, only about 30 percent of the area was free of concrete and asphalt. The park's namesake, Warren G. Magnuson, fought from his Senate seat in the 1970s for this land to become what it is, prevailing over local pilots who wanted a county airstrip.

WINDSTORM!

Transplants to Seattle from elsewhere are always amused by the drama: "Windstorm 200X!" TV broadcasters blare in their best "disaster's looming" tones. "Lock up your cats! Put away your patio furniture!" Wind events are even branded with their own news logos. Without tornadoes, hurricanes, or month-long snowstorms (well, not usually), are windstorms just an attempt to drum up drama from the depths of another rainy winter?

According to Seattle's Northwest Weather Forecast Office, the excitement is mostly justified. This city is surprisingly non-windy over much of the year considering how close it is to the Pacific, which spins off storms and pressure systems like a pop star churns out hits. We're generally protected by our two mountain ranges. In late fall and winter, however, we sometimes get a taste of the coastal weather that so dismayed Lewis and Clark when they reached the inaccurately named Pacific Ocean in southwest Washington in the fall of 1805. There they recorded ceaseless, miserable rain and "tremendious [sic] wind." Such storms, when they reach us, can be intense, causing huge power outages and lost lives. In addition, the topographical turbulence makes such events much harder to predict than would be possible in flatter places—it's hard to know whether the wind will blow north of the Olympics and head for British Columbia, or go south and then turn in our direction.

One such tempest was named by the National Weather Service as Washington state's top weather event of the twentieth century. Called the Columbus Day Windstorm, it struck along the West Coast from British Columbia to Northern California on October 12, 1962—"the strongest widespread non-hurricane windstorm to strike the continental U.S. this century," with gusts to one hundred miles per hour recorded in Renton.

The National Weather Service's list of top Washington State Weather Events for the Twentieth Century is a fascinating catalogue of nature's disasters. From Seattle's Greatest Snowstorm, in 1916, when 21.5 inches of snow fell on the city in twenty-four hours, to the May 18, 1980 eruption of Mount Saint Helens, this list proves that more than rain falls from Seattle skies. Find the list online at *http://seawfo.noaa.gov/WATOP10.htm.*

Some rare summer wind excitement took place in 2001, when the *Seattle Times* reported a dramatic moment on a rainy June day, when a teacher and several children at a West Seattle daycare were thrown into the air by violent gusts. Local atmospheric scientists can't explain the incident, but suggest it may have had something to do with the Puget Sound Convergence Zone, when ocean winds divided by the Olympic Mountains reconnect again, usually near the King–Snohomish county line, before moving south through the city. This effect tends to happen most in late spring and early summer, and late in the day. It doesn't usually cause liftoff, though—just wind movement and rain showers.

The winds we do have play an important role in everyday city life. Boaters raise a wetted finger before taking to the water. And locals sometimes attempt to forecast by wind direction, noting that when the wind is coming from the south, wet weather is often approaching, whereas sunny weather seems to come on the tails of winds from the north. North winds tend to be continental, whereas Pacific winds generally come from the south. This kind of prediction is not new: the South Wind was long ago described by Native Americans as the bringer of rain, and the story goes that it was partially brought under control by animals who got fed up and beat the Wind until he agreed to bring sunny days, too. Something to consider in the depths of another soggy February.

The HistoryLink website at *http://historylink.org* describes early settler encounters with Puget Sound weather, including a "gale so strong it blew seven railway cars off a trestle into the bay" February 9, 1882, and the 1880 "big snow," historically the largest in Seattle history.

Today, the only things taking off are birds, and kites lifting off from the top of "kite hill," a grassy mound near the shoreline.

Enter the park at NE Sixty-fifth Street and Sand Point Way NE. Pass Radford Student Housing on your right and veer right at the fork, following signs for Promontory Point. Park at the first lot, and walk to the Education Pavilion (1), the metal-roofed structure to the west. This is one of many park improvement projects by local volunteer groups, most prominently MESA, the Magnuson Environmental Stewardship Alliance.

The fifteen acres of this former rifle range, from the shoreline to the top of the bluffs in front of you, are being developed as a wildlife habitat preserve. Beside the pavilion, children from Northwest Montessori School have been helping to create a garden using native plants to attract native butterfly species. The gardeners have seen parnassians, swallowtails, whites, blues, and several other butterfly species here in summer, flitting among lupines, native irises, yarrow, and grasses. An innovative irrigation system diverts rainwater runoff from the pavilion roof to keep things watered. Anna's hummingbirds are known to perch near the pavilion—keep alert for them buzzing past. The bark path behind the pavilion leads to a paved path heading uphill. Follow this to Kingfisher Basin, behind which rise crumbling bluffs. EarthCorps volunteers have rappelled down them to remove English ivy and clematis, invasive, nonnative plants that allowed rodents access to the nesting holes of kingfishers. A path leads up above the bluffs where you can explore the mixed forest, and look for such woodland birds as Northern flickers, sparrows, Bewick's wrens, and spotted towhees. Rectangular nest boxes on your way up are here to attract some of these species. Placards offer more information on various promontory restoration projects and plant species.

California Quail

When you're done exploring here, drop back down to the water, returning the way you came or following the chain-link fence down another trail going east. On a clear day, Mount Rainier shimmers just out of reach from the tip of Promontory Point (2). This stretch of shoreline is quieter than the rest of the park and its benches offer a great stopping point. In winter, watch these waters for ducks such as the American wigeon, common goldeneye, bufflehead, greater and lesser scaup, common mergansers, and

Magnuson Park has a varied habitat, including unmowed grasses where birds such as the Savannah sparrow nest.

canvasbacks. Sea lions and seals are also occasionally viewed from the Sand Point Magnuson shoreline—the mammals sometimes make their way through the locks and come here to feed on fish.

Now, head north by foot, bike, or skates along the 12-foot-wide Lakeshore Promenade. This park has approximately forty-five acres of shoreline, prime frolicking territory for humans but also a crucial area for wildlife. Birds hunt and nest here; fish find shelter under the shade of shoreline trees.

Keep watch for the boat launch on your right. Just past this spot huge patches of blackberries and grasses create what one park volunteer calls the "raptor brunch line." Watch for red-tailed hawks swooping down on a scurrying vole or mouse here and elsewhere at the park, joined occasionally by the Northern harrier in fall, or the Cooper's and sharp-shinned hawks, which prey on other park birds in winter. To your right, as you continue along the promenade, mowed lawn is a prime nesting site for the park's killdeer in spring and summer. Look for this leggy shorebird with a longish tail and two black chest bands. Also watch for its "nest," a clutch of three or four eggs laid unprotected on flat ground. Volunteers try to cordon off the eggs when they spot them, using stakes and ribbon, but the best way to avoid inadvertent bird infanticide is to keep yourself and your dog on the path during breeding season March through July.

If you wonder why some areas at the park are maintained like a golf course while others are exuberantly weedy, you're not alone. The question of when and whether to mow the park's lawns, or how much grassland should be left untouched, is hotly debated by maintenance staff and park activists. While the killdeer (and some parkgoers) might prefer a flat lawn, most park wildlife need bramble and cover. One of Magnuson's migratory songbirds,

Near the north entrance to Magnuson Park you'll find the innovative Community Gardens, with features such as a garden designed by disabled people, a plot of native plants, and one area designed by Children's Hospital based on kids' drawings of dream gardens.

the Savannah sparrow, nests only in long grass, and mowing during breeding season puts the eggs in jeopardy (as does wandering off trail).

Just past the pale green cinderblock bathrooms on the left of the trail, a cross-park path leads inland, toward signs for tennis courts and athletic fields (3). For those who advocate for the park's natural areas, proposed plans for eleven new, lighted ball fields with synthetic turf abutting wetland habitat (debated in 2002) raised hackles. Adult sportsplayers in Seattle say the city lacks enough designated ball fields, while nature advocates decry the habitat lost to athletic events, and the impact of bright, late-night lighting on wildlife in the park.

Not long after the bathrooms along the promenade thorn-shaped metal objects seem to emerge from a bark path—this "fin art" is intended to look like an orca whale pod, and was created from parts recycled from decommissioned submarines. From here until you reach the path's end you'll be kept busy watching for birds in the three different habitats: meadow, lawn, and lake. Something to watch for is a covey, or family, of California quail—a whimsical sight on a summer evening. An adult bird takes the lead with up to a dozen little chicks trailing behind, all with comical knots bobbing atop their heads. Watch for the males in spring, when they sit atop blackberry bushes and call females with a loud "Chi CA go!"

You may also see cliff swallows, swooping over the trail and water, catching insects in midair. These birds nest on a couple of the park's rooftops, and can be seen in mid-spring gathering mud to create their nests.

You will soon dead-end at the gates of NOAA (4). (See the note at the end of this tour for information about entering NOAA grounds.) The grounds of NOAA contain a shoreline artwork path that draws attention to the natural environment. From where you are standing, on even a mildly windy day, you'll likely be distracted by an eerie moaning and high-pitched fluttering like the soundtrack to Lost in Space. This artwork, the "Sound Garden" by Doug Hollis, appears as a cluster of tall steel structures in front of you, which channel winds through organ pipes. Another work consists of a pair of shoreside seats hewn from boulders pulled from Lake Washington. NOAA is also a haven for owls: Barn owls live in the NOAA hangars and hunt at night over the park. Short-eared owls used to winter every year here, too, but as of 2002 had not been seen for a couple of years. Sand Point's shores have also been a destination for snapping turtles. Likely introduced to Lake Washington by people who got tired of feeding them, these nonnatives have inhabited these waters for years. The turtles have used the area as a breeding ground, and Sand Point boasts one of the highest recorded snapping turtle clutch counts anywhere, numbering some seventy-eight eggs.

To the left and right of the main path, wooden gates and chain-link fencing delineate the off-leash area for dogs—just one more controversial issue. Dogs are allowed shoreline access here, though the area would otherwise provide habitat for migrating salmon, which require the shelter such places provide.

Turn onto the paved path (5) just before the dog fence, and follow the trail uphill. Take the second dirt trail on your right. This leads you up a hillside blooming with Scotch broom and lupines in late spring and summer. Cresting the hill you'll see a mowed lawn on your left where kites are flown. Soon after this is a bark path on your left (6). Take it and admire the swath of native plantings by MESA, EarthCorps, and the Starflower Institute. Red currants, Oregon grape, ocean spray, shore pine, and Indian plum are just some of the species you'll find. Meander on the bark trail as it veers gently right, where it devolves into a dirt footpath. Continue on this, veering left where there's a fork, passing a thicket of alders on your right, and crossing a lawn that ends at a sidewalk. Turn left on this to return to the lakeshore promenade, or right to roam farther through the park. The map also shows the location of a nearby tree frog pond (7).

> Bird lovers urge all walkers to stay on trail in all parks with bird habitat from April through July. During breeding season many birds make nests on the ground, and roaming around significantly ups your chances of stepping on eggs.

Note that access to NOAA has been restricted since September 11, 2001. If the access gate near the "Sound Garden" is closed, you can still visit from the NOAA access road off Sand Point Way NE. You can't bring your car onto the grounds, but you may walk or bike. To do this, walk, pedal, or drive to Magnuson Park's north entrance at NE Seventy-fourth Street. From here, head right out the entrance about one and a half blocks to the Department of Commerce/NOAA entrance at NE NOAA Drive. You will need to show picture identification to the guards, who will give you a pass to the grounds. The site is open from 5:00 A.M. to 7:00 P.M. For updates call the security office at (206) 526-6653.

34. Places for Pondering: Meadowbrook's Wetlands

Where:	Near Lake City, at the corner of Thirty-fifth Avenue NE and 105th Street. The detention pond is across the street.
Phone:	(206) 684-7522
Internet:	Meadowbrook Community Center, *http:// ci.seattle.wa.us/parks/centers/meadowbrookcc.htm*; Seattle Public Utilities, *www.ci.seattle.wa.us/util/planning/ meadowbrook/SETTING.HTM*
Hours:	Community Center, Monday–Friday 9:00 A.M. to 9:00 P.M., Saturday 10:00 A.M. to 5:00 P.M., closed Sunday. Wetland and detention pond are open dawn to dusk.
Disabled Access:	Parts of the wetland and all of the detention pond
Dogs:	On leash
Driving:	From downtown Seattle, take I-5 north about 4.5 miles to Exit 171, S.R. 522 toward Bothell and Lake City Way. Keep left as the ramp forks. Stay straight onto S.R. 522 East. Turn slightly right onto Lake City Way NE. Follow this street through several lights to NE 110th Street. Turn right, then turn right again onto Thirty-fifth Avenue NE. Turn into the Meadowbrook Community Center parking lot on the right.
Bus:	64, 65
Special Note:	Good birding here, bring binoculars

Here at this corner in northeast Seattle two natural sites lie hidden behind unassuming facades just across the street from each other. One, the Meadowbrook Community Center wetlands, is small, shady, and a little wild; the other, the Seattle Public Utilities' Meadowbrook detention pond, is larger, wide-open, and well stocked with benches and overlooks. Together they can be easily walked in an hour, but leave enough time to explore.

First, the wetland. Nothing about the low, squared-off building or flat green ball fields beside the Meadowbrook Community Center suggests a place for nature adventure. But get away from the parking lot up the sloped sidewalk (1) to the right of the Center, and pay attention—what's the trickle of water you're hearing, and where is it headed? Are the tips of fir trees in the distance in a local backyard? Or are they hints that maybe, past the asphalt and pavement, a wilder Meadowbrook exists? As you walk along this sidewalk and pass behind the building, notice the mix of native trees and ground covers. Follow a woodchip path that leads toward a small wooden bridge and the sound of moving water. From here you will take a winding westward route, always on the woodchip path, along a series of these channels and ponds overhung by alders, where grasses rustle and yellow iris bloom. You'll return this way for the next part of the tour.

As you go, stop to notice what's around you. Watch these first ponds in the growing season for arrowhead, known as wapato by Native Americans, or commonly as "duck potato," which emerges from the middle of the water on thin stems with leaves that are, indeed, like arrows pointing around the pond. Ducks like to root around among these underwater tubers. Their white flowers generally bloom in late July. Other pond plants include grass-like slough sedge, which has long, drooping dark brown flower spikes, and huge clumps of the nonnative yellow flag iris. Don't fret about a rusty scum in the water—it's not toxic bloom but a natural pond algae that feeds on iron springs underground. The native name for it is "Licton," also the name of a springs and a neighborhood in the area.

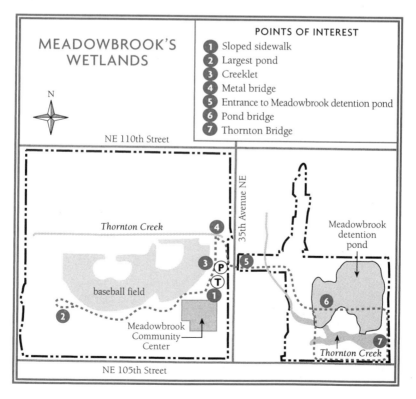

MEADOWBROOK'S WETLANDS

N

NE 110th Street

POINTS OF INTEREST
1 Sloped sidewalk
2 Largest pond
3 Creeklet
4 Metal bridge
5 Entrance to Meadowbrook detention pond
6 Pond bridge
7 Thornton Bridge

35th Avenue NE

Thornton Creek

Meadowbrook detention pond

baseball field

Meadowbrook Community Center

Thornton Creek

NE 105th Street

SKIMMING THE SURFACE: POND LIFE

Science fiction filmmakers might lose interest in life on Mars if they took the time to consider a pond's peculiarities. Some inhabitants of your average watering hole make little green men sound like plausible next-door neighbors.

Take the neuston, for instance. From the Greek word for "swimming," this is the community of organisms that spend their time at or just under the surface of the water. Skittering among the larvae deposited on leaves and twigs are such creatures as the whirligig beetle—the only beetle in the neuston community, and blue-black and shiny as cosmic nail polish. These members of the true bug or Hemiptera family twirl frantically over the water, using their two pairs of eyes—one pair focused above the water, and one below—to locate their next meal.

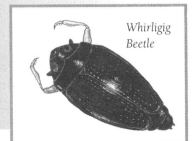

Another "true bug" is the water strider, which rushes across the water on its six legs with astonishing speed, its miniscule leg hairs keeping the bug from sinking. This and other true bugs have ferocious mouthparts with which to pierce and suck prey. Up above the neuston you'll find clouds of midges,

Water Strider

gathering in the evening to mate, and perhaps unwittingly become an evening snack for the swallows dipping gracefully past. Below the neuston, at pond bottom, worms, snails, and larvae burrow, joined by frogs, turtles, and pond beetles in winter. The larvae of dragon and damselflies, known as nymphs, forage here. Nymphs can expel water in a kind of jet propulsion that moves them forward a few inches at a time.

Few pond visitors are as captivating as the full-grown dragonfly, and his near kin the damselfly. Damselflies can be distinguished by their smaller size, more widely separated eyes, and wings nearly always held closed up over the abdomen. Both of these members of the Odonate order are among the fastest of insects—the dragonfly can fly forward and backward at speeds up to

Whirligig Beetle

sixty miles per hour. They are most likely to be at the water when mating and egg-laying, where their activities can be easily observed. Many males stake claim to territory, which they aggressively defend against other males, while others skim the water's surface searching for females. You may spot the insects mating in flight—they attach themselves one behind the other like tandem bicyclists. Sunny summer days are best for dragon- and damselfly watching, and freshwater wetlands such as the ponds and shallow lakes found in northeast Seattle are a good place to find them when they come to the water to breed. One species you might see is cardinal meadowhawk, astonishingly scarlet down to its big, close-set red eyes. Others include the blue-eyed darner, paddle-tailed darner, eight-spotted skimmer, Pacific forktail, and tule bluet. Identify these and more using the booklet *Dragonflies of Washington* by Dennis Paulson, sold by the Seattle Audubon Society and available at some local bookstores.

The green darner dragonfly (*Anax junius*) is Washington's official state insect. It's identified by its bright green head and thorax. Abdomen colors vary, but an adult male's is aqua blue. Students at Crestwood Elementary School in Kent suggested the idea of a state insect, and students around Washington voted for this widespread, shimmery species.

This may feel like a remnant wetland somehow spared development, a result of artist and designer Peggy Gaynor's artful design for the space, as well as nature's volunteer efforts. A decade or so ago this land was just a soggy, unusable extension of the baseball field—the kind of place outfielders might get stuck in the mud. Neighbors pressed for wild habitat, and put in long hours (one year they held work parties here every other weekend) to plant, mulch, and weed. Water levels vary little from year to year, as the wetland is fed by springs from the hillside behind it, keeping pools replenished and plants moist. There's also a lighthearted aspect to this design: Gaynor planned for each pond to have a different geometric shape. Though the edges have blurred as plants have grown, you might be able to pick out such shapes as a square, hexagon, and isoceles triangle. The project has been so successful that several trees and plants have self-seeded here, including the plentiful, shading alders. The sheltered nature of this wetland is one reason it is excellent off-channel habitat for salmonids—both juvenile chinook and coho have been seen here. It is suspected that trout and salamanders may be visiting as well. You'll probably quickly notice how alive the area is with birds—songbirds such as chickadees, Bewicks wrens, kinglets, brown creepers, and dark-eyed juncos have all been seen here. Cedar waxwings, most obvious in late summer, travel in flocks seeking out fruit and insects—their nutmeg-colored crests and black eye mask are distinguishing features. Dragonflies also criss-cross the path and ponds.

The walk continues alongside enormous native spirea (hardhack) hedges, more than 10 feet tall and blooming pink in summer, and huge billowy clumps of Arctic willow. At one point the trail opens out next to the ball field, which was previously a tennis court, and before that a dairy farm, and originally wetland, too. When a project-related problem required digging two feet deep into part of the field, the hole immediately filled with water. Don't stop walking until you get to the end of this trail—right before the tennis courts in front of you—to find the largest pond (2). It's the archetype of ponds, the kind of place where fairies might gather in a children's book. It's shallow, shaded by trees, and often visited by waterfowl and their downy young. Be sure to walk partway into the pond on the big stepping stones placed here during restoration, to get a bird's-eye view of pond life. In a breeze, tree leaves rustle. On a sunny day, shafts of light penetrate this shadowy spot, and the water dapples, ripples, and shimmers. Water skimmers dimple the surface, and dragonflies skim by. All is right with the world as long as you stand here.

But don't fall into a trance. There's much more to see. Turn around and return the way you came. As you emerge to the parking lot, turn left and walk alongside the log fence to your left, beside a small creeklet (3). This piece of restoration, added after the main wetland, connects it with the south fork of Thornton Creek, providing access for juvenile salmon. They use this and other placid backwaters when flood conditions on the creek during rainy autumn days threaten to batter and possibly kill them. If you're alert and moving discreetly, you may very well catch sight of a muskrat (*Ondatra zibethicus*) here. This native rodent, bigger than a rat, with rich brown fur and partly webbed hind feet, will dive under the surface of the water if it gets wind of you. Muskrats eat sedges, rushes, and other aquatic plants, and also some frogs and fish. They usu-ally build lodges constructed from reeds in a dome shape. At the end of the fence, head to the two foot-bridges before you. The south fork of Thornton gushes under the metal bridge (4), sometimes touching the bridge bottom in winter. Watch for chinook, coho, cutthroat, and sockeye

Cardinal Meadowhawk

Part of Meadowbrook's Reflective Refuge, the Flood Pool fills seasonally and contains a secret fountain.

in fall, passing by on their way to where Thornton spills into Lake Washington at Matthews Beach, not far from here. The sockeye are the most vividly colored, in shades of red and orange.

An interesting counterpart to the Meadowbrook wetland project is just across the street—the Seattle Public Utilities' detention pond facility, also known as "Meadowbrook Pond." Return to the parking lot and cross Thirty-fifth at the crosswalk that intersects the lot, to where the entrance (5) to this facility is flanked by large boulders and a sign.

Long ago, the land here was also wetland, providing natural flood control for Thornton. In the 1950s the Lake City Sewage Treatment Plant was built on this site, and later it was used as a sort of junkyard for various scrap from city projects. After years of flooding increases in the area, and problems with sediment washing into Lake Washington, the utility company planned for a holding pond to catch excess stormwater during the rainy season. With input from the local community, the project evolved into a site useful not just for humans, but for wildlife, too.

Soon after you enter the grounds, you pass over the creek itself, which

To learn more about Meadowbrook's natural and neighborhood history, go inside the community center and take a look at the Meadowbrook Book, a large scrapbook of clippings, photos, and other memorabilia created by a local family.

winds south and east in a "J" around the detention pond in the center. Man-made hills are covered in native wildflowers like yarrow and lupine. Peggy Gaynor, whose wetland design you just walked through, collaborated with artists and architects Lydia Aldredge and Kate Wade on most of the earthforms and other artistic additions here, collectively entitled "Reflective Refuge." Their vision was to create a protected and quiet series of outdoor "rooms." The berms, or hills, provide shelter from freeway noise and block views of houses. In one area a tufa wall, looking like melted concrete and made of peat moss, sand, granite grit, oyster shells, and Portland cement works both as noise barrier and growing medium for lichens and plants. Explore this spot, then rejoin the main path when you're ready, crossing the long, pond bridge (6) made of recycled plastic. To the south of the bridge a rock weir built across the pond is where sediment filters out from the water—ducks like to use it as a sunbathing spot in summer. Continuing across you're likely to see plenty of waterfowl, including green-winged teals and hooded mergansers. Below the south side of the bridge, nearly at its end, a beaver lodge is usually built up to bridge level.

By this time you have probably noticed tangible differences between this habitat and the wetland—some of them are aesthetic, while others affect what kinds of wildlife use one place or the other. For many people, the site you're standing in is more palatable than the wetland area across the street. It's wide open, sunny, and carefully maintained and signed here. There's no question that this is a good place for many animals, too, particularly mammals and diving ducks that need deeper water. But if the other wetland's thicker plantings seem too shaded or messy by comparison, remember that those qualities attract brush-loving songbirds. The gentle slopes and minimal water fluctuations of the wetland across the street also are good for amphibians, which lay their eggs on or near the water. Even for humans, the wetland provides some amenities not offered by the detention site, such as a sense of mystery and a chance to explore, appreciated especially by children.

At the end of the bridge, turn right on the path and continue circling the pond. A bridge crosses a part of Thornton Creek (7). Look upstream here—those lodge-building beavers are sometimes seen here at dawn or dusk, and sometimes build a dam on this waterway. Continue on the path and turn right at the fork, walking along the site until another right turn takes you back into the facility.

✳ 35. Evening Chorus at Paramount Park Open Space

Where: Shoreline neighborhood at NE 148th Street and Eleventh Avenue NE

Phone: Park, (206) 546-5041; Paramount Park Neighborhood Group, (206) 365-4477

Internet: *http://cityofshoreline.com/parks*

Hours: Dawn to dusk

Disabled Access: Wood-chip paths

Dogs: On leash

Driving: Take I-5 north just over eight miles from downtown Seattle to Exit 175, S.R. 523/NE 145th Street. Turn right at the light onto NE 145th Street. Go two blocks to Eight Avenue NE and turn left. Turn right onto 147th Street. Follow this to its end. Park in a lot on the left. As you cross the park entrance, the restoration project is located along the path to your right (east).

Special Note: The frog population is still getting established, so please respect this important project and do not collect frog eggs, tadpoles, or mature frogs at this site. Also, consider wearing mosquito repellent or long sleeves and pants if you'll be waiting for the frog carols at dusk. Spring and summer evenings are the best time to hear them.

The creation of Paramount Park's open-space wetland began in the early 1990s as a collaboration of King County Parks and the Paramount Park Neighborhood Group. But it wasn't truly complete until someone showed up with a beer can.

You think you've had hoppy beer? This particular brew was made up of the eggs of Pacific tree frogs (*Hyla regila*) collected in a wild area near Seattle as starter material for the new wetland. The tree frog, native to the West Coast and generally abundant in our state, is a dwindling species in urban environments due to habitat degradation, collecting of full-grown frogs as pets—the usual list of woes. But visit this small Shoreline park, just blocks from I-5, on a spring or summer evening (usually starting at dusk), and the ponds reverberate with their songs.

Paramount Park, at the end of a small residential street, has long been a respite for neighbors, who spearheaded the move to acquire and restore this adjacent filled-in wetland, fed by nearby springs, into good habitat for wild-life and nature lovers. Turn right as you walk onto Paramount grounds, and a trail and map of the wetland and ponds can be found to your right (south). A short walk through the lovingly reclaimed site, just shy of two acres, is scented with wild roses and shaded by fir trees and hemlocks planted by volunteers. Woody debris, such as snags, root wads, and the limbs of dead trees, has been carefully placed to interest insects, amphibians, birds, and other animals. About forty-five species of birds have been seen at the park so far, including hum-mingbirds, kingfishers, pileated woodpeckers, and a peregrine falcon, and mammals from bats to coyotes have paid visits.

The original look of the wetland had been lost, but the designer came up with a layout that fit the space, helps with water detention and filtration into a nearby tributary of Thornton Creek, and is also romantically pretty. Reflec-tive pools are partially shaded by alders, and planted with such natives as the tall, spiked hardstem bullrush, the smaller, fresh-green beaked rush, and grass-like slough sedge. Though the freeway fizzes in the background, this is a tranquil spot.

But these ponds were not actually designed for humans—everything about their size, depth, and orientation was chosen with the preferences of amphib-ians in mind. Take a seat on the log bench on the east side of the farthest pond, and listen for the chorus of our region's most widespread and musical frog. This caroler is the park's star attraction, with a song that can sometimes be heard for more than a mile. If its hearty call has you looking for a bullfrog-size amphibian, however, you'll miss this 2-inch long critter, concealed, most likely, under rushes or pondside jetsam. Pacific tree frogs range from bright chartreuse green (juveniles) to a variety of darker colors, with a black stripe

The distinctive caroling of Pacific tree frogs can be heard at Paramount Park's ponds.

running from snout to shoulder. It is thought that they can even change their coloring, going darker or lighter over a few minutes' time. Their feet aren't webbed, but have bulbous, spreading tips that aid in climbing. As with all frogs,

> Paramount Park Open Space boasts a hibernaculum, which is an underground structure created out of rock and wood to help native reptiles overwinter.

singing is done only by males, drawing females in to mate, and has been described variously as a high-pitched "ribbet," a "kree-eek," or, when in chorus, "the jingle of bells." Listen carefully and you'll be able to count how many frogs are at the pond—each voice sounds slightly different, and, like people singing "Row, Row, Row Your Boat" in rounds, they stagger their voices. If you make a noise while they're chorusing they may stop, but will soon start up again, one by one, once it's quiet. The best time to hear them is after a rain on a warm evening.

The mating rites of the tree frog are more entertaining than any movie (though tree frog song is actually widely used in films when frog noises are needed). The females do all the choosing of mates and are most likely to go for those with the longest and loudest songs. Females have actually been observed watching males before deciding which one to approach. Once she hops up to him, he doesn't waste time. Jumping aboard, he wraps his front arms around her in what is called amplexus. They then go underwater, where they may remain for several hours, breathing through their skin. But no fertilizing occurs now—the female must release the jelly-encased eggs, perhaps hours later, on pondside grasses or other soft material. Then the male inseminates the eggs—and goes right back to singing. About three weeks later the tadpoles emerge.

The number of male frogs (more easily counted because of their songs) has reached about fifteen thus far. Though reintroduction of this species has been tried in several places throughout the city, Paramount is the most successful project at this point. One reason is that the ponds were built specifically with amphibians in mind. The bottom topography, orientation to the sun, and water levels were all designed to provide good habitat for frogs and salamanders to breed and rear. Another is that there are no bullfrogs here—this nonnative species is a major predator of tree frogs and other amphibians. Also, the presence of nearby forest is essential for frogs and salamanders, which actually spend only a small portion of the year at the water. The rest of the time, in fall and winter, they retreat to shrubs, trees, and neighboring

Gelatinous Egg Mass

backyards. These frogs are often found in gutters and downspouts as well. Tree frogs are the park's most noticeable amphibian, but not its most notable. Brian Bodenbach, a volunteer with the Paramount Park Neighborhood Group, has worked to reintroduce several more sensitive species of native frogs and salamanders into the pond area. Harder to locate, salamanders are usually found under dense forest debris or ferns. A good way to find evidence of them is to poke around here in spring—the long-toed salamander (*Ambystoma macrodactylum*), which is slender with a green or yellow stripe on its back, leaves its gelatinous egg mass, around the size of a small plum, near the shoreline on wiry vegetation. The Northwestern salamander (*Ambystoma gracile*), which is stockier and has a swollen gland behind its eyes, leaves a much bigger egg mass like a grapefruit-size ball of jelly on stout branches, or floating in the water. The red-legged frog (*Rana aurora*), another native introduced here, is not yet established. It is hoped that the restoration project will be enough advanced by spring of 2003 to begin reintroducing native reptiles such as northwestern garter snakes and northern alligator lizards.

36. North Seattle Community College Wetlands

Where:	West of I-5 near Northgate Mall
Phone:	(206) 528-4597 or (206) 528-4516
Internet:	*www.northseattle.edu*
Disabled Access:	The main campus and oil-water pond are accessible. The wetland has dirt trails.
Dogs:	On leash
Driving:	From downtown Seattle, take I-5 approximately 4 miles north to Exit 173, Northgate. Turn right (south) onto First Avenue NE. Turn right onto College Way North. The college is on the right. Park at the marked visitor's lot at the south end of campus off College Way between North Ninety-fifth Street and North Ninety-seventh Street. Register with the security office just east of the lot. Then go to the last parking lot at the north end of campus, where you'll see the natural area.
Bus:	16, 75, and 302. Or go to the Northgate Transit Center and transfer to the Metro shuttle (Route 318) to campus.

Harvard and Princeton are decked in ivy; Stanford has its towering eucalyptus. But how many schools can boast of their very own wetland? Here at

North Seattle Community College (NSCC), the stuffy rules of traditional college landscaping, favoring foreign-bred trees, wide lawns, and invasive vines, have been upended, exchanged for a nationally recognized native habitat that provides its own first-rate education. Science instructors take classes here to study the physical, chemical, and biological environment. Art, writing, and history classes also make use of this landscape.

Since the 1980s, the college has been increasingly planted with native species, a move led by head groundskeeper, Michael Brokaw, who decided to make his work a reflection of his environmental values. In the 1990s he and his crew turned their attention to several acres of land at the north end of the college, a semi-wild area squeezed between I-5 and S.R. 99 providing a habitat of ponds and thickets.

In literary terms, you might call this wetland area a palimpsest. A Greek word that means something like "scraped again," a palimpsest is a manuscript that has been written on more than once, with one set of words incompletely erased to make room for another. The college's land lies on the site of a former neighborhood, a former dairy farm, and also a former bog where local Native American groups once harvested cranberries. Volunteers have found (and encouraged) native salmonberries growing behind blackberry bushes, and uncovered a kitchen floor beneath a layer of woodland duff. A walk around the wetland makes clear that none of the site's histories has been covered over completely.

ROCK OF AGES

You think the old-growth trees in Schmitz Park are old? Try telling that to the Wedgwood Boulder, a gigantic rock in this northeast Seattle neighborhood that's been around for 163 million years. At 19 feet tall and 75 feet in circumference, this incredible hulk only came to what is now our city between 15,500 and 17,000 years ago, hitching a ride on the Puget Lobe, ice that once covered much of this area and created what is now Puget Sound.

"Big Rock," as the boulder has sometimes been called, is thought to have been a Native American gathering place, and since the founding of Seattle has functioned a bit like a "pet rock" for locals. It has been decorated with Christmas lights on holidays, and its surrounding greenery pruned and pampered by neighbors. In a memory book from the nearby Bryant School, one former student described taking an overnight camping trip here in the 1930s, when the area must still have been partially forested. In the 1970s, hippies gathered at the rock and often perched on it (supposedly to smoke marijuana), a source of disgruntlement for some neighbors, who urged police to forbid the practice.

Though you can't legally climb on the boulder now, you can learn much about local geology from studying its history. It is considered a "glacial erratic," a type of rock that is unlike those around it. This particular erratic is greenstone, a basaltic lava that's been metamorphosed by extreme heat and pressure. It was "plucked"—a term that refers to the ability of glacial ice to yank bedrock blocks from the side of a large protuberance or knob, much as a dentist might pull out a molar—from Fidalgo Island, which lies about 75 miles north of Seattle.

In this case, the ice sheet flowed up and over the island's 1273-foot Mount Erie. The ice warmed and softened as it moved uphill, then chilled again on its way down, taking chunks of the mountain's knob, including our own boulder, with it. Geologists are able to determine how the ice sheet flowed by looking at Wedgwood Boulder—the fact that it is longest from north to south, for instance, reveals just how it would have been positioned by the ice flow, which itself was moving north to south.

Recently, a University of Washington geologist used the rock, because its age was already known, to calibrate a new type of geologic dating. For further study, you can visit Wedgwood's siblings plucked from the same mountaintop, most prominently two even bigger erratics on Whidbey Island, one of which is in the town of Coupeville. The Wedgwood Boulder is found on the 7200 block of Twenty-eighth Avenue NE.

The 163-million-year-old Wedgwood Boulder is thought to have been a meeting place for pre-Seattle Natives.

The "top" or most recently added layer of NSCC's living palimpsest is the restoration project, which is being approached from two directions. First, the south fork of Thornton Creek starts on this land, and must be managed both for its own health and for flood control. In midsummer you'll walk on dry paths and lowlands here, but in winter things drip, seep, and shimmer with moisture. The I-5 freeway, which rushes along right beside the college, would be submerged in winter had it not been elevated with fill—it's on land originally 10 to 15 feet below the current level of the college. Thornton Creek is culverted beneath the interstate, and also beneath Northgate Mall on the other side of I-5. To maintain the health of the waterway, the city and the college have been experimenting with such ideas as a holding pond near the north parking lot. Oil and other toxins picked up in runoff water from surrounding roads can be separated from the creek before its waters continue their way east.

Another aspect of the restoration involves careful decision-making about regrading the earth or tinkering with the current eccentric mix of plant species. The school thinks carefully before replacing nonnative plants with natives—sometimes existing plantings, even if not ideal, are being used by local species and would not be easily replaceable. For example, the wetland's rampant blackberries provide shelter and food for songbirds. In addition, former human inhabitants of this green corner have left behind cultural remnants that might warrant preservation. After all, Brokaw himself has promoted to the college's instructors the idea of accessing this natural site through a variety of "doorways," including literature and history. Viewed this way, the nonnative ornamental plum trees planted here by a Japanese farmer, or the old baseball backstop and defunct fire hydrant at the corner of two footpaths, become potential teaching tools. Try visiting the grounds in several different seasons to see the dramatic changes in the landscape. Some spots to stop:

1. **The Settling Pond.** Walk the sidewalk west along the natural area and you'll eventually come to this small pond lined with rocks. The pond allows fine particles to settle before the water reaches the wetland. This might be your first place to hear the resident Pacific tree frogs. The population of this native species, which has survived more than a century of human-engineered upheaval, is considered remarkable. The wetland also shelters native long-toed salamanders. To the north and east of this pond you can see restoration plantings of evergreens. Soil, concrete, and blackberries were removed from this area, which was then "paved" in 12 to 18 inches of woodchips as restorative mulch. The mulch and evergreens suppress weeds to allow planted native shrubs and perennials, such as garrya, mahonia, and salal to gain a foothold.

2. **Pondo Nuevo.** Native Americans called the kind of wetland you're walking in a "*Slo'q'qued.*" This word, meaning "bald-headed marsh," describes a low area of wetland surrounding a drier area. Walking north on the dirt trail into the restoration area you can get some sense of this topography. As you enter you quickly find yourself on a ridge path elevated above the surrounding ground. If it's summer, the field to your right quickly fills with invasive reed canary grass, kept mowed and under control. Brokaw and Lortz affectionately call this area Pondo Nuevo after having been surprised by the "new" ephemeral pond that springs up here in winter. Pondo Nuevo is perfect habitat for tree frogs and salamanders. Bullfrogs, one of those species' major predators, spend more than a year as tadpoles and therefore can't survive in an ephemeral pond. Tree frogs and long-toed salamanders are tadpoles only a few months, right when the pond is in season. When mature, they become mainly terrestrial, sheltering among soil debris.

3. **Cultural curiosities.** If you split off the main path, keep an eye out for a few features of cultural significance. One is the stand of lodgepole pines, 8 feet tall or more, growing near one of the paths. The Native American Student Council donated these trees. When they eventually need thinning, the harvested pines will be used as poles for an on-campus teepee. Also keep watch for the old fire hydrant, left behind from the former neighborhood, at a fork in two paths. Near this hydrant is another remnant from an earlier time, what appears to be a small orchard of Italian plum trees. The "orchard" is actually a thicket of plums growing from one "mother tree." The plant spreads not by seeds, but underground runners. Very little is ever sprayed with herbicides in this wetland, and then only in controlled, marked locations. You are free to pick blackberries, pears, plums, or hazelnuts.

4. **Surge Pond.** Next to the freeway, this is the biggest campus pond and regularly holds eight to ten species of waterfowl in the winter, as well as the three-spined stickleback, a native fish, in its depths. Common here in winter are buffleheads, ring-neck ducks, gadwalls, pied-billed grebes, wood ducks, and Northern shovelers. Other birds at NSCC include bushtits, black-capped chickadees, flickers, finches, juncos, and sparrows. There have been rarer sightings of great blue herons, green herons, and Cooper's hawks.

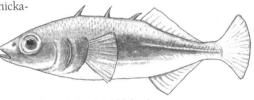

Three-Spined Stickleback

LICTON SPRINGS

Just a couple of blocks west of North Seattle Community College is a park that offers both a pleasant retreat and a history lesson. Licton Springs Park has significance in Native American history as a gathering site for ceremonies. The springs are called Licton, for the Salish word *Lee-uk-tid*, which refers to the red oxide that emerges from the ground here, and provided pigment for Native American painting and mineral-rich mud for healing rituals. The location was the site of a spa in the 1930s. Visitors from all over the area came to soak in thermal baths and drink the Licton waters. Though the springs are now piped from here to the city's sewage treatment plant, you can still see the water emerging and rub the same rusty mud between your fingers. This leafy, one-block park with its ponds and spring is a small remembrance of the network of wetlands that once covered much of this area. Licton Springs Park is located at 9536 Ashworth Avenue North.

FAIRWAYS OR FOWL?

What if resident orca populations, instead of declining, were on the rise? What if they were clogging waterways, causing accidents, and eating every last salmon? Would they still be local icons? Or would we consider killing killer whales?

If our response to Western Canada goose populations is any clue, the answer to that last question is yes. Some Canada goose subspecies, such as the midsize chocolate brown "dusky," are currently so threatened they are protected by refuges. Few people realize that the Western Canada goose—those imposing black, white, and brown "honkers" at every waterside park—also nearly went extinct only a few decades ago. Eastern Washington migrants, they were brought to Western Washington in the 1960s by wildlife biologists to help repopulate.

The honkers quickly took to our expanding suburbs, with their emerald green lawns and easy water access, and have now become as common on golf courses and boat docks as Starbucks on street corners. In Seattle, parks with shoreline lawns, such as Matthews Beach in northeast Seattle, have also been inundated. In 1999, figures showed more than 20,000 satisfied Western Canadas were strutting the shorelines of the Puget Sound region (2000 or so in the city). Their population growth rate may be 15 percent a year.

Somewhere along the way, the romance of fluffy yellow goslings and goose couples pairing up (they mate long-term, and possibly for life) paled. So comfortable were the birds that they ceased their natural migration patterns and, unlike those honking V-formations of migrants that pass through our area in spring and fall, began breeding here.

Goose–human conflicts arise during breeding season. The geese molt their feathers then and are unable to fly. Irritated park visitors and homeowners complain of angry ganders (the male goose can be aggressive in his protection of the female) and lawns chicken-poxed with a rash of green goose excrement. When fecal coliform levels in public wading areas get too high, Western Canadas are charged with fouling our waterways.

The U.S. Department of Agriculture (USDA) Wildlife Services began thinning the population in the late 1990s, at first oiling eggs to prevent hatching, and then taking the more controversial approach of gassing adult geese in a portable killing chamber. Year 2002 reports suggest Puget Sound goose numbers have fallen perhaps 20 percent since 1999. The Humane Society advocates for non-lethal solutions to this conflict. Visit *http://geesepeace.org* for more information.

THORNTON CREEK WATERSHED

The name "creek" just doesn't do justice to a waterway with such huge significance for Seattle. The largest watershed in the city, the Thornton Creek drainage covers 11.6 square miles in northeast Seattle, providing habitat for untold numbers of birds, mammals, bugs, and humans. The creek has also historically supported salmon and trout, including chinook salmon, currently listed as threatened under the Endangered Species Act.

The waterway flows through yards, parks, into pipes, and underground. Wherever it goes it seems to inspire citizens to act on its behalf. Currently, three separate groups are devoted to its well-being. The Thornton Creek Project, based at North Seattle Community College, brings teachers and students together with the creek for educational purposes. The Thornton Creek Alliance works on improving creek health. And the Thornton Creek Legal Defense Fund wades into the deep end of the water: This group is engaged in a legal struggle with the owners of Northgate Mall over the shopping center's south parking lot, located over a historic stretch of the creek's south fork. The mall owners made plans to expand into the area without raising this stretch of Thornton back aboveground, destroying any possibility of reconnecting it. Mall representatives have argued that the creek may not exist if it's already buried. When is a creek not a creek?

There are several public access points for visiting the creek. Some are detailed in this chapter (Meadowbrook, Paramount Park, and North Seattle Community College) and the rest can be found by visiting the Thornton Creek Alliance website and printing their restoration site tour, at *http://scn.org/earth/tca/tcatour.htm*.

PACIFIC FLYWAY: WHO MIGRATES THROUGH?

Some Seattle birds, such as black-capped chickadees and Canada geese, are content to spend their lives here in the city. Other more peripatetic avian species come through only during certain seasons—some to over-winter and others merely stopping by on their way elsewhere.

Many naturalists and scientists originally believed that migrating birds stuck pretty faithfully to one of several fairly specific routes, known as "flyways," which followed coastlines, mountain ranges, and major river systems. In North America, these are known as the Atlantic, the Mississippi, the Central, and the Pacific Flyways. Today, it is understood that, although these four general passageways do exist, they are broad categories within which each migrating bird species follows its own specific route, and may even cross several flyways. Located on protected saltwater near the outer Pacific Coast, we are ideally located on the Pacific Flyway and many other migration routes. The Pacific Flyway reaches north to the western Arctic, Alaska, and the Aleutian Islands, and south to where it meets the other flyways in Central and South America.

Other migrations are east–west, or altitudinal, meaning those species that move from mountains to lowlands and back according to season. Many Western grebes, east–west migrants, nest in Eastern Washington in spring and summer, and visit here in the other seasons. The varied thrush, a wood-land bird with a haunting voice that sometimes visits backyards in Seattle, moves high up into the Cascades in breeding season to nest, an example of altitudinal migration. This type of migration is slightly different from the others, as it tends to involve species, such as the varied, which are actually residents of our area but travel back and forth.

But the largest patterns here tend to follow north–south lines, and can occur in any season of the year. In fall and winter many waterfowl, raptors, and gull species come here after nesting elsewhere to enjoy good hunting and the protected waters of Puget Sound. After a rather slow birdwatching period in midsummer, enthusiasts anticipate these seasons with excitement. In fall and winter sharp-shinned hawks and other raptors might pay a visit to your backyard to prey on smaller birds. The farthest traveling bird, the Arctic tern, also visits Puget Sound in fall while migrating the enormous distance between the Arctic Circle and the tip of South America. A variety of shorebirds, such as sanderlings, overwinter on our urban beaches.

Spring brings a different crew, such as many warbler species, which might have passed through unnoticed in fall, but now make a dazzling appearance at parks and neighborhood yards, decked out in their breeding plumage. The rufous hummingbird is another spring arrival. Swallows, easily noticed as they swoop and dive for insects overhead, arrive in spring, stay here for the summer, and leave in the fall for warmer climates. Once you learn which birds are coming and going in local parks and backyards, you will anticipate the first warbler, raptor, or shorebird of the season like others anticipate big movie openings or the start of baseball season.

Farther Afield

Outside the city, opportunities for encountering the wild increase exponentially. Included here are some popular destinations such as Bellevue's Mercer Slough, and lesser-known locales with excellent credentials, such as Everett's Jetty Island and Renton's Waterworks Gardens. Among the selections, you'll find the forested walks and beach excursions for which the Northwest is famous, plus a few surprises including a sewage treatment plant where you may want to picnic, and a bird sanctuary formed from a harbor's dredging spoils. Each of the choices makes a satisfying day trip in and of itself, or can be combined with another excursion in the same area. The sites in this chapter can be reached within a twenty- to sixty-minute drive from downtown Seattle.

37. Renton: Waterworks Gardens

Where:	The East Division Reclamation Plant is at 1200 Monster Road SW
Phone:	(206) 684-2400
Internet:	*http://dnr.metrokc.gov/WTD/waterworks/index.htm*
Hours:	Dawn to dusk
Disabled Access:	Yes
Dogs:	On leash but not conducive to wildlife viewing
Driving:	From downtown Seattle, head south on I-5 to Exit 157, Martin Luther King Jr. Way. Follow Martin Luther King Jr. Way to the second stoplight at Sixty-eighth Avenue South. Turn right. Go 1 mile to Monster Road SW. At the intersection there is a small parking area to the left signed "Black River Riparian Forest." Park here, cross the road, and walk a short way up the hill to the Waterworks entrance just before the white water tower.
Bus:	Take Route 150 to the Southcenter Mall, then change to Route 140 and get off at Oakesdale Avenue SW and Grady Way SW. Walk north on Oakesdale about 0.5 mile to Monster Road.

The forested ravine at O. O. Denny Park is home to eagles, owls, salmon, and huge cedar trees.

It's the first day of spring in Renton's Waterworks Gardens and the cattails are bursting at their seams, hawks are courting overhead, and the frogs are resonantly awake. Just off I-405 beyond the fast food restaurants and chain superstores is a public art space that acts as a bridge between industry and nature. Looking over Waterworks' tranquil pools and a significant stretch of wetland, the paradoxical distant views include a cement-recycling plant, heron rookery, box factory, Mount Rainier, and King County's largest secondary sewage treatment plant.

When the East Division Water Reclamation Plant applied for a $229 million expansion in the late 1990s, the permitting process required cleansing stormwater runoff from the site. Had it not been for some visionary thinking (and King County's Metro Arts Program), huge cement tanks surrounded by cyclone fencing would be treating the oil-polluted water from the eighty-five–acre plant's roadways and parking lots. Instead, an eight-acre sanctuary created next door invites people to walk through a natural water purifier, watch birds and other wildlife, or just shake off the developed world.

Artist Lorna Jordan says she masterminded this unusual mix of art, nature, and technology in an effort to "connect people to the cycles and mysteries of water." To help visitors experience the process of natural water treatment, she created a series of five "rooms" that teach by way of bubbling streams, calming ponds, and thriving wetlands.

"The progression of rooms engages the visitor on an intimate scale and follows the story of the water's cycle: impure, working, mysterious, beautiful, and life sustaining," says Jordan. If you flew above the grounds you'd see the artist's abstract interpretation of a large-scale flowering plant shaped through landforms, plantings, water bodies, and the garden rooms—symbolic of a plant's filtering power to cleanse water.

The story begins at the plant's "roots"—an overlook named The Knoll marked by large basalt pillars. Here, untreated runoff bubbles stream-like underfoot, covered by an iron grate that affords the rare opportunity to walk inches above running water. From here, it flows into The Funnel, a chain of leaf-shaped ponds linked by a path representing a stem. Lined with clay and recycled glass pulverized into sand, particle pollution settles to the bottom of the ponds. Next the water seeps into The Grotto, the sun-collecting core of the garden where river rock–studded benches frame a mosaic tile seedpod below cave-like walls of cascading plants. The Grotto leads to The Passage, a line of poplars and three circular ponds meant to symbolize fruit. Next comes The Release, which includes the last of the treatment ponds and a meandering wetland. By the time the water reaches the final pond, most of the pollutants and sediments have settled out. In the wetland, remaining surface water contaminants are absorbed or broken down by plants and microscopic organisms. The marsh helps decompose organic matter, bringing nutrients back into the food chain, as well as helping to prevent flooding during storms. The water passes through islands of native plantings via a series of channels to Springbrook Creek, which feeds into the Black River Wetland and finally the Green River. The pathway connects to a regional bike path system.

BLACK RIVER RIPARIAN FOREST HERON COLONY
Just across Monster Road SW is the Black River Wetland, home to an established heron colony with more than thirty-five active nests. Early spring is the best time to visit before new leaves block views into the sky-scraping black cottonwood trees where they nest. Follow the bike path to Springbrook Creek, then walk quietly along the grassy trail by the creek to the colony. The herons have been brooding here since the early 1980s. More than fifty species of birds have been counted here, as well as coyotes, raccoons, beaver, moles, voles, skunks, weasels, frogs, salamanders, and snakes.

❋ 38. Vashon Island: Winter Bird Wonderland

Where:	Jensen Point is at 8900 SW Harbor Drive, the eastern tip of the Burton Peninsula in Quartermaster Harbor
Phone:	NA
Internet:	NA
Hours:	Dawn to dusk
Disabled Access:	Yes, except for Burton Acres Trail
Dogs:	On leash, but not conducive to bird watching
Driving:	From the Fauntleroy Terminal in West Seattle, take the ferry to Vashon Island. Drive off the ferry onto Vashon Highway SW and continue 9 miles to Burton. Turn left onto Southwest Burton Drive and continue for 0.6 mile. The road comes to a T at Ninety-seventh Avenue SW. Turn left. Continue 1 mile around the peninsula to the Burton Acres Boat House and Jensen Point. To reach Shawnee Beach, turn right out of the boat house parking lot and return to Burton. At the highway, turn left and follow the road along Quartermaster Harbor. Drive 0.7 mile to public parking on the harbor side of the highway near an Important Bird Area sign. Access the beach via the metal stairs.
Bus:	118 via Fauntleroy Ferry

In various circles, Vashon Island is famous for its skis (K2), its coffee (Seattle's Best Coffee), and its tofu (Island Spring)—but among bird lovers, the thirty-square-mile green space is renowned for its Western grebes. While populations of this red-eyed, swan-shaped aquatic bird have declined by up to 95 percent in other areas of Puget Sound, they have remained stable on Vashon, whose waters are spawning grounds for its favorite delicacy, Pacific herring.

Western Grebes

Designated in 2001 as one of the first Important Bird Areas in the state by the National Audubon Society, Vashon's Quartermaster Harbor is the wintertime home of thirty-five species of waterfowl—including thousands of duck-size Western grebes, which account for 8 percent of the state's wintering population. An Important Bird Area is a site deemed essential to one or more species for breeding, wintering, or migration—earmarking areas key to bird conservation. Vashon is at least a part-time home to more than one hundred bird species.

Eelgrass beds where herring and other small fish lay their eggs are crucial to the health of Quartermaster Harbor's ecosystem. To find a school of herring, look for a large "raft" of Western grebes shadowing the unlucky fish as they move about the harbor. Large grebes can eat up to a pound of fish in one day!

To see wintering birds, the best time to visit Quartermaster is from November to April when thousands of waterfowl—including the threatened marbled murrelet, common loon, and Brandt's cormorant—gather here from breeding grounds on small lakes and reservoirs in Alaska and Canada. Two good viewpoints are Jensen Point at the west edge of the Burton Peninsula and Shawnee Beach.

Sometimes described as "more fish than feathers," Western grebes will dive rather than fly away from intruders. They are streamlined for swimming, with large feet set way back on their bodies. Perhaps the most legendary of the Western grebe's behaviors is its inimitable courtship display. The male and female face each other with necks outstretched, then turn together to literally run on water, necks arched high. The dance ends with a synchronized dive. This show usually only occurs in their northern breeding grounds, but sometimes in April, when the winter is long and hard up north, visitors spy grebes practicing their moves on Quartermaster. The Puget Sound Kayak Company, (206) 463-9257, rents kayaks from the Burton Acres Boat House if you would like to join the grebes on their own "turf." Open seasonally or by reservation.

BURTON ACRES PARK

Across the road from Jensen Point is the trailhead for a walk through Burton Acres Park. A tranquil 1-mile loop winds through second-growth native maple, cedar, fir, hemlock, and alder trees—some more than seventy-five years old. Old-growth stumps are scarred with marks where loggers would insert springboards where they would stand to swing their axes. These boards were placed high enough to avoid the lower root crown, the hardest part of the tree.

39. Bainbridge Island: IslandWood

Where:	4450 Blakely Avenue NE
Phone:	(206) 855-4333
Internet:	www.islandwood.org
Hours:	Public tours are held the last Saturday of every month 9:30 A.M. to 12:30 P.M. Designed for adults and kids age thirteen and up, tours include the main campus buildings and a hike to some of the natural areas. To reserve a spot, call (206) 855-4333 or send email to registrar@islandwood.org.
Disabled Access:	Yes
Dogs:	No
Driving:	Take the Seattle-to-Bainbridge ferry from the Seattle Terminal at 801 Alaskan Way on the waterfront in downtown Seattle. On Bainbridge, drive up the hill from the ferry to the first stoplight. Turn left onto Winslow Way. Continue to the first stop sign at Madison Avenue, turn right. Continue to the next stop sign at Wyatt Way, and turn left. Continue around Eagle Harbor on Wyatt until the road forks. Take the right fork up the hill, following signs to Port Blakely. You are now on Blakely Avenue. Continue approximately 1 mile until you see the Blakely Elementary School on your left. After you pass the school, IslandWood is the first driveway on your left.
Bus:	No convenient access

There's a one-of-a-kind school on Bainbridge Island where you can practice drawing like John James Audubon or taking photos like Art Wolfe, learn to track local mammals and how to read trees to unravel a forest's life history. IslandWood inspires exploration and stewardship of the natural world by linking science, technology, and the arts in an incredibly diverse outdoor classroom. Miles of fir needle–cushioned trails wind through an enchanting 255 acres of second-growth forest to a bog, pond, marsh, stream, and ravine. For saltwater studies, the property connects to the Blakely estuary and Blakely Harbor. In outdoor school programs for Seattle school students and public workshops for children, adults, and families, IslandWood students can track a barred owl as it flies through the forest, look a long-toed salamander in the eye, learn how to build photovoltaic systems, or plant an organic garden.

Here even the buildings have something to teach. Though they have the look and feel of traditional Northwest lodges, they are models of sustainability constructed and finished with reused or recycled building materials, equipped with solar-heated hot water, and heated and cooled naturally. No opportunity is missed to subtly—and with an artistic playfulness—model ways to live with less impact on the earth. In the cafeteria, students weigh their leftovers in friendly competitions to waste the least food, and sinks are lined with pictures of salmon to remind people that what goes down the drain flows into fish habitat. Each of five fireplaces tells a different geologic story of Puget Sound, wetland plants treat wastewater in the living machine, and solar power lights up classrooms installed with cork and bamboo floors.

You can visit IslandWood on a public tour, sign up for a volunteer project such as bird banding, or take a class. Call to request a catalog.

BLAKELY HARBOR PARK

South of IslandWood is an undeveloped waterfront park (closest cross streets are Country Club and Blakely Harbor Roads)—a great place to launch a kayak or canoe to explore Blakely Harbor. The former site of Port Blakely Mill, one of the world's largest sawmills in the late 1800s, the now quiet beach is a good spot for a picnic. As of 2003, plans for trails are underway.

Pileated woodpeckers leave large rectangular holes in trees as they chip away bark in search of their preferred food, carpenter ants.

40. Bellevue: Wild Wetland in Mercer Slough

Where:	South Bellevue
Phone:	(425) 452-2752
Internet:	*http://cityofbellevue.org*
Hours:	Park, dawn to dusk. Visitor's center, April–October, Monday–Saturday 10:00 A.M. to 4:00 P.M., Sunday noon to 4:00 P.M.; November–March, Monday–Friday 10:00 A.M. to 4:00 P.M., Saturday 10:00 A.M. to 2:00 P.M., closed Sunday.
Disabled Access:	Winter's House and some trails accessible
Dogs:	On leash
Driving:	From downtown Seattle, head south on I-5. Merge onto I-90 East toward Bellevue and Spokane. In 6.5 miles, take the Bellevue Way exit and stay on it north to Bellevue Way SE. In about 1.3 miles, watch for a Park-and-Ride sign on your right. Just past here, turn in at the blue Winter's House sign on your right.
Bus:	550; get off at Bellevue Way SE and SE Nineteenth Street. Walk a few blocks south to the Winter's House entrance.
Special Note:	Canoes and kayaks can be launched from Sweyolocken Park Boat Launch, the first right off Bellevue Way, north of I-90.

Just blocks from Bellevue Square and the I-90 freeway, the 320 acres of the Mercer Slough Nature Park pulse with lush, primordial life. It's the largest stretch of wetland left on Lake Washington, a habitat so rich it is easy to understand why Salish Indians located longhouses here in centuries past. Later, while other wetlands on the shores of Lake Washington were filled in and built over, the slough's peat soils were claimed by farmers, eager to grow such acid-loving plants as blueberries and strawberries. Only a remnant of this time exists at the Mercer Slough historic Blueberry Farm at slough's edge, owned by the City of Bellevue. The ground here is so waterlogged that pumps are used to keep the land viable for growing.

Much of the land and waters here were once heavily abused, directly or indirectly, by nearby cattle grazing, the use of the property for bulb farming, and the construction of I-90 and I-405. In the 1970s the Bellefields Office Park was built on slough shores, which involved filling in a whopping 130 acres of wetland and excavating a stretch of the waterway. The slough was eventually reduced to only a shallow stream, and invasive species such as reed canary grass and blackberries were squeezing out native plant species. The City of Bellevue, which has been buying land along the slough since the 1950s, has made restoration of this park an ongoing project.

Coyote

The slough and its more than 5 miles of trails are now a treat for the city escapist. Walk through the deciduous woodlands thriving in this damp soil, a mix of trees such as paper birch, red alder, Oregon ash, vine maple, and cottonwood, and you'll likely hear the music of thrushes and kinglets. Huge, tropical-looking skunk cabbages the size of ottomans hunker on the forest floor, and garter snakes rustle under leaf litter. Quietly cross a footbridge spanning the winding waterway, and you might glimpse a green heron or great blue heron staking out territory for hunting, or spot resident waterfowl such as kingfishers, grebes, mergansers, and wood ducks. At least one hundred birds, including winter visitors such as buffleheads and goldeneyes, use the park as a home or stopping place. Underwater, salmon and steelhead migrate up- and downstream.

The land is used by a diverse list of animals, from Pacific tree frogs and salamanders to mammals such as red foxes, coyotes, and porcupines, creatures you'll be most likely to glimpse if you're here and very alert at dusk or dawn. Watch for bald eagles and osprey overhead.

A visit will likely whet your curiosity for more information about the place—be sure to sign up for one of the park's nature walks or, even better, a guided canoe trip of the slough. At Winter's House, the park's visitor center, you can ask questions and pick up a list of park species. Whatever you do, don't miss this link to the region's greener, wilder past.

Porcupine

LAKE TO LAKE TRAIL AND LAKE HILLS GREENBELT

The Mercer Slough is a part of the Lake to Lake Trail and Greenway, a linked series of trails that can be walked from Lake Washington to Lake Sammamish. One park on the route is the Lake Hills Greenbelt, 140 acres of wetlands, woods, and meadows that connect Phantom and Larson Lakes. A ranger station at the park offers more information on the habitat. The station is also home to a lush demonstration garden, with native and drought-tolerant plantings, bat houses, a butterfly garden, and other great ideas to incorporate into your own backyard. For more information, contact the ranger station at (425) 452-7225.

To get to the park by car, take the 148th Avenue SE exit off I-90, turn right onto SE Sixteenth Street, and go to the intersection with 156th Avenue SE. The ranger station is on the northeast corner.

✳ 41. Kirkland: Orion's Lush Legacy

Where:	Denny Park on Holmes Point Drive NE
Phone:	(206) 296-4232
Internet:	*http://metrokc.gov/parks* or *dennycreek.org*
Hours:	Dawn to dusk
Disabled Access:	To the beach only
Dogs:	Leash and scoop. Not allowed on beach.
Driving:	From downtown, take I-5 north and merge onto S.R. 520 East toward Bellevue and Kirkland. In about 6.7 miles, merge onto I-405 North toward Everett. Take Exit 20A, NE 116th Street. Turn left at the bottom of the ramp onto NE 116th Street. Follow this through a large intersection at Ninety-eighth Avenue NE, as it becomes NE Juanita Drive. In about 2 miles make a sharp left at the light for Seventy-sixth Place NE (also known as Holmes Point Drive NE), and wind your way down to the lakeshore. Beachside parking is on your left. An overflow parking lot, next to trailheads, is on your right.
Bus:	260 to the intersection of Holmes Point Drive NE and NE Juanita Drive. Walk down Holmes Point to the park.
Special Note:	As of 2002, major shortfalls in King County's budget left Denny Park and many others in the county without funding, leading to cutbacks in park operation. Check websites or call the county for details.

It's a rare local park that offers lush wilderness abutting a sweet semicircle of beach, all tucked into a quiet lakeside neighborhood. But that's what you'll get on a visit to Orion O. Denny Park, informally known as Denny Park, and named for the son of Arthur Denny, one of Seattle's first settlers. Set in Kirkland's Finn Hill area, the park makes a good kayak launch site or picnic spot. But even if you're here to dip your toes in Lake Washington, you won't want to miss the forested ravine across the street, where a couple miles of trail pass by a cool, clear salmon stream and beneath huge trees where bald eagles and barred owls nest.

To visit this enchanting place, start at the north end of the loop trail, which begins at the back of the lawn next to the overflow parking lot. The trail, which can be mucky after rain, follows the north side of Denny Creek, sheltered by huge bigleaf maples, red alders, Western red cedars, and Douglas firs, and flanked by green explosions of sword- and ladyferns. For much of the twentieth century, this park contained the largest Douglas fir in King County, until it was blown down by a windstorm—the stump still stands beside the trail.

Watch for a faint footpath to the left of the trail; if you come to a more recent blowdown that crosses the path, you've gone a little too far. This path leads you north up a dry valley with bigleaf maples and mixed conifers. Watch for pileated woodpeckers here. (Keep in mind that side trails quickly lead to private property, so avoid trespassing.) Back on the main trail watch out for a fallen Douglas fir that has not yet settled. Walk around, not under, this tree. Soon after this you'll come to Denny Creek, site of a fish restoration project instigated by the Denny Creek Alliance, a group that actively works to preserve park habitat. Beneath the bridge—a 1930s Work Projects Administration project—a fish ladder compensates for erosion caused by building the bridge. North of the bridge, a path leads beside the stream past a defunct pumphouse. To follow it, you need to cross the stream three times by stepping on rocks. The stream is also the site of a salmon egg incubator, where the alliance hatches coho for the creek.

Staying on the main trail, cross the bridge and continue south to climb a gravel service road and visit the park's "high ridge" area, where there has been an active eagles' nest. It's not really visible from ground level, but watch for the birds in flight. Other park birds include barred owls nesting on the north side of the creek, red-tailed hawks, and hairy and downy woodpeckers. Varied and Swainson's thrushes visit in spring and summer, responsible for otherworldly singing in the brush. Other woodland birds such as Hutton's vireos, golden-crowned kinglets, spotted towhees, and black-capped and chestnut-backed chickadees are here all year, moving among park greenery such as salmonberry, huckleberry, and Pacific blackberry shrubs, and an ever-changing carpet of bleeding heart, vanilla leaf, foamflower, and other native plants.

An information kiosk south of the picnic shelter back on the beach side of the park offers information on the Alliance, some history, and breaking park news.

42. Everett: Jetty Island

Where:	Jetty Island is off the Everett waterfront, about 30 miles north of Seattle
Phone:	(425) 257-8304
Internet:	*http://everettwa.org/parks/recreation/jetty/jettyinfo.htm*
Hours:	Jetty Island may be visited year-round with your own boat. Free passenger ferry service, a trip that takes only a few minutes, is available July 5–Labor Day, Wednesday–Saturday 10:00 A.M. to 5:30 P.M., and Sundays 11:00 A.M. to 5:30 P.M. The island is also open until 9:00 P.M. on four Saturdays each summer. Ferries leave from the Tenth Street Boat Launch about every half-hour.
Disabled Access:	There is access onto the ferry, but if the tide is out, the on-ramp can be quite steep. Terrain on the island is wide, packed dirt trails or sand.
Dogs:	No pets allowed
Driving:	From downtown Seattle, take I-5 north approximately 28 miles to Exit 193. Turn right onto Everett Avenue. Continue all the way to the waterfront and turn right onto West Marine View Drive. Go north approximately 17 blocks to the Tenth Street Boat Launch and Marine Park on the left. Jetty parking is on your left as you enter.
Bus:	From Fourth and Union downtown take Sound Transit Routes 510, 512, or 513, signed for Everett. Get off at the Everett bus station at Thirty-third and Broad. From here you will need to take a taxi or a couple more buses. For schedule information, call Community Transit at (800) 562-1375.
Special Note:	Visit the kiosk near the water for free passes onto the island ferry. To paddle to Jetty Island during or outside regular ferry access hours, you can put in a kayak or canoe at the southwest corner of Marine Park, the ferry departure point.

The only nature experience most people headed to Jetty Island seem in search of is poking their toes in the sand. As you ride across the Everett harbor to the island on the jam-packed ferry, toddlers bounce on knees and kids are lathered up with banana-scented sunblock for a swim in the shallow, warm waters, the island's main draw.

But among the crowds you'll also spy quieter types with binoculars and bird books. Follow them, and you'll find the island's grassy dunes and saltwater lagoon, a destination for area birders who come to look for a long list of birds with a preference for ocean beach habitat. If you've never seen a Caspian tern, a spotted sandpiper, or a black-bellied plover, you might find them here, along with many other shorebirds. In winter, a wide array of ducks visit, including gadwalls, northern pintails, ruddy ducks, northern shovelers, and American and Eurasian wigeons. Birding visitors record their sightings in a logbook at the on-island kiosk, a useful place to start for advice and guidance. It is located near the ferry dock. Twice daily interpretive walks teach about island animal and plant life, and other programs, geared especially toward children, focus on mollusks, bugs, fish, and other nature topics.

The island is the unnatural result of a failed attempt to create a freshwater harbor. Dredging spoils from the mouth of the Snohomish River plus leftover construction waste turned a 2.4-mile dike into the island it is today. Clean dredging materials are still placed here to prevent erosion and create intertidal habitat.

Particularly interesting to note are the many dune-loving plants that have made their way to this new territory, where they thrive in the salty, sandy soil. Several of them are edible, including seaside plantain (*Plantago maritima*), whose leaves grow to a foot long, peppergrass (*Lepidium oxycarpum*), which has peppery-tasting seeds in late July and August, and beach asparagus (*Salicornia virginica*), also known as pickleweed, which looks a little like supermarket asparagus and has a wild, salty taste. Ask a naturalist or ranger at the island kiosk to point these plants out to you, or go on one of the scheduled nature walks.

You can also gather your own information at the Discovery Hut, a veritable cabinet of wonders with bugs in jars, a pickled octopus, miscellaneous unlabeled bones, and assorted information on island life.

Man-made Jetty Island attracts many species of shorebirds and ducks to its sandy shoreline and saltwater lagoon.

43. Everett: Spencer Island

Where:	Everett is about 30 miles north of Seattle
Phone:	(425) 388-6600
Internet:	*www.co.Snohomish.wa.us/parks*
Hours:	Dawn to dusk
Disabled Access:	Yes. There is a handicap parking lot next to the main entrance. Conditions on the boardwalk interpretive trail are good; conditions on the island loop trail can be variable with the compacted trails soft and damp in places in wet weather.
Dogs:	Only on the island's north end, which is also a hunting area
Driving:	From Seattle, take I-5 north about 28 miles to Exit 195, Marine View Drive. Go left on East Marine View Drive and follow this about 2 miles or less to S.R. 529 North (Pacific Highway). From here, cross the river and take the first exit on your right (Smith Island Access/ Frontage Road) and follow signs to Langus Riverfront Park and Spencer Island. Past Langus Riverfront Park is a parking lot just past the left curve in the road. Continue by foot down the gravel road a few hundred feet to the park entrance.
Bus:	From Fourth and Union downtown take Sound Transit Routes 510, 512, or 513, signed for Everett. Get off at the Everett bus station at 3201 Smith Street. From here you will need to take a taxi or a couple more buses. For schedule information call Community Transit at (800) 562-1375.
Special Note:	Kayaking is another great way to see the area around Spencer Island. A put-in site is at Langus Riverfront Park.

More than fourteen hundred acres of the Snohomish River estuary, where the waters of the river meet the saltwater of Possession Sound, are a home for more than three hundred birds and a variety of mammals, and critical habitat for salmon species, all of which thrive in and around the brackish wetlands. It's a place naturalists could spend years getting to know. One way to visit the estuary and perhaps spot a wide range of species, is to take to a kayak or canoe through the area. To this end, county and local paddle groups are working to develop a network of "water trails" here, designated water routes set up with boat access and rest stops. The trails should be accessible some time in late 2003. Contact the Parks and Recreation Department number above for more information.

Another great way to explore the estuary is to visit Spencer Island, a renowned birdwatching destination and excellent spot for an easy day hike. The northern part of the island is managed by the Washington Department of Fish and Wildlife, and is open to seasonal hunting. South Spencer Island is former pastureland that is being restored to its original state of grassy marshland with seasonal ponds. A footpath encircles the entire island—a 3.5-mile loop. A boardwalk near the park entrance heads into the cattails and offers interpretive panels for learning more about the property. Late winter and spring are a great time to see a wide variety of ducks and other waterfowl. Deer, beaver, river otters, and even seals are sometimes spotted in the area.

✳ APPENDIXES

NATURE IN THE CITY: VOLUNTEER OPPORTUNITIES
If the places in this book inspire you, consider joining the enthusiastic individuals who work to protect Seattle's natural heritage.

Restoration and Animals
King County Department of Natural Resources
(206) 296-0100
www.metrokc.gov, dnr.metrokc.gov/wlr/pi/commstew.htm

King County has the following environmental volunteer programs:
Beach naturalist: (206) 296-8359
Lake steward: (206) 296-8008
Restoration planting: (206) 296-1923
Adopt-a-road: (206) 296-3807
Adopt-a-park: (206) 296-2990

Progressive Animal Welfare Society (PAWS)
(425) 787-2500
http://paws.org
15305 44th Ave. W
Lynnwood, WA, 98037
The Progressive Animal Welfare Society (PAWS) is an animal advocacy organization based in Lynnwood. PAWS advocates for animals through the operation of a companion animal shelter, a wildlife center, and an advocacy department.
The PAWS Wildlife Center in Lynnwood is a world-renowned wildlife rehabilitation facility. Formerly known as HOWL, it receives more than five thousand injured or displaced wild animals every year. The center houses and rehabilitates wild animals, and prepares them for eventual release back into the wild. The center has cared for bears, coyotes, opossums, seals, starlings, bobcats, squirrels, and many other species of wild animals that populate the Pacific Northwest. There are a variety of volunteer opportunities such as the care and feeding of injured and orphaned wildlife, including raising orphaned songbirds.

Seattle Audubon Society
(206) 523-8243, ext. 11
www.seattleaudubon.org
8050 35th Ave. NE
Seattle, WA 98115

Founded in 1916, the Seattle Audubon Society is the oldest natural history organization in the Northwest. They have classes, youth programs, work on conservation issues, and field trips. Volunteers can teach children about conservation and help with the newsletter. The Audubon Society also has chapters in Snohomish, South King, and Pierce Counties and in the Bellevue/Redmond area.

Seattle Public Utilities Creek Steward Program
(206) 684-4163
www.ci.seattle.wa.us/util/urbancreeks/creeksteward.htm
The Creek Steward Program provides opportunities to learn about creek systems and get involved in restoring and sustaining Seattle creeks.

Gardens, Trees, and Plants
Center for Urban Horticulture
(206) 543-8616
www.urbanhort.org
3501 NE 41st St.
Seattle, WA 98105
Plant Answer Line: Call with your gardening questions Monday–Friday 9:00 A.M. to 5:00 P.M. at (206) 897-5268 (206-UW-PLANT).

The Center for Urban Horticulture's mission is to apply horticulture to natural and human-altered landscapes to sustain natural resources and the human spirit. It is the first and largest program in the world devoted to addressing questions about plants in cities. The center manages the plant collections and interpretive programs of the Washington Park Arboretum, comprising more than five thousand species on two hundred acres, as well as its own collections. Volunteers lead tours or teach classes at the arboretum, collect and process herbarium specimens, help to maintain the gardens and natural areas, and assist with plant production, plant records, and seed exchanges.

City of Seattle P-Patch Program
(206) 684-0264
www.cityofseattle.net/neighborhoods/ppatch/default.htm
700 Third Ave., 4th floor
Seattle, WA 98104
More than forty-six hundred urban organic gardeners work on more than nineteen hundred p-patch garden plots on twelve acres of land in the Seattle area. Special programs serve low-income, disabled, youth, and non-English speaking populations. Gardeners supply seven to ten tons of produce to Seattle food banks each year.

Seattle Tilth Association
(206) 633-0097
tilth@seattletilth.org
www.seattletilth.org
4649 Sunnyside Ave. N
Seattle, WA 98103
Seattle Tilth is a volunteer organization of gardeners interested in eco-
logical food production, urban ecology, composting, and recycling. Volunteers can work at educational events and plant sales, teach in the children's
garden, and work in the beautiful association gardens.

Washington Native Plant Society
(206) 527-3210
wnps@blarg.net
www.wnps.org/cps/
7400 Sand Point Way NE
Seattle, WA 98115
The Native Plant Society is a volunteer-run program with nearly nine
hundred members. Volunteers help with bog restoration, trail maintenance,
leading nature walks, and can work in the herbarium on the University of
Washington campus. The chapter conducts an annual Native Plant Stewardship
Program wherein participants receive free training in native plant–related
issues and, in return, provide volunteer service in their community.

Environmental Justice
  Community Coalition for Environmental Justice
  (206) 720-0285
  justice@ccej.org
  www.ccej.org
  105 14th Ave. Suite 2-D
  Seattle, WA 98122
  The Coalition for Environmental Justice is a people-of-color led nonprofit that investigates and educates the public about environmental justice
concerns in the greater Seattle area. Volunteer projects include planting trees
in South Park, reducing local air pollution hazards, and pressing for the closing of incinerators in residential areas.

  EarthCorps
  (206) 322-9296, ext. 217
  www.earthcorps.org
  7400 Sand Point Way NE, Bldg. 30
  Seattle, WA 98115

EarthCorps' mission is to create a global community through local environmental service. Their programs focus on four main areas: environmental restoration, training and education, cross cultural understanding, and volunteerism. Thousands of volunteers work on EarthCorps restoration projects every year.

People for Puget Sound
(206) 382-7007
www.pugetsound.org
911 Western Ave., Suite 580
Seattle, WA 98104
People for Puget Sound promotes actions that benefit the Puget Sound environment and economy. Volunteers speak at community events and participate in restoration projects.

Washington Toxics Coalition
(206) 632-1545, ext. 20
www.watoxics.org
4649 Sunnyside Ave. N, Suite 540E
Seattle, WA 98103
The Washington Toxics Coalition works to reduce society's reliance on toxic chemicals. The Coalition is active on a wide range of issues including pesticide reform, ground water protection, use of household products, and industrial pollution. Volunteers assist in dispensing information and educating civic groups through slide show presentations.

Youth

Earth Service Corps
(206) 382-4966
www.yesc.org
Metrocenter YMCA
909 4th Ave.
Seattle, WA 98104
Earth Service Corps is an innovative program of environmental education, leadership development, and student-organized service to the community. Volunteers help teens organize service projects and educational events.

Student Conservation Association
(206) 324-4649
www.sca-inc.org
1265 S. Main St., Suite 210
Seattle, WA 98144

The SCA fosters environmental stewardship by offering opportunities for education, leadership, and personal development through volunteer work in natural resource management, environmental protection, and conservation. Programs include the High School Program for volunteers sixteen to eighteen years old, the Resource Assistance Program for older volunteers, and the International Youth Program which brings Canadian and U.S. volunteers together on restoration projects.

Teens for Recreation and Environmental Conservation (TREC)
(206) 684-7097
www.seattletrec.org
100 Dexter Ave. N
Seattle, WA 98109

TREC is a program designed to expose multi-ethnic teens to environmental education, conservation, and stewardship, while creating an environment for community leadership and empowerment. Volunteer opportunities include supervising outdoor excursions (backpacking, river rafting, and rock climbing), facilitating plant restoration projects, or conducting science research in Seward Park.

Wilderness Volunteer Corps
(206) 633-1992, ext. 101
wvc@wawild.org
www.wawild.org/youthvolunteer
4649 Sunnyside Ave. N, #520
Seattle, WA 98103

WVC provides low-income and at-risk high school students with challenging wilderness trips, year-round mentoring, urban service opportunities, and individual support in their lives at school and at home. During the school year, volunteers help Seattle high school students with service projects focused on environmental justice.

NATURE CENTERS IN THE SEATTLE AREA

Carkeek Park
(206) 684-0877
carkeek@ci.seattle.wa.us
www.cityofseattle.net/parks/parkspaces/carkeek.htm

The Environmental Education Center here offers free and low-cost environmental education classes for children and adults.

Camp Long
(206) 684-7434
www.camplong.org
On Saturdays throughout most of the year, individuals and families can join a park naturalist for a free interpretive walk or rock climbing class.

Discovery Park
(206) 386-4236
www.cityofseattle.net/parks/Environment/discovparkevents.htm
discovery@ci.seattle.wa.us
Take a guided beach walk, go on a meadow safari, or join the Adopt-an-Area stewardship program.

Seward Park
(206) 684-4396
parksinfo@ci.seattle.wa.us
www.cityofseattle.net/parks/parkspaces/sewardpark.htm
The nature center leads programs on urban owls, eagles, bats, and more.

CITY OF SEATTLE URBAN FOREST AND TRAILS PROGRAMS

Nature in the city wouldn't happen without these programs. If you're interested in urban forest restoration or would like more information on Seattle Parks trails, visit Seattle Parks and Recreation at the following websites, or call (206) 684-4075 for more information.

Seattle Parks Urban Forest Restoration
www.cityofseattle.net/parks/horticulture/forestrestoration.htm
Seattle Parks Trails Program
www.cityofseattle.net/parks/environment/trails/trailsprogram.htm

SELECTED READING LIST

A list of all the enticing natural history books out there would be a book in itself. The sampling here includes those that were most useful to our research, and our favorites, old and new. Most, if not all of these books are available through Seattle Public or King County libraries. Plus, the well-stocked shelves of Pioneer Square's Flora and Fauna Books qualify as an honorary field trip.

Local Natural History

Kruckeberg, Arthur R. *The Natural History of Puget Sound Country.* Seattle: University of Washington Press, 1995.

Larson, Suzanne B. *"Dig the Ditch!" The History of the Lake Washington Ship Canal.* Seattle: Western Interstate Commission for Higher Education, 1975.

Laskin, David. *Rains All the Time: A Connoisseur's History of Weather in the Pacific Northwest.* Seattle: Sasquatch Books, 1997.

Saling, Ann. *The Great Northwest Nature Factbook.* Seattle: Alaska Northwest Books, 1991.

General Field Guides

Alden, Peter. *National Audubon Society Field Guide to the Pacific Northwest.* New York: Knopf, 1998.

Kozloff, Eugene. *Plants and Animals of the Pacific Northwest.* Seattle: University of Washington Press, 1978.

Matthews, Daniel. *Cascade-Olympic Natural History: A Trailside Reference.* Portland, Oregon: Raven Editions, 1999.

Plants and Fungi

Arno, Stephen F., and Ramona Hammerly. *Northwest Trees.* Seattle: Mountaineers Books, 1977.

Arora, David. *All That the Rain Promises and More . . . : A Hip Pocket Guide to Western Mushrooms.* Berkeley, California: Ten Speed Press, 1991.

Cooke, Sarah Spear, ed. *A Field Guide to the Common Wetland Plants of Western Washington and Northwestern Oregon.* Seattle: Seattle Audubon Society, 1997.

Jacobson, Arthur Lee. *Trees of Seattle: The Complete Tree-Finder's Guide to the City's 740 Varieties.* Seattle: Sasquatch Books, 1990.

Jacobson, Arthur Lee. *Wild Plants of Greater Seattle.* Seattle, 2001.

Kruckeberg, Arthur R. *Gardening with Native Plants of the Pacific Northwest.* Seattle: University of Washington Press, 1996.

Link, Russell. *Landscaping for Wildlife in the Pacific Northwest.* Seattle: University of Washington Press, in association with the Washington Department of Fish and Wildlife, 1999.

McKenny, Margaret et al. *The New Savory Wild Mushroom.* Seattle: University of Washington Press, 1987.

Moore, Michael. *Medicinal Plants of the Pacific West.* Sante Fe: Red Crane Books, 1995.

Pojar, Jim, and Andy MacKinnon. *Plants of the Pacific Northwest Coast*. Redmond, Washington: Lone Pine, 1994.

Taylor, Ronald. *Northwest Weeds*. Missoula, Montana: Mountain Press Publishing Company, 1990.

Vitt, Dale H., Janet E. Marsh, and Robin B. Bovey. *Mosses, Lichens and Ferns of Northwest North America*. Renton, Washington: Lone Pine Publishing, 1991.

Geology

Alt, David, and Donald Hyndman. *Roadside Geology of Washington*. Missoula, Montana: Mountain Press Publishing Company, 1998.

Birds

Field Guide to the Birds of North America. 4th Edition. National Geographic Society, 2002.

Fisher, Chris C. *Birds of Seattle and Puget Sound*. Renton, Washington: Lone Pine Publishing, 1996.

Kaufman, Kenn. *Birds of North America*. New York: Houghton Mifflin, 2000.

Sibley, David Allen. *The Sibley Guide to Bird Life and Behavior*. New York: Alfred A. Knopf, 2001.

Sibley, David Allen. *The Sibley Guide to Birds*. New York: Alfred A. Knopf, 2000.

Other Animals

Arnett, Ross, and Richard Jacques. *Simon and Schuster's Guide to Insects*. New York: Simon and Schuster, 1981.

Brown, Herbert et al. *Reptiles of Washington and Oregon*. Seattle: Seattle Audubon Society, 1995.

Corkran, Charlotte C., and Chris Thoms. *Amphibians of Oregon, Washington and British Columbia: A Field Identification Guide*. Renton, Washington: Lone Pine Publishing, 1996.

Eder, Tamara. *Mammals of Washington and Oregon*. Renton, Washington: Lone Pine Publishing, 2002.

Levi, Herbert. *Spiders and Their Kin*. New York: Golden Press, 1987.

Maser, Chris. *Mammals of the Pacific Northwest: From the Coast to the High Cascades*. Corvallis: Oregon State University Press, 1998.

Mitchell, Robert T. et al. *Butterflies and Moths: A Golden Nature Guide*. New York: Golden Press, 2001.

Paulson, Dennis. *Dragonflies of Washington*. Seattle: Seattle Audubon Society, 1999.

Pyle, Robert Michael. *The Butterflies of Cascadia*. Seattle: Seattle Audubon Society, 2002.

Sea Life

Angell, Tony, and Kenneth C. Balcomb III. *Marine Birds and Mammals of Puget Sound*. Seattle: University of Washington Press, 1982.

Harbo, Rick. *Shells and Shellfish of the Pacific Northwest*. Madiera, British Columbia: Harbour Publishing, 1997.

Kozloff, Eugene. *Marine Invertebrates of the Pacific Northwest*. Seattle: University of Washington Press, 1987.

Kozloff, Eugene. *Seashore Life of the Northern Pacific Coast*. Seattle: University of Washington Press, 1993.

Osborne, Richard. *A Guide to the Marine Mammals of Greater Puget Sound*. Anacortes, Washington: Island Publishers, 1988.

Creative Nonfiction and Poetry

Egan, Timothy. *The Good Rain*. New York: Random House, 1990.

Haupt, Lyanda Lynn. *Rare Encounters with Ordinary Birds: Notes from a Northwest Year*. Seattle: Sasquatch Books, 2001.

Hugo, Richard. *Making Certain it Goes On: The Collected Poems of Richard Hugo*. New York: W. W. Norton and Co., 1991.

Levertov, Denise. *The Life Around Us: Selected Poems on Nature*. New York: New Directions, 1997.

Luoma, Jon R. *The Hidden Forest*. New York: Henry Holt and Company, 1999.

Peterson, Brenda. *Living by Water: True Stories of Nature and Spirit*. New York: Fawcett Columbine, 1994.

Pyle, Robert Michael. *The Thunder Tree: Lessons from an Urban Wildland*. New York: Lyons Press, 1993.

Roethke, Theodore. *The Collected Poems of Theodore Roethke*. New York: Anchor Books, 1975.

Children's Books

Arnold, Katya, and Sam Swope. *Katya's Book of Mushrooms*. New York: Henry Holt and Co., 1997.

Birman, Linda. *Stewart: The Skyscraper Falcon*. Surrey, British Columbia: Hancock House, 1997.

Bjork, Christina, and Lena Anderson. *Linnea's Almanac*. New York: Farrar Straus & Giroux, 1989.

Boring, Mel, and Linda Garrow. *Birds, Nests, and Eggs*. Milwaukee, Wisconsin: Gareth Stevens Publishing, 1998.

Swanson, Diane. *Safari Beneath the Sea: The Wonder World of the North Pacific Coast*. San Francisco: Sierra Club Books for Children, 1994.

Weidensaul, Scott. *Birds, National Audubon Society First Field Guides*. New York: Scholastic, 1998.

NAME	TELEPHONE	BEST TIME TO GO	REST-ROOMS	DISTANCE/TERRAIN (TOURS ONLY)*
1. Seattle to Bainbridge Island: The Watery Wilderness	(206) 464-6400	Spring-Fall	Yes	*1 hour 10 minute round-trip ride
2. Danny Woo International District Community Gardens	(206) 624-1802	Summer-Fall	No	Less than 1 mile, dirt paths
3. Suite 5600: Peregrine Penthouse	(206) 461-6475	Spring	Yes	NA
4. Space Needle: Cloud Viewing	(206) 905-2100	Spring	Yes	NA
5. On (and Under) the Water-front: Myrtle Edwards and Elliott Bay Parks	(206) 684-4075	Fall-Winter	Yes	1.25 miles, path
6. Frink Park: Woodland Revival	(206) 684-4075	Spring-Summer	No	*0.75 mile loop/steep trails
7. Washington Park Arboretum Winter Garden	(206) 543-8800	Winter	Yes	Less than 1 mile, paths
8. Nora's Woods: Hushed Tribute	(206) 684-4075	Winter-Spring	No	Less than 1 mile, trails
9. Interlaken Park: Making Natural History	(206) 684-4075	Winter-Spring	No	1 mile or more, paved and dirt trails
10. Walking the Boulevard	(206) 684-4075	Clear days	No	*4 RT or 4.5-mile loop/sidewalks
11. Good Tiding: Beach Walk at Discovery Park	(206) 386-4236	Low tide, year-round	Yes	*About 3 miles/trails, sidewalk, beach
12. Kiwanis Ravine Heron Colony	(206) 684-4075	Spring	No	NA
13. Magnolia's Madrones	(206) 684-4075	Summer-Fall	No	1 mile RT
14. Eternal Bloom	(206) 282-1270	Fall-Winter	No	Less than 1 mile/paved, grass
15. Carkeek Park Salmon	(206) 684-0877	Fall	Yes	*Under a mile or more/beach, path
16. The Big Dig: Hiram M. Chittenden Locks	(206) 783-7059	Late Summer-Fall	Yes	*Less than 1 mile/sidewalks
17. Shilshole Bay: Sea Lions	(206) 684-7249	Late Summer-Spring	Yes	Short dock + 87.8 acre beach/park
18. Paddling Lake Washington	(206) 543-9433	Spring-Summer	at dock	NA/boating
19. Green Lake's Birding Bounty	(206) 684-4075	Year-round	Yes	*2.8-mile circuit/flat path
20. Raising the Dead: Ravenna	(206) 684-4075	Year-round	Yes	Less than 2 miles of trail
21. Green Days: UW Campus	(206) 543-2100	Spring-Fall	Yes	4+ miles avail./sidewalk, grass
22. Reclaiming Paradise: Union Bay	(206) 543-8616	Fall-Spring	Yes	50 acres with gravel and dirt trails
23. Dead Horse Canyon: Wild Plant Walk	(206) 684-4075	Fall	No	*0.5-mile loop/steep in parts
24. Kubota Garden: Idealized Nature	(206) 684-4584	Winter-Spring	Yes	*About 1 mile, mostly gravel paths
25. Bradner Gardens Park: Waiting for Butterflies	(206) 684-4075	Summer-Fall	Yes	Less than 1 mile, sidewalk, paths
26. Seward Park Natural History: From Bedrock to Eagles	(206) 684-4396	Spring	Yes	1 mile or more, some steep trails
27. Dearborn Park Elementary School	(206) 252-6930	Fall-Spring	No	Less than 1 mile, trails
28. West Seattle Beach Chronicles	(206) 684-4075	Low tide, year-round	No	*2 miles/sidewalk and beach
29. Duwamish River Restoration Bike Tour	(206) 382-7007	Summer-Fall	No	*4.5 miles, bike paths and streets
30. Mushrooming at Camp Long	(206) 684-7434	Fall	Yes	1 mile or more, trails

DOGS OK	WHEELCHAIR	BEST FOR KIDS	SPECIAL FEATURES	PLAYGROUND
In cars only	Yes	X	Puget Sound views, ferry ride, birding	
On leash	Partial		Gardens, city view	
No	Yes	X	Peregrines	
No	Yes	X	Views	
On leash	Yes	X	Puget Sound views, fishing, birding	X
On leash	No		Forest, wetlands, stream	
On leash	Yes	X	Gardens, birding	
On leash	Partial		Native plants	
On leash	Partial		Forest, stream, birding	
On leash	Yes		Views, trees	
Not on beach	Partial	X	Beach, tide pools	X
On leash	Yes	X	Heron colony	
On leash	Yes		Views, madrones	
Discouraged	Yes		Lichens, trees	
On leash	Partial	X	Beach, creek, salmon	X
On leash	Yes	X	Salmon, garden	
On leash	Yes	X	Beach, sea lions	X
Yes	Partial	X	Boating, birds	
On leash	Yes	X	Birding, trees, lake	X
On leash	Partial	X	Wooded ravine, creek	X
On leash	Yes		Trees, observatory, herb garden	
On leash	Yes		Birding, open meadow	
On leash	No	X	Forest, creek	
On leash	Yes		Gardens, waterfall, creek	
On leash	Yes	X	Gardens, city view	
On leash	Partial	X	Old-growth, Lake Washington access	X
On leash	Partial	X	Forest, wetlands	
On leash	Partial	X	Beach, views, birding	
On leash	Partial		River, birding, salmon	
On leash	Partial	X	Forest, creek	

NAME	TELEPHONE	BEST TIME TO GO	REST-ROOMS	DISTANCE/TERRAIN (TOURS ONLY)*
31. Roxhill Bog: Headwaters of a Legacy	(206) 233-2046	Spring-Fall	Yes	Less than 1 mile, gravel paths
32. Schmitz Park Preserve: Seattle's Forest Past	(206) 684-4075	Year-round	No	1 mile or more, trails
33. Wide Open Spaces: Magnuson	(206) 684-4946	Year-round	Yes	*3+ mile RT/dirt trails and paved path
34. Places for Pondering: Meadowbrook	(206) 684-7522	Summer-Fall	Yes	*About 0.75 mile, paths and paved
35. Evening Chorus at Paramount	(206) 546-5041	Spring-Summer	No	Less than 1 mile/woodchip paths
36. North Seattle Community College	(206) 528-4597	Year-round	Yes	Less than 1 mile/sidewalks, paths
37. Renton: Waterworks Gardens	(206) 684-2400	Fall	No	Less than 1 mile, gravel paths, trails
38. Vashon Island: Winter Bird Wonderland	None	Fall-Spring	No	Less than 1 mile, trails
39. Bainbridge Island: IslandWood	(206) 855-4333	Year-round	Yes	1 mile or more, trails
40. Bellevue: Wild Wetland in Mercer Slough	(425) 452-2752	Year-round	Yes	5+ miles avail./boardwalks, trails
41. Kirkland: Orion's Lush Legacy	(206) 296-4232	Summer-Fall	Yes	About 2 miles/boardwalk, rugged trail
42. Everett: Jetty Island	(425) 257-8304	Summer	Yes	2+ miles avail./paths, beach
43. Everett: Spencer Island	(425) 388-6600	Year-round	Langus Pk	3.5-mile loop/boardwalk, dirt trail

*Those distances with an asterisk are the total distance of the outing as mapped. Those without offer the total amount of trail available.

DOGS OK	WHEELCHAIR	BEST FOR KIDS	SPECIAL FEATURES	PLAYGROUND ACCESSIBLE
On leash	Yes	X	Wetland, bog plants, birding	X
On leash	Partial	X	Old growth, stream, birding	
On leash	Mostly		Lakeshore, meadows, trees	
On leash	Partial	X	Creek, pond, artwork	
On leash	Partial	X	Frogs, ponds	
On leash	Partial		Wetand, waterfowl	
On leash	Yes	X	Gardens, wetlands, heron colony	
On leash	Partial		Island, birding, forest trails	
No	Partial		Forest, creek, bog, marsh, pond	
On leash	Yes	X	Slough, wildlife	
Not on beach	To Beach		Dense forest, creek, beach	
No	Partial	X	Beach, lagoon, shorebirds	
North end only	Partial		Island, estuary, bird habitat	

INDEX

A alcids, 23
alder, red, 163
alga, algae, 27, 65, 97
Alki Point, 19, 78, 79, 185, 186, 188, 192
anemones, 86–87
Aquarium, Seattle, 26, 42, 192
arachnids, 124–126
arrowhead (wapato, duck potato), 178, 233
Astronomical Society, Seattle, 146
avens, large-leaved, 164
Avenue of Stars, 189

B Backyard Wildlife Sanctuaries, 69–71
Bailey Peninsula, 157, 175, 178, 179
Bainbridge Island, 166, 188, 257–258, 280
Ballard, 103, 116, 124, 202
barnacles, 84
bats, 63, 67–69, 141, 157, 186, 205
Bat Conservation International, 69
Bats Northwest, 69
beaches: Bainbridge Island, 258; Carkeek
Park, 104–105; Discovery Park, 82–89;
Golden Gardens Park, 120–123; Jetty
Island, 263–265; Me–Kwa–Mooks, 186,
191–192; O.O Denny Park, 262–263;
Vashon Island, 255–256; West Seattle,
186–192
Beacon Hill, 73, 116, 195
bear, black, 12, 30, 78
beaver, American, 129, 135, 176, 178–179
Bellevue, 259–260
birds: feeding flock, 138; hawking behavior,
57; migration, 249–250, nesting, 16, 22,
33–36, 56–57, 62, 69, 71, 81, 88–89,
90–92, 95, 97, 100, 132, 135, 138–141,
152–153, 168, 175–177, 190, 200–201,
205, 228–231, 249, 255, 262; rare, 151
Black River Riparian Forest Heron Colony, 255
Blake Island, 79
blackberries, 82, 224, 229, 245–246
blackbirds, red–winged, 137–138, 140
(gaping behavior), 201, 212; Brewer's 139
Blakely Harbor Park, 258
boating, 130, 200, 258, 259, 262, 263, 266
bugs, 133,192, 209–212, 211 (bog plants),
243, 258, 259
Botanical Gardens, Carl S. English Jr., 113
Bradner Gardens Park, 171–174, 278
Burke Museum, 125, 145
Burke–Gilman Trail, 116, 154
Burton Acres Park, 257
bushtits, 50, 135, 138, 151, 205
butterflies, butterfly gardens, 171–174, 261
Butterfly Association, Washington, 172

C Camp Long, 79, 101, 179, 186, 191, 273
Capitol Hill, 30, 38, 45, 48, 53, 60, 63–65,
73, 97, 151, 154
Carkeek Park, 104–111, 105, 272, 278
Carkeek Watershed Community Action
Project, 108
Cascade Mountain Range, 12, 38, 77, 84, 97,
168, 170, 249
cattails, 57, 131–132, 140, 178, 196
Cedar River Watershed, 30
cedar, Western red, 99, 163, 217, 220
Center for Urban Horticulture, 149, 150, 152, 269
cetaceans: Dall's porpoise, 24–25; harbor
porpoise, 25; orca whale, 25, 26, 28, 84, 122
cherry trees, 64, 65, 136, 145
chestnut, Spanish, 94
chitons, 85, 192
Colman Pool, 192
coltsfoot, 160
Constellation Park and Marine Reserve, 186,
189–190
coots, American, 11, 137, 138
Cormorant Cove Park, 186, 190–191
cormorants, 83–84, 190
cougars, 30, 84
coyotes, 83, 260
crabs, 25, 85, 124
creeks and creek restoration: Denny, 262;
Hamm, 197; Mahteen, 74; Mapes, 166–
167, 166, 170; Mohlendorph, 105, 106;
Longfellow, 202, 212, 213; Piper's, 103,
104–110, 105; Puget, 200; Ravenna, 129,
132, 142–43; Ross, 103, 115, 117; Taylor,
158–159; Thornton, 112, 223, 233, 236,
238, 240, 245, 248; Venema, 105, 106, 112
crows: 81, 95, 205 (nesting), 135 (roosting)
crustaceans, 27, 84

D damselflies, 234–235
Danny Woo International District
Community Gardens, 30–32, 278
Dead Horse Canyon, 158–164, 159, 278
Dearborn Park Elementary School, 180–183,
278
Denny Creek Alliance, 262
Denny Creek, 262
Denny Hill, 19, 64, 73, 76
Department of Fish and Wildlife, 67, 69, 71,
122, 177, 267
Discovery Park, 82–89, 83, 100–101, 174,
179, 273, 278
dove, rock, 36, 41
dragonflies, 234–235
duck, harlequin, 191

Duwamish River, 13, 19, 21–22, 91, 116–117, 193, 194, 198–199, 212, 278

E eagle, bald, 88, 89, 112, 139, 176–177, 177 (habitat preservation), 201, 260, 262
eelgrass, 88, 256
Elliott Bay, 13, 21, 22, 26, 79
Elliott Bay Park, 40–43, 278
Emerald Necklace, 48, 60
Everett, 121, 263–267

F falcon, peregrine, 33–35, 41, 205, 278
Falcon Research Group, 33
ferns: deer, 59; licorice, 163; sword, 161, 182
fir, Douglas, 176, 188, 204, 217, 219
Fisherman's Terminal, 35, 73
fishing, 41, 139, 201
flickers, Northern, 62, 95, 151
forests, old-growth, 52, 62, 164, 176, 217
Foster Island, 131, 132, 134, 135
fox, red, 205, 208, 212, 217
Fremont Cut, 114, 117
fringecup, 61, 217
Frink Park, 46–52, 47, 278
frogs, 231, 239–242, 246; bullfrogs 135, 241, 246
fungi, 49, 94, 146, (see also Mushrooms)

G gardening for wildlife: 204, 218–219; urban gardening, 151, 152, 230, 261, 269–270; (see also Backyard Wildlife Sanctuaries)
gardens: Bradner Gardens Park, 171–174, 278; butterfly gardens, 171–174, 228, 261; Carl S. English Junior Botanical Gardens, 113; Cascade Garden of Happiness, 29; Danny Woo International District Community Gardens, 30–32, 278; Greek Garden, 145; Japanese Garden, 55; Japanese gardening, 165, 166, 167, 168, 170; Kubota Gardens, 165–171, 278; Medicinal Herb Garden, 144, 146; Parsons Gardens, 78–79; p–patches, 29; Renton Waterworks Gardens, 253–255, 280; Sound Garden, 230; Washington Park Arboretum Winter Garden, 54–56, 278; Woodland Park Rose Garden, 111–112
Gas Works Park, 116
Golden Gardens Park, 103, 120–123
goldeneye, Barrow's, 191
goldfinch, American, 152
geese: Brant, 191; Canada, 139, 247–248, 249
gopher, Western pocket, 63
grebes: pied–billed 135, 137, 140–141; Western 249, 256, 278
Green Lake Park, 53, 68, 136–142, 137, 146, 152
guillemot, pigeon, 23, 89
gulls, 22–23, 137, 141, 249

H Hamm Creek City Light, 194, 197

Harbor Island, 116, 199, 200
hawks: Cooper's, 41, 229; red–tailed, 35, 41, 229; sharp–shinned, 59, 229, 249
hazelnut, 50, 182
hemlock, Western, 217, 220
Herbarium, University of Washington, 146
Heritage Tree Program, 64
herons: 150 (baitfishing); great blue, 90–92, 129, 132, 136, 137, 149, 255, 260, 278; green, 129, 132, 152, 260
herring, 22 (herring balls), 41, 200, 256
Herring's House Park, 193, 194, 200–201
Herschel, 121–122
honeysuckle, 55, 174
horsetail, 109, 160, 167
huckleberry, red, 164
hummingbirds: 56–57, 95; Anna's, 172, 228; rufous, 150–151, 200, 250

I Indian plum, 110, 182
insects, 35, 57, 67, 95, 109, 139, 140, 143, 150, 172–174, 197, 211, 234–235, 250
Interbay, 73, 74
Interlaken Park, 60–63, 64, 65, 278
International Dark Skies Association, 147
invasive species, 51, 61, 123–124, 149
IslandWood, 257–258, 280
Ivy OUT, 51

J jay, Steller's, 49, 50
jellyfish, 23–24, 27, 86
Jetty Island, 263–265, 280

K Kellogg Island, 194, 200
Kerry Park, 73, 74, 75, 76
killdeer, 211, 229
kingfishers, 89, 228
kinnikinnick, 49
Kiwanis Ravine Heron Colony, 90–92, 278
Kiwanis Ravine Heron Habitat Helpers, 92
kokanee, 157
Kubota Garden, 165–171, 166, 278

L lahars, 77
Lake Hills Greenbelt, 261
Lake to Lake Trail, 261
Lake Union, 13, 28–29, 103, 114, 117, 226
Lake View Cemetery, 64, 97
Lake Washington, 13, 19, 45, 48, 49, 52, 53, 59, 60, 65–66, 114, 116, 117, 119, 122, 130–135, 148, 157, 160, 198, 223, 226, 231, 237, 259, 261, 262, 278
landslides, 48, 63, 77, 185, 189
lichens, 96–99
Licton Springs, 233, 247
light pollution, 147–148
Lighthouse, West Point, 84
limpets, 85

Little Tahoma, 78
Locks, Hiram M. Chittenden, 113–119, 114, 121–122, 278
Longfellow Creek Legacy Trail, 212–213

M madrones, 52, 92–95
Magnolia Boulevard Viewpoints, 93
magnolia, 53, 73, 82–89, 90–92, 124, 188, 278
Magnuson Environmental Stewardship Alliance (MESA), 224–228
Magnuson Park, 101, 223, 224–231, 225, 280
Mahteen Creek, 74
mammoth, Columbian, 191
Mapes Creek, 166–167, 166, 170
maple, bigleaf, 161, 163
marine mammals, (see Cetaceans)
Marshall Park, 75, 79
Meadowbrook, 232–238, 233, 248, 280
Medicinal Herb Garden, 145–146
Me–Kwa–Mooks Park, 186, 191–192
Mercer Slough, 259–261, 280
merlins, 95
middens, shell, 26, 80, 185, 192, 200
milfoil, 123, 153
millipedes, 217, 218
Mohlendoph Creek, 105, 106
Montlake Fill, 132, 148–152
moon snails, 89
moths, 124, 172, 174
Mount Pleasant Cemetery, 75, 96–99, 278
Mount Rainier, 37, 76, 77, 78, 80, 144, 145, 228
Mount St. Helens, 227, 228
mountain beavers, 110, 178–179
murre, common, 23
mushrooms, 83, 202–205, 278
muskrats, 87, 135, 179, 236
Mycological Society, Puget Sound, 203
mycorrhizae, 218–219
mycelia, 203
Myrtle Edwards Park, 35, 40–43, 278

N Native Plant Society, Washington, 270
nature centers, 272–273
nettles, 86, 160, 179, 182, 205
NOAA (National Oceanic and Atmospheric Administration), 25, 225, 226, 230, 231
Nora's Woods, 57–59, 278
North Seattle Community College, 242–246, 248, 280
North Wind's Weir, 195, 196
nudibranchs, 192
nurse logs, 164, 217

O Observatory, University of Washington, 130, 144–145, 146
octopuses, 26, 42, 43, 189, 192
Olmsted Brothers, 30, 50, 52, 53, 60, 62, 63, 65, 45, 48, 74, 76, 80, 136

Olympic Mountain Range, 31, 37, 41, 76, 79, 80, 93, 120, 191, 227
Olympic Sculpture Park, Seattle Art Museum, 43
opossums, 66–67
Oregon grape, 54
O.O. Denny Park, 261–263, 280
ospreys, 190, 200, 201
otters, 179, 193, 267
owls, 100–101, 135, 152, 157, 166, 175, 205, 217, 230–231, 258, 262

P Pacific Flyway, 249–250
Pacific Water Sports, 200
Paramount Park, 239–242, 248, 280
parrots, 176
Parsons Gardens, 75, 78–79
People for Puget Sound, 27, 271
periwinkles, 85
pesticides, 26–27, 35, 112, 172, 177, 208, 271
pigeon, band–tailed, 36, 62
piggy–back plant, 161
Pioneer Square, 19, 40, 273
Piper's Creek, 103, 104–110, 105
plankton, 27–28, 84
polypores, 49, 204
pond life, 234–235
Potlatch Meadows, 78
Powwow Tree, 78, 99
p–patches, 29, 31, 171, 269
Puget Creek, 200
Puget Lobe, 78, 87, 152, 243

Q quail, California, 228, 230
Queen Anne, 53, 73–74, 74–81, 96–99
Queen Anne Boulevard, 74–76, 75

R rabbits, 111
raccoons, 66–67
rats, 66
Ravenna Creek, 129, 132, 142–43
Ravenna Creek Alliance, 143
Ravenna Park, 129, 142–143, 278
recycling, 170, 217, 218, 270
Reflective Refuge, 237, 238
rhododendrons, 50, 59, 93
rodents, 79, 81, 87, 110, 151, 178–179, 208, 236
Ross Creek, 103, 115, 117
Roxhill Bog, 209–212, 280

S salamanders, 108, 205, 206–208, 241–242, 245, 246, 258
Salmon Bay, 73, 74, 103, 114, 124
salmon, 22, 25, 26, 27, 30, 41, 88, 104–108, 112, 117, 118, 119 (ID chart), 132, 159, 195–198, 200, 212–213, 235, 248, 260, 262, 266, 278

sand dollar, 190, 192
Sand Point Magnuson Park, 223, 224–231, 225, 280
sapsucker, Red–breasted, 137, 141
Sarvey Wildlife Center, 68
Save Magnolia's Madrones, 93
Scarab Society, The, 126
Schmitz Park Preserve, 125, 190, 214–217, 219, 280
scotch broom, 123
sea cucumbers, 27, 192
sea lions, 24, 84, 103, 120–122, 229, 278
sea stars, 85, 88, 189
seals, 24, 84, 122, 198, 229
Sealth, Chief 19, 21, 79
Seattle Fault, 175, 188–189, 192
Seattle Metro, 65–66, 87
Seattle Parks and Recreation, 69, 106, 109, 141, 158, 166, 215, 273
seaweed, 192
sedge, 196, 211, 233
Seola Park, 93
Seward Park, 45, 53, 69, 93, 101, 157, 175–179, 273, 278
shellfish, 26–27, 28, 42, 80, 89, 185, 197 (clam "necklaces"), 200
Shilshole Bay, 120–122, 278
Shilshole Marina, 103
Shoreline Street Ends, 201–202
skunk cabbage, 143, 182, 215, 260
slugs, 205, 217, 218, 219
snags, 69, 137, 141, 177, 201, 217, 240
snails, 85, 89
snakes, 205, 242
Snohomish River, 265, 266
Space Needle, 37–38, 76, 78, 278
sparrows, 71, 200, 230
Spencer Island, 266–267, 280
spiders, 124–126
springs, 49, 73, 94, 142–143, 223, 233, 235, 240, 246, 247
squids, 41–42
squirrels, 79, 80–81, 151
starlings, 33, 35, 71, 136, 140, 200
stars, 146, 147–148, 174, 189
steelhead, 118, 121, 122, 195, 260
strawberries, 59, 259
sturgeons, 132–133
sundials, 154
sundew, round–leaved, 211–212
sunflower stars, 85
Sunset Hill, 120
sweet box, 55

T Taylor Creek, 158–159
thimbleberries, 182
Thornton Creek, 112, 223, 233, 236, 238, 240, 245, 248

thrushes: Swainson's, 262; varied, 249, 262
tides: 21–22, 86, 106, 115, 195, 196, 197; red, 28; flats/lands, 26, 74, 80, 117, 201; pooling, 82–89, 187, 189, 190, 191, 192; records, 25; zones, 84
towhee, spotted, 52
tree frogs, Pacific, 109, 205, 231, 239–242, 245, 246
trees: Capitol Hill, 63–65; conifer ID, 219–220; Green Lake, 136–137; Heritage Tree Program, 64; madrones, 92–95; Powwow Tree, 99; Seattle's oldest, 176; University of Washington Brockman Memorial Tree Tour, 144–145; (see also individual parks)
Turning Basin, 194, 196–197
turtles, 134–135, 149, 231

U Union Bay Natural Area, 132, 148–152, 278
Union Bay, 130–133
University of Washington Campus, 129, 144–146

V Vashon Island, 255–257, 280
Vashon till, 78
Venema Creek, 105, 106, 112
viburnum, 55
volcanoes, 77, 189
Volunteer Park, 45, 53, 64, 65
vulture, turkey, 79

W Washington Park Arboretum, 45, 54–57, 131, 133–134, 278
Washington State Ferries, 21
Washington Trout (organization), 107, 108
water striders, 234
waterfalls, 40, 52, 168, 169, 170
Waterfront Activities Center, University of Washington, 130, 131
Waterworks Gardens, 253–255
waxwing, cedar, 235–236
weather, 37–39, 191, 226–227
Weather Watch Park, 186, 191
Wedgwood Boulder, 243–244
West Point Sewage Treatment Plant, 74, 87, 143, 188
West Queen Anne Wall, 75, 80
Wetlands Network, Washington State, 206
wigeons, 138–139
Winter Garden, Washington Park Arboretum, 54–56, 278
witch hazel, 54, 55
Woodland Park, 53, 100, 111–112
woodpeckers, 52, 62, 95, 141, 150, 151, 175, 205, 258
wren, Bewick's, 62, 63

Z Zoo, Woodland Park, 111–112, 135, 139

ABOUT THE AUTHORS

MARIA DOLAN is an essayist and nonfiction writer in Seattle. She has written for *Salon.com*, *Seattle Weekly*, *Seattle Magazine*, *Audubon*, and elsewhere. As a former research assistant for nonfiction books and articles, she investigated topics from biometeorology to professional volleyball. Her favorite mode of transportation is her sea kayak, which has kept her buoyant in such wild places as Glacier Bay, Alaska, Desolation Sound, British Columbia, and the bustling waters of Lake Union. An avid supporter of outdoor urban life, she is a backyard gardener and a member of Seattle's organic gardening organization, Seattle Tilth. She also belongs to the Washington Water Trails Association, which promotes small craft access to local waterways.

KATHRYN TRUE lives with her family on Vashon Island near Seattle. Before starting her own writing and editing business, she was associate editor of *In Context* (now called *Yes!*), a journal that explores sustainability issues. Her writing has appeared in *Simple Living*, *Seattle Weekly*, and the *Seattle Times*. She was the editor of Seattle Tilth's *Maritime Northwest Garden Guide*. Kathryn writes to help people find their connection to the natural world. She is active in her local Audubon chapter, and spends her free time visiting forests in the rain and beachcombing Puget Sound shores with her husband and young daughter.

Kathryn True and Maria Dolan

THE MOUNTAINEERS, founded in 1906, is a nonprofit outdoor activity and conservation club, whose mission is "to explore, study, preserve, and enjoy the natural beauty of the outdoors. . . . " Based in Seattle, Washington, the club is now the third-largest such organization in the United States, with 15,000 members and five branches throughout Washington State.

The Mountaineers sponsors both classes and year-round outdoor activities in the Pacific Northwest, which include hiking, mountain climbing, ski-touring, snowshoeing, bicycling, camping, kayaking and canoeing, nature study, sailing, and adventure travel. The club's conservation division supports environmental causes through educational activities, sponsoring legislation, and presenting informational programs. All club activities are led by skilled, experienced volunteers, who are dedicated to promoting safe and responsible enjoyment and preservation of the outdoors.

If you would like to participate in these organized outdoor activities or the club's programs, consider a membership in The Mountaineers. For information and an application, write or call The Mountaineers, Club Headquarters, 300 Third Avenue West, Seattle, WA 98119; 206-284-6310.

The Mountaineers Books, an active, nonprofit publishing program of the club, produces guidebooks, instructional texts, historical works, natural history guides, and works on environmental conservation. All books produced by The Mountaineers Books fulfill the club's mission.

Send or call for our catalog of more than 500 outdoor titles:

The Mountaineers Books
1001 SW Klickitat Way, Suite 201
Seattle, WA 98134
800-553-4453
mbooks@mountaineersbooks.org
www.mountaineersbooks.org

The Mountaineers Books is proud to be a corporate sponsor of Leave No Trace, whose mission is to promote and inspire responsible outdoor recreation through education, research, and partnerships. The Leave No Trace program is focused specifically on human-powered (nonmotorized) recreation.

Leave No Trace strives to educate visitors about the nature of their recreational impacts, as well as offer techniques to prevent and minimize such impacts. Leave No Trace is best understood as an educational and ethical program, not as a set of rules and regulations.

For more information, visit www.LNT.org, or call 800-332-4100.

Other titles you might enjoy from The Mountaineers Books

These books are available at fine bookstores and outdoor stores, by phone at (800) 553-4453, or on the Internet at www.mountaineersbooks.org.

Animal Tracks of the Pacific Northwest by Karen Pandell and Chris Stall. $6.95 paperbound. 0-89886-012-1.

Mac's Field Guide: Northwest Park/Backyard Birds by Craig McGowan, illustrations by David Sauskojus. $4.95 laminated card. 0-89886-246-9.

Northwest Trees by Stephen F. Arno and Ramona P. Hammerly. $14.95 paperbound. 0-916890-50-3.

Washington State Parks: A Complete Recreation Guide, 2nd Edition by Marge and Ted Mueller. $16.95 paperbound. 0-89886-642-1.

Best Hikes with Children® in Western Washington & the Cascades, Volume 1, 2nd Edition by Joan Burton. $14.95 paperbound. 0-89886-564-6.

Best Hikes with Children® in Western Washington & the Cascades, Volume 2, 2nd Edition by Joan Burton. $14.95 paperbound. 0-89886-626-X.

Kids in the Wild: A Family Guide to Outdoor Recreation by Cindy Ross and Todd Gladfelter. $12.95 paperbound. 0-89886-447-X.

Best Winter Walks and Hikes: Puget Sound, 2nd Edition by Harvey Manning and Ira Spring. $15.95 paperbound. 0-89886-822-X.

Best Short Hikes in™ Washington's North Cascades & San Juan Islands, 2nd Edition by E.M. Sterling. $14.95 paperbound. 0-89886-813-0.

Best Short Hikes in™ Washington's South Cascades & Olympics, 2nd Edition by E.M. Sterling and Ira Spring. $14.95 paperbound. 0-89886-869-9.

Best Rain Shadow Hikes: Western Washington by Michael Fagin and Skip Card. $16.95 paperbound. 0-89886-863-7.

Mountain Flowers of the Cascades and Olympics, 2nd Edition by Harvey Manning, photographs by Bob and Ira Spring. $9.95 spiral bound. 0-89886-883-1.